Old Ship of Zion

Religion in America Series
Harry S. Stout, General Editor

A Perfect Babel of Confusion
Dutch Religion and English
Culture in the Middle Colonies
Randall Balmer

The Presbyterian Controversy
Fundamentalists, Modernists,
and Moderates
Bradley J. Longfield

Mormons and the Bible
The Place of Latter-day Saints
in American Religion
Philip L. Barlow

The Rude Hand of Innovation
Religion and Social Order
in Albany, New York 1652–1836
David G. Hackett

Seasons of Grace
Colonial New England's Revival
Tradition in Its British Context
Michael J. Crawford

The Muslims of America
edited by Yvonne Yazbeck Haddad

The Prism of Piety
Catholick Congregational Clergy
at the Beginning of the Enlightenment
John Corrigan

Female Piety in Puritan New
England
The Emergence of Religious Humanism
Amanda Porterfield

The Secularization of the Academy
edited by George M. Marsden
and Bradley J. Longfield

Episcopal Women
Gender, Spirituality, and Commitment
in an American Mainline Denomination
edited by Catherine Prelinger

Submitting to Freedom
The Religious Vision of William James
Bennett Ramsey

Old Ship of Zion
The Afro-Baptist Ritual
in the African Diaspora
Walter F. Pitts

Old Ship of Zion

The Afro-Baptist Ritual in the African Diaspora

WALTER F. PITTS

With a Foreword by Vincent L. Wimbush

New York   Oxford

OXFORD UNIVERSITY PRESS

Oxford University Press

Oxford   New York

Athens   Auckland   Bangkok   Bogota   Bombay
Buenos Aires   Calcutta   Cape Town   Dar es Salaam
Delhi   Florence   Hong Kong   Istanbul   Karachi
Kuala Lumpur   Madras   Madrid   Melbourne
Mexico City   Nairobi   Paris   Singapore
Taipei   Tokyo   Toronto

and associated companies in
Berlin   Ibadan

Copyright © 1993 by Leroy Davis

First published in 1993 by Oxford University Press, Inc.
198 Madison Avenue, New York, New York 10016

First issued as an Oxford University Press paperback, 1996.

Library of Congress Cataloging-in-Publication Data
Pitts, Walter F., 1947–1991.
Old ship of Zion : the Afro-Baptist ritual
in the African diaspora / Walter F. Pitts.
p.   cm. — (Religion in America series)
Includes bibliographical references and index.
ISBN 0-19-507509-9
ISBN 0-19-511145-1 (Pbk.)
1. Afro-American Baptists.   2. Blacks—Africa—Religion.
3. Public worship—Baptists—History.
I. Title.   II. Series:
Religion in America series (Oxford University Press)
BX6443.P58 1993
264'.06'0089960730764—dc20
92-15256

Portions of chapters 5 and 6 were adapted from previously published
articles and are acknowledged on pages 154 and 175, respectively.

1 3 5 7 9 8 6 4 2

Printed in the United States of America
on acid-free paper

To the memory of Walter, Sr.,

who used to tell me:

"Don't play it if you don't mean it."

and

To Leroy,

A signpost,

A leaning post.

A bright and shining star.

"Throw the ball Retha!"

ACKNOWLEDGMENTS

I would like to thank the numerous churches in central Texas that willingly let me tape record and play for their worship services, thereby encouraging my study as well as teaching me how to play gospel music. Above all, I acknowledge the congregation of St. John Progressive Baptist Church in Austin, whose doors were always open for my research. I also acknowledge the congregation of Good Hope Baptist Church in Round Rock, Texas, who were equally supportive of my efforts to write about the Afro-Baptist experience. I am indebted to Lucien Johnson for taking me to his church, Paradise Baptist. This visit began my involvement with the Afro-Baptist ritual, its sound, and its followers.

I would like to thank John Bordie of the University of Texas at Austin for strongly encouraging me to publish my research when I was in doubt; and Jane Atkinson at Lewis and Clark College for reading an earlier draft of the manuscript and offering helpful comments and encouragement. In 1987, while I was studying as a President's Fellow at the University of California, Berkeley, my mentor Alan Dundes gave invaluable assistance by meticulously reviewing the theoretical issues that I argue. In the Department of Geography and Anthropology at Louisiana State University, my colleague Miles Richardson made insightful literary suggestions for Chapter 1, while Jill Brody and Joyce Jackson were supportive listeners. I would like to thank Mervyn Williams of the Ministry of Culture of Trinidad and Tobago for taking me during the summer of 1989 to several rituals in Trinidad, which were important to my fieldwork.

I owe much to Bradley Phillips, the painter, for his unyielding insistence that I begin writing. I am also indebted to the congregation of Israelite Divine Spiritual Church in New Orleans for allowing me to participate in their rituals. I feel a special indebtedness to Israelite's Bishop E. J. Johnson, Deacon Carlos Washington, organist Hillary Dozier, and Sister Wilma Brooks, who welcomed me warmly into their midst.

I am thankful for the support my sister Jeanne and my mother Inez have always given me, whether I was right or wrong, or whether they knew what I was doing or not. I am also thankful for the warmth of the family of C. T. and Mattie Davis of Giddings, Texas. Each of their children—Nancy, Wallace, Lena Ann, Kathryn, Leroy, Alma, Vera, Cynthia, and Clyde—is like a refraction of Olodumare, God, in that from each I learned something valuable and different about life. I thank Leroy for helping me type the manuscript and for proofreading it, as well as for his constant comments about its subject matter. I finally thank Rufina, the spirit of an old Cuban slavewoman, who told me through possession trance fourteen years ago that I had a book to write. I take it, Rufina, that this is the book. I only regret that many of my friends, whom I took for granted as a "support system," will not read it. Their lives have ended prematurely as a result of AIDS, other illnesses, and random violence. I miss them for themselves and for their reactions, had they been able to read *Old Ship of Zion*.

W. F. P.

CONTENTS

FOREWORD

Walter F. Pitts died July 20, 1991. I did not know him personally; I came to know only a part of him through the manuscript—obviously an important part of his life—that has been transformed into the book now before the reader. If that which is created is in the image of its creator, I suspect that had I met Walter Pitts I probably would have liked him very much; I know I would have been impressed by him, and would have learned a great deal from him.

At first, when I was asked by Oxford University Press to review Pitts's manuscript while it was under consideration for publication, I remember thinking that I really could not afford the time to take on more commitments. Besides, although I have taught courses in, read widely, and pursue scholarship in African-American religious traditions, it is not my primary field of specialization, and I very much needed to stick to my primary scholarly agenda in New Testament and Christian Origins.

But the title of the manuscript was my undoing—*Old Ship of Zion: The Afro-Baptist Ritual in the African Diaspora.* "Old Ship of Zion"? "Afro-Baptist"? "Ritual"? The "Old Ship of Zion" metaphor immediately struck a chord; it reminded me of the old song that was a favorite of my grandparents in their worship experiences ("prayer band") at home and in church. During visits, my sisters and I were often allowed on the sidelines at such events. We were awe-struck observers, picking up on the rhythms, the harmonies and idiosyncracies of the worshippers. "Old Ship of Zion" was one of the haunting songs I recall from those days. It is associated with so powerful and vivid a memory that after reading only a few pages of Pitts's manuscript I could not restrain myself from humming the tune, the tune that I recognized as part of the devotional period of my grandparents' Afro-Baptist folk church and house worship experiences. So I knew I had to know more about the manuscript. Once it was atop my desk I could not put it aside. It was, after all, in some sense about me and the sacred world to which I was introduced in my youth.

Actually, there are several reasons why many—sociologists, anthropologists, Americanists, Africanists, scholars of religion, theologians, literary and cultural critics—should read this book. As a historian of religion with special interests in how religions both ancient (especially Christianity) and modern (especially African-American) developed (in Geertzian terms) their ethoses and world views, my interests represent something of a bridge between social-scientific studies of religion and culture and more traditional historical and literary studies. Given this position, I can assert that there are wide-ranging and provocative implications in the arguments of the book for what is likely to be the wide categories of readers with different interests and agendas. There are, for example, enormous implications for the general critical study of culture, and of religion as a vital dimension of it; for the study of African-American religious traditions and culture as well as those of other African diaspora; and for the study of American religious traditions and culture.

This book is an example of a type of social-scientific and phenomenological study of a culture that assumes religion to play a major role in the shaping of ethos and world view. In addition, it is an excellent model of a type of new scholarship that ignores entrenched disciplinary and field boundaries, prerogatives, and prejudices. In order to do full justice to the subject matter—religion—Pitts had to employ a range of different questions and angles, raise a number of different issues that go beyond any one field or discipline, and thereby risk vulnerability to the usual criticism from the "experts" and disciplinary purists.

But what seems to make the book so interesting is the author's evident enjoyment of and relish for raising and pursuing questions and issues, whatever their traditional homes—theology, sociology, comparative religions, African studies, sociolinguistics, to name a few—that help him to understand and explain the complexity, texture, and rhythms of the world of an African-American community in central Texas. Although Pitts did not declare himself a card-carrying member, his scholarship certainly has affinities with the tendencies of the loosely defined movements associated with the "New Historicism," in which, among other things, focus is placed upon describing culture ("thick description") as event or action serving as a springboard for a wide-ranging analysis of society and culture (H. A. Veeser, ed., *The New Historicism*). In this view, anthropology is understood as cultural critique in

which ethnography is seen not as an end in itself, but as a foundation
for theoretical play and experimentation and as an opportunity for critique of the assumptions of our larger culture (G. E. Marcus and
M. M. J. Fischer, *Anthropology as Cultural Critique*).

By focusing upon ritual as an important index of ethos and world
view, Pitts seemed to share some of the assumptions of these movements. There is certainly evidence—for example, in the attention given
to relating the ritual of Afro-Baptists to larger currents in American
religious history, and to African and African diaspora communities—
of Pitts's genuine interest in exploring further the larger issues and
questions toward which ritual frames point. So I see the book as one
good piece of evidence for the revitalization of the critical function of
ethnography, as well as its growth beyond focus on the static "ethnographic present" (E. Ohnuki-Tierney, ed., *Culture Through Time*).

As applied to African-American communities, not nearly enough of
the type of work that this book represents—emphasis on ritual and structure, and on "little communities"—has been done. (Nearly all the exceptions are graciously acknowledged and expanded upon by the author.)
Much general academic scholarship on African-Americans has been
and remains focused upon the history, literature, and criticism of great
figures, institutions, and movements. In scholarship on religion and theology in particular, it is still the case that emphasis is placed primarily
upon great founding figures, denominational movements, and congregations, and upon the systematization and criticism of the thinking,
rhetoric, and actions of the great figures. (Martin Luther King, Jr.,
immediately comes to mind as one figure who in death has not lacked
attention or support.) Its sophisticated sociological analysis notwith-
standing, even the C. E. Lincoln/L. Mamiya book, *The Black Church
in the African American Experience*, billed as the "largest nongovern-
mental survey of urban and rural churches ever undertaken," falls back
upon the artificial construct of denomination for its organizing framework and concluding arguments about the "black church."

Although focus upon gathering "qualitative data" from the African-
American religious experience is not new, the sustained attention to
ritual (not in general, but within a particular community) and to its
implications for African-American self-understandings is not common.
Moreover, in its rather consistent and fair-minded attention to the matter
of origins and functions, the book models an approach to the study not

only of religion in general but of African-American religious self-understandings that has enormous potential. In the spirit of the historian of religion Charles Long, for Pitts it is neither their theology, their philosophy, nor their ethics, but rather their rhythms that reflect most accurately and dramatically the "world" of a large segment of African-Americans.

Those rhythms, Pitts came to understand, were learned and preserved not in the large and prestigious institutions, but in the little institutions and communities—of the "folk"—in which accommodation to the styles, rhythms and rhetorics of the larger world was not considered important. Such communities deserve much more attention than they have received. But such attention, Pitts argues, should be characterized by respect and sensitivity, judicious gathering and weighing of data, and empathy, not by impressionistic explanations, uncritical defensive jargon, or idealization and stereotyping by African-Americans themselves or by Hollywood.

It seemed terribly important to Pitts to attempt to present something of the complexity—the richness of the aesthetics, the poignancy, profundity, and inconsistencies of world view—reflected in the ritual frames of the Afro-Baptists he studied. Perhaps, "studied" is too weak a word to describe what Pitts did; he actually became a part of the communities that were the object of his study. Over a period of several years, he came to know individuals and their personalities, and the impact of the structural frames of the worship experience on them. He became a part of the worship experience that he describes and analyzes. Little or no concern about the needed detachment of the scientist is registered. Are there implications here for the scientific study of religion?

I suspect many readers will agree with me that this book provides a picture of a significant segment of African-American culture that is more provocative and at the same time more realistic than any book in recent years. In my opinion, few scholarly treatments about African-American religious experiences appear to reflect the sensibilities of the many, of the "folk." Many of us will recognize the personalities, the rhetoric, the communal rituals described in the book. All of us will greatly appreciate the author's empathetic and critical analysis. Might there be implications for the study of American and African-American religious traditions? Might there be in the book something of a challenge to shift perspective or focus?

The major thesis of the book is that, in Afro-Baptist worship, there are two ritual frames ("Devotion" and "Service") that correspond to some African initiation rites, and that these two contrasting frames, as retained in Afro-Baptist worship experience, function, as in some African contexts, to transport worshippers psychically from a hostile and precarious world to a smaller and more secure one that will equip them to face that hostile environment again. Pitts argues this thesis persuasively, with help from Victor Turner and by virtue of his own full initiation into the mysteries of the Afro-Baptist world. There is in the analysis of the function of the ritual much that can inform discussions about whether and in what ways African-American religions represent resistance or critique. Too much such discussion has been based upon the presence or absence of political rhetoric and direct confrontation of institutional powers. Pitts's book reminds us of the power—psychic, social and political—of the experience of communitas and of ritual as a part of it. Insofar as the ritual frames isolated by Pitts "transform" the emotions and psyches of participants, and insofar as such transformation sustains the alternative social formation that is the Afro-Baptist world, resistance is evident and powerful.

Nowhere is the power of the resistance clearer than in the metaphor of the ship of transport for the initiation ritual and its effects. Each participant in the ritual is transported from one world (of emotional and psychic challenges) to another world (of emotional refreshment). The folk communities of Afro-Baptists can, therefore, be understood to practice the "arts of resistance" that constitute their ritual; as alternative communities, their very existence constitutes resistance. But this means that these alternative communities must be understood in all their complexity, not as simple babble and farce. Pitts's book goes a long way toward helping us understand that they are very complex indeed.

At any rate, this book's revelation of the complexity of the folk communities among Afro-Baptists presents implications for the understanding of religion in America. To the extent that academics and journalists often categorize American religion as liberal, mainline, fundamentalist, and so forth, according to perceptions about orientations to the centers of socio-economic-political powers, they need to reconsider. If Pitts's arguments are taken seriously, the challenge is to rethink what the accommodationist response really is, and who the dissenters are.

Because the book contains so many implications for so many considerations and types of readers, it is in its own right a fascinating, powerful "ship" of intellectual and conceptual transformation. For this and many other reasons, in the words of the song that supplies the book's title, it is well worth readers' time and effort to "get on board."

VINCENT L. WIMBUSH
Professor of New Testament and Christian Origins
Union Theological Seminary
New York City

Old Ship of Zion

The preacher tells of days long ago and of a people whose sufferings were like ours. . . . What we have not dared feel in the presence of the Lords of the Land, we now feel in church . . . our eyes become absorbed in a vision. . . . The preacher begins to punctuate his words with sharp rhythms, and we are lifted far beyond the boundaries of our daily lives . . . until drunk with our enchanted vision . . . we do not know who we are, what we are, where we are. . . . We go home pleasantly tired and sleep easily, for we know that we hold . . . a possibility of inexhaustible happiness. . . . We take this feeling with us each day and it drains the gall out of our years, sucks the sting from the rush of time, purges the pain from our memory of the past, and banishes the fear of loneliness and death. . . . Some say that, because we possess this faculty of keeping alive this spark of happiness under adversity, we are children. No . . . for we know that there will come a day when we shall pour out our hearts over this land.

RICHARD WRIGHT, Twelve Million Voices

INTRODUCTION

Although baptized, confirmed, and practically raised in the Episcopal Church, I was irresistibly drawn to the rhythms and sounds of another church from which people came away apparently more vitalized from their Sunday morning experience than I from mine. As a teenager in New Haven sitting in the cold, quiet pews among a reserved congregation, I would hear the swinging, hard beats of Daddy Grace's sanctified brass band next door drift through the open windows of the church in which I found myself. With the hidden glee of a captive audience, I savored those interruptions of the somber sermon and the even more somber choir singing. When I moved to New York City at the age of twenty, a close friend invited me to his small church, Paradise Baptist, that stood on a Harlem streetcorner. From that day on, I resolved always and only to attend the folk church.

Perhaps my decision was the result of the Reverend Cooke's chanted preaching style. As pastor of Paradise, he hummed his sermon with such feeling that the whole congregation would give in to the impulse to clap and sway so that Monday morning would still reverberate with joy. Perhaps my decision owed something to the gospel piano player, Sister Anna M. Walker, who insisted that her middle initial stood for "Music" and who, from her piano bench, would beat the rhythms into the choir, making them dip and sway as they moved up the center aisle to the choir stall.

Imitating her style, I found myself more than a decade later on the Chisholm Trail in Round Rock playing piano for Baptist worship services there and throughout central Texas. Whole Sundays, from early morning to dusk, would be spent in a series of church services where, in order to stay awake, I would sometimes peer out the window at the windings of a slow-moving creek during a slow-moving sermon. When the mood of the service changed, I would be drawn into a vortex of excitement—the pounding of keyboards, drums, and electric guitar building the crescendo that would end in a state of trance.

3

After five years of attending and playing for Texas church services, I began to wonder about the nature of the rituals I had become part of. I also began making mental comparisons between these Protestant services and those of Afro-Cuban origin in which I had participated. As an avid reader of Melville J. Herskovits's theories on African retentions in the Americas, I suspected that certain cultural connections between the two rituals existed. But what were they? How strong were the links between black Baptist worship in Texas and the rest of the African diaspora? Aside from casual observations of the similarity in motor behavior of those in trance, or the common importance of water symbolism, Herskovits notes very few connections among the various religious rituals in Afro-America. Taken as a whole, they seemingly form a disparate mosaic, or, better yet, a cultural kaleidoscope of incongruous parts.

The focus of this book, therefore, is to locate those connections which other scholars, from W.E.B. DuBois ([1903] 1973) to Amiri Baraka (Leroi Jones 1963), have argued so forcefully with mostly qualitative evidence. What we now need to balance this perspective is quantitative data. Such an effort is necessarily interdisciplinary, relying in part on linguistics, American history, ethnomusicology, and cultural anthropology. In the process of establishing historical and cultural ties between various Afro-American rituals whose commonalities ultimately lie in Africa, I hope to bring to the reader a better understanding to dispel the stereotyping and mystification that surround black folk Baptist churches. How many more movies and television situation comedies do we need to see in which the black preacher is a buffoon or the members themselves, shouting and fanning uncontrollably, the comic relief?

It is also my intention to respond to another kind of misunderstanding of the black church. In 1944 Gunner Myrdal, in "The Negro Church: Its Weakness, Trends, and Outlook," stated that the black church had become an outdated, impractical, dysfunctional institution whose conservative politics supported black poverty. Setting the stage for negative views, Myrdal's work was followed seven years later by William Pipes's analysis of black Baptist sermons called *Say Amen Brother! Old-Time Negro Preaching: A Study in Frustration.* Linking the black sermon to the superstitions and ignorance of Africa, Pipes, himself a black preacher, concluded like Myrdal that assimilation into mainstream American culture would fortunately seal the doom of the old-time church with its distinctive preaching style (Pipes 1951). At the end of the 1960s some scholars were still predicting the demise of the black church as a development favorable to the black community's survival (Cone 1971: 349; Washington 1971: 301–09).

The impact of the black church within African-American society is richly documented; no significant sociological study ignores the role of the church, whether dysfunctional or not, within that community. The black folk Baptist ritual owes its distinctive character to the crossing paths of American history and the African slave trade. W.E.B. DuBois was the first scholar to look at cultural links between Africa and the black Baptist church. In his collection of essays, *Souls of Black Folks*, he suggested that certain African practices had been transformed in black Baptist worship, such as the African's sacred regard for water, which led to the institution of baptism by total immersion. However, it was not until the publication of James Weldon Johnson's *God's Trombones* in 1927 that serious attention was drawn to the black church, the black preacher, and his sermons. Although travelers to the American South had reported the singing of Negro Spirituals and ringshout worship during and immediately following slavery (see Higginson 1960: 187–213), Johnson's poetic work, appearing six decades after the emancipation of slaves, was the first collection of African-American sermons rephrased in the form of verse. Johnson recognized the sociological importance of black preaching. In his preface he wrote: "It was the old-time preacher who for generations was the mainspring of hope and inspiration for the Negro in America. This power of the old-time preacher . . . is still a vital force. . . . The Negro today is, perhaps, the most priest-governed group in the country" (Johnson 1927: 2).

Another landmark was the publication in 1934 of Zora Neale Hurston's biographical novel *Jonah's Gourd Vine*. In a letter to Johnson, Hurston explained why she had chosen her father, a country Baptist preacher, as protagonist and the Baptist church as background for her story: "I do not speak of those among us who have been tampered with and consequently have gone Presbyterian and Episcopal. I mean the common run of us who love magnificence, beauty, poetry, and color so much that there can never be too much of it" (Hurston [1934] 1971: 5).

After Hurston's novel, other collections and sociological tracts appeared on Negro folk religion and sermons. Charles S. Johnson, a renowned figure from the Harlem Renaissance, recorded nine sermons for Fisk University's Department of Social Sciences; and in 1942 Alice

Jones wrote her thesis, "The Negro Folk Sermon: A Study on the Sociology of Folk Culture." During this same time the Julius Rosenwald Fund supported research on black sermons in Louisiana (Wright 1976: 2). In 1940, John Henry Faulk based his master's thesis for the University of Texas on ten Negro sermons that he recorded in central Texas for the Library of Congress with the support of the Julius Rosenwald Fund. Testifying in his own defense before the New York State Supreme Court during his spectacular 1962 lawsuit against those who had blacklisted him a decade earlier, Faulk stated that his thesis was significant because it was

> the first of its kind ever accepted at the University of Texas. It con-
> sisted of ten sermons that I had transcribed as they were preached
> by ten Negro ministers. . . . I told [my attorney] of my consuming
> interest in the folklore of the Southwest, how I had been attracted
> by the epic quality of the Negro sermons, an art form rapidly dis-
> appearing at the time. . . . I described the imagery and the grandeur
> of the Negro folk sermon. (Faulk 1983: 170)

During the 1970s and 1980s an increasing number of books and dissertations appeared on the subject of black folk worship, many expressing an interest in its music. Two significant historical works focusing on black Baptists were published in 1978 and 1979. The first was Albert J. Raboteau's *Slave Religion: The "Invisible" Institution in the Antebellum South*, which provided a detailed history of the black Baptist church from the clandestine slave meetings to recognized congregations formed during the antebellum period. The second was Mechal Sobel's *Trabelin' On: The Slave Journey to an Afro-Baptist Faith*. This was an historical account of the development of a black Baptist worldview hewn from an African system of philosophy and theology. What most later studies share is the recognition of a strong, undeniable African presence in the folk worship of African-Americans.

Bruce Rosenberg's 1970 collection of black sermons, *The Art of the American Folk Preacher*, was a landmark in the analysis of the black preaching style. His study was the first attempt to understand the mechanics of poetry preachers use in constructing their chanted sermons. Following his lead, Faye Vaughn-Cooke, in her linguistic analysis of the black preaching style, discusses its attraction: It "is considered one of the most important speaking styles used by blacks, and . . . one of the most unique styles in the United States" (Vaughn-Cooke 1972: 28).

As a biographer of Martin Luther King, Jr. wrote about his preaching style: "His rich religious imagery reached deep into the Negro psyche, for religion had been black people's main source of strength and survival since slavery days" (Oates 1982: 80). The importance of the preaching style, according to one of its observers, is that it is the "heart and soul of the Black church" (Wright 1976: 2).

Black preaching and religious music styles have a wide popular appeal because of the excitement their performances spark. Since the early 1950s Mahalia Jackson and other pioneering black gospel singers propelled the music of the religious black masses into the national spotlight so that the black church, along with its ecstatic preaching and singing, has become a regular feature on Broadway and in Hollywood productions (Hughes and Meltzer 1967: 164–68). In 1963 Langston Hughes's *Tambourines to Glory* established the first connection between Broadway and gospel music. James Baldwin's *Amen Corner* followed in 1965 (Hughes and Meltzer 1967: 226).

Hollywood's interest in the black church began much earlier. In 1929 King Vidor directed the first all-black cast in *Hallelujah*, and *Green Pastures* appeared seven years later (Hughes and Meltzer 1967: 298). In the 1970s and 1980s we saw gospel extravaganzas such as *Black Nativity, Purlie, Your Arms Too Short to Box with God, Bubbling Brown Sugar*, and a revival of *Amen Corner* on Broadway. During the same period two films—*Cotton Comes to Harlem* and *The Blues Brothers*—featured gospel extravaganzas. The famous Clara Ward Singers even had a Las Vegas nightclub review in the 1960s. In the late 1980s the television industry showed the weekly sitcom *Amen*, whose characters and plots seemed very far removed from the reality of the black church. It seems that no Christmas season can pass without a gospel mass choir in a televised special. Even the relatively new medium of the musical video has found use for gospel backgrounds to enhance the appeal of its stars. In a blatant travesty, tour buses bringing white spectators into Harlem on Sunday mornings have included black churches in their stops.

The sincerity of religious experience is compromised by tourism and the burlesque and minstrelsy of popular entertainment capitalizing on the excitement that black religious performance creates. To the outsider the events of the black folk church may seem hyperbolically ecstatic or stereotypically noisy and out of control, if not ludicrous. This view of the black church is not confined to popular opinions. Most scholarly research on the black church has focused exclusively on those features of black worship that lead to emotional climax. All the linguistic studies mentioned earlier are concerned with the climactic black folk sermon. There are moments within black religious ritual, however, that are not climactic at all but subdued, melancholic, even monotonous. Many scholars either ignore or are unaware of these aspects of black church services while they exploit the more ecstatic speech and music events, thus reinforcing the common impression that nothing of a somber nature occurs in black folk worship.

I would like to refute the impression, both scholarly and popular, that ritual behavior in the American black church is an ecstatic jumble. As we will see in the following chapters, in which I make connections between black Baptist ritual and rituals of Africa and other Afro-American groups, both somber and climactic events are required to produce the ritual structure found in the black Baptist church. Two "ritual frames" combine to create the total ritual structure. Earlier scholars focused on the climactic sermon to illustrate the "magnificence, beauty, poetry, and color" of the black church. This book will look at the speech of both sermons and prayers, the songs of excitement and melancholy, and the gestures enacted by congregational members, all of which are needed to construct the frames. By moving from frame to frame in sequence, the ritual participant is emotionally—and spiritually—satisfied at its end.

The origin of these ritual frames is African: the frames are carried over from secret African initiation rites and the ritual public display of possession trance. Evidence of their African source, however, is not apparent, and the search to uncover African retentions must begin with some clue provided by congregational members themselves. As pianist for six years in one of these churches, I was able unobtrusively to record many worship services with a portable tape recorder resting on my piano bench. I recorded preaching, singing, and conversations from as many as sixteen different congregations in central Texas who worshiped with each other on special occasions during my tenure as church musician. In my observations of these events, the variation in ways of speaking at different points in the ritual was a start in the search for clues. One notices that in the beginning of the ritual the first frame uses both standard twentieth-century English and Jacobean English in the prayers, while the second frame—the sermon—draws on Black Vernacular English. This manipulation of speech styles is parallel to the manipulation of music styles within the same frame. In addition to hearing seventeenth-century English in the deacons' prayers, the observer also hears eighteenth-century hymns "raised" or "lined" in the fashion of Puritans in colonial America during the first frame, in which each line is first spoken by a deacon or prayer leader, then sung by the congregation. The second frame, however, exploits the rhythms of black composers and sacred folk songs, commonly called spirituals and gospel songs. No longer raised and a cappella, these black songs are accompanied by piano, organ, synthetic keyboards, drums, guitars, and handclapping.

The variation of vernacular speech and song styles that define the two distinct frames have been crucial in preserving an oral ritual for nearly three hundred years without a written liturgy. By experiencing the contrasting moods of each frame in sequence and becoming emotionally transformed, ritual participants are restored to a state of ideological stability within a mainstream society hostile to their social, economic, and political needs.

The dichotomous structure of the black folk, or "Afro- Baptist," ritual has shown up consistently throughout the African Western Hemisphere. By connecting the two-frame ritual with Brazilian and African initiation practices and attitudes, the reader is more likely to understand that the Afro-Baptist ritual is an extension, as well as a reinterpretation, of African religious custom.

As an object of study, the Afro-Baptist ritual as it still exists in some parts of the American South offers a chance to explore the process of acculturation. In changing and assimilating to mainstream American religious practice, the Afro-Baptist church—to use the words of the noted anthropologist Ruth Benedict—selects "from among the possible traits in the surrounding regions those which it can use, and discards those which it cannot" (Benedict 1934: 47). Focusing on the challenge of cultural assimilation and adjustment, Melville Herskovits developed a method for comparative study of Afro-American cultures in the Americas in *Myth of the Negro Past* ([1941] 1958). Believing that Afro-American cultures were disoriented—or uprooted—from their African past, Herskovits argued that their study could become a laboratory for testing theories of cultural change and African retentions. Starting from Herskovits's recognition of African retentions, this book looks at the Afro-Baptist ritual as a rare opportunity for assessing the plasticity and cultural adjustments of an initially disoriented people—that is, an assortment of enslaved Africans—in their efforts to construct a new religious worldview. As Herskovits discovered, and as this study again demonstrates, anthropologists no longer have to guess at the creative solutions a truly disoriented culture would have to devise in order to maintain its identity and strength. The survival of Afro-Baptist ritual in North America, like Afro-American rituals elsewhere, is a living testament.

1

"Magnificence, Beauty, Poetry, and Color": The Afro-Baptist Church, Its Ritual, and Frames

Afro-Baptist Worship

"I love the Lord, He heard my cry," Deacon cries out. The newly gathered congregation, now seated in their pews, echoes his words in a plaintive tune. They do this without the support of piano, organ, or hymnal. Another Sunday morning worship service has begun at St. John Progressive Baptist Church, which, like many working-class Baptist churches in the black community of Austin, Texas, is home to a small congregation. Why the adjective "Progressive" has been inserted into the church's title is a mystery—and not a very interesting one to its members. Unlike "Free Will" or "Missionary," it connotes no sectarian leanings or history.

"And pitied every groan!" The deacon, not waiting for his chorus to finish the first line, bellows the second from a hymn composed by Dr. Isaac Watts at the beginning of the eighteenth century. Again the congregation resumes their mournful melody, overlapping the deacon's last verse with their chorus. This form of response singing "has been advanced as the basis of all African polyphony" (Waterman 1943: 78). As the interaction between deacon and congregation unfolds, mothers wrestle with their smaller children to sit still while beckoning to their older ones to come into the sanctuary.

11

"As long as I live and trouble rise," Deacon Simon continues, "I'll hasten to His throne." The congregational chorus swells to each new line, in a nasal drawl, until the hymn is sung in its entirety.

Deacon Simon, a strong, balding man in his sixties who wears blue-jean overalls and flannel shirts outside of church service, needs no hymnbook to recall the verses to these old tunes which he raises, or lines out, from the deacon's bench. A tattered copy of *Gospel Pearls*, a collection of sacred songs that the all-black National Baptist Convention first published in 1921, rests by his hand as a ready reminder of any hymn he might have overlooked. As usual, the congregation performs Watts's "I Love the Lord, He Heard My Cry" in such a dragging manner that a newcomer would have difficulty deciphering the text. So slurred are the words, drawn over an almost rhythmless but highly embellished melody, that they bear little resemblance to those called out by the deacon. The opening hymn is not quite rhythmless, however. As they echo Deacon Simon's call, congregational members keep the dirge-like beat with the tapping of their shoe heels upon the wooden floor, like the steady thud of the ax heard in work songs.

No matter which hymn a deacon chooses, the congregational melody always seems to be the same, or at least a close variant of some basic, underlying melody. This melody consists of five to six notes, including the flattened "blue notes" so characteristic of African-American song. Its overall effect is one of sadness mixed with hope. Because it seems to shift illusorily between minor and major modes with passing tones, the tune is difficult to notate. But notation is no problem for a congregation who has memorized the basic melody—and its variants—and passed the tunes, as well as the manner of echoing them, down to each generation.

Church attendance at St. John Progressive averages fifty members on any given Sunday, except the first one of the month when attendance increases considerably because Holy Communion is offered and monthly tithes are due. Housed in a small, T-shaped whitewashed structure, the church has a little open porch at the front door. The once vinyl-stripped windows that imitated a stained-glass mosaic are gone. They have been replaced with immovable orange-tinted plexiglas shields that glow with the growing morning light. Unfortunately, the fresh breezes that once wafted freely through the opened windows are now stifled. Only two new white ceiling fans stir the air trapped in the sanctuary. The field of bluebonnets off to the building's side has been covered over with asphalt to make room for a parking lot. Both plexiglas and parking lot are thought to be improvements. They are features pointed to with pride by a few members and all of the deacons who helped to install these indicators of progress.

Each Sunday ritual at St. John Progressive begins at eleven-thirty in the morning when a deacon, noticing that several congregational members have assembled in their pews, begins to line out a hymn from the deacon's bench. As the ritual begins, a concerned mother will go to the church's front porch to beckon her teenage offspring to come into the opening of worship. Sister Sally Clark, a stout, pleasant woman who directs the children's Angel Choir, leaves the sanctuary to round up her two children and other choir members, giving them a brief scolding for loitering about. Obviously reluctant to attend this part of worship, called Devotion, where prayers and hymns will be heard, the youth prefer to remain outside to hear the latest gossip. Even members in their twenties and thirties tend to avoid Devotion by arriving at church twenty minutes late after this part of the ritual has nearly run its course. With coaxing and prodding, the teenagers slowly join Devotion. The ultimate prodder, however, is the Reverend R. L. Pearson, pastor, who chastises his young members from the pulpit about their lateness. In his late sixties, gray-haired, and balding Pastor Pearson reminds his musicians, who do not play their instruments during Devotion, that attendance at this part of worship is mandatory.

Pastor Pearson, a part-time carpenter as well as the leader of his flock, is especially proud of the new glowing plexiglas windows he and the deacons installed. The glow they create spreads over the blood-red carpet covering the center aisle that leads to the dais and the pulpit. Directly behind the pulpit sit three high-backed chairs, upholstered in plush red velvet to match the carpet, for the pastor and guest preachers. Behind these is the choir stall on whose rear wall hangs an inexpensive but colorful tapestry of Leonardo Da Vinci's *Last Supper*. In front of the pulpit stands the communion table engraved with Christ's words to his disciples: "This do in remembrance of me." Off to the left of the pulpit, an organ and a set of snare drums and cymbals stand, while the piano and deacon's bench sit to its right. On top of the pulpit itself rests an enormous Bible containing the sacred Word that draws the congregation together once a week.

On any given Sunday, the congregation ranges in age from infants to the middle-aged and elderly church members who preside over the deacon bench, church organizations, and pulpit. The women constitute the majority of the congregation. Roughly one-third of the members attending are men and boys who come dressed in suits and ties. At least half of the membership consists of persons under the age of thirty-five, many of whom are teenagers dressed in the latest fashions or young children. Nearly all of St. John's members are Austin natives. Indeed all of them are natives of Texas—this usually stated assertively; and most of these members come from some central Texas county. The members work in service-related jobs as city or state maintenance personnel, nursing home attendants, domestic help in private white homes, or in low-paying clerical positions. Most of these members work at least six days a week; some, like Sister Evelyn Reese, regard Sunday's service as a break from a week-long routine of work. Younger members often work after school at fast-food franchises. A few younger members have middle-income, skilled jobs, working at the local IBM or Motorola plant. An even smaller number attend the nearby colleges and universities in Austin.

Today's opening hymn belongs to the repertoire of "Old One Hundreds"—to use the black Baptist terminology—whose origins date back to the eighteenth and early nineteenth centuries. This particular hymn, "I Love the Lord, He Heard My Cry," an improvisation on Psalm 116, became very popular on both sides of the Atlantic when English composer Isaac Watts included it in his *Hymns and Spiritual Songs* in 1702. The deacon calls out the first hymn line in a singsong recitative, and the congregation repeats the line in a dirgelike melody, each member carefully embellishing each syllable. Because every hymn is sung with nearly the same melody, the hearer gets the impression of endless monotony accentuated only by the thud of feet thumping the floor in time with the slow beat. No wonder the youth prefer their livelier conversations out on the front porch.

When the congregation reaches the last line of the final hymn stanza, the Devotion continues in prayer. During prayer, the church is at its stillest. Mothers gather their younger children to restrain their fidgeting, while giving older offspring reproachful glances should they move or talk. A deacon, not waiting for the end of the verse, kneels before the deacon's bench. With his back turned to the congregation, he prays in what is an amalgamation of seventeenth-century English and contemporary standard American English:

Lord Jesus,
  You said if you look to the hills from whence cometh all of our help,
There You would be in the midst.

Though some of his prayer verses are spontaneously addressed to specific personal problems, most of the lines are often-heard verses from Old One Hundred hymns, gospel songs, Scripture, and lines from the prayers of other speakers (see Pitts, W. 1988: 83–91).

Sister Pearson, wife of the pastor, whom many members address as "Mother Pearson," is especially effective at praying. Wiping away tears as she kneels before her pew, she begins to chant her prayer. Praying louder as she continues, Sister Pearson moves other congregants to sway to the rhythm of her voice, keeping time with their church fans and responsive Amens:

> This evening,
>   O Heavenly Father,
> I come to You in the humblest manner that I know how.
> I come,
>   Lord Jesus,
> with a humble heart and a bowed head.
> I call upon Your name,
>   Lord Jesus,
> because I know no other name to call.
> Lord Jesus,
>   bless the ones that are here under the sound of my weak voice.
> O Heavenly Father,
>   we might be few, Lord, but You said where there are two
>   or three gathered in My Name,
> You would be in the midst.

While the congregation conducts Devotion, church ushers wearing white gloves fold their arms before the doors of the sanctuary. They guard them to make sure that no one enters or leaves while this part of worship is taking place. Although the hymn-singing and praying may swell in intensity, no one "shouts," that is, goes into trance, during this period. In fact, church members who feel on the verge of trance will run out of the sanctuary rather than let a premature "descent of the Spirit" disturb Devotion. The only time the ushers will open the sanctuary doors is to allow the member to exit before he shouts. If a member, moreover, should shout before removing himself, the ushers or deacons will carry the entranced congregant out of the sanctuary. Church members will describe with amusement and some chagrin how a certain member shouted before Devotion was finished and had to be "packed" out. Sister June Whitaker, a young supervisor at Motorola, occasionally talks about the time when her mother shouted during Devotion. What was once a terribly embarrassing incident is today an amusing anecdote when Sister Whitaker, chuckling through her laughter, recounts, "Mama shouted during Devotion, y'all." Elder members at St. John Progressive talk about a time "way back yonder" when church members shouted "a while" during Devotion as well as the rest of the worship service.

The prayer finished, another deacon or congregant starts lining a second hymn, "Guide Me, O Thou Great Jehovah," which Thomas Hastings, the New York composer of "Rock of Ages," wrote in the early nineteenth century. Before the congregation finishes the hymn, this time a member of the congregation or deacon stands to let everyone know he or she will offer the next prayer. Before the singing ends, the prayer will begin, as before, with the speaker kneeling before the pew or bench. Brother Leroy Davis, a young man in his thirties, speaks the ornate language of prayer whose lines, though never written, are familiar to every black Baptist. They closely resemble the verses spoken by Sister Pearson:

This evening,
   O Heavenly Father,
      I come to You in humblest manner that I know how.
I come,
   Lord Jesus,
      with a humble heart and a bowed head.
I come,
   Lord Jesus,
      because I'm standing in the need of prayer.
I call upon Your name,
   Lord Jesus,
      because I know no other name to call.
I come tonight,
   O God,
      asking that if You will, Lord Jesus, to have a blessing upon us right now.
Lord Jesus,
   bless the ones that are here under the sound of my weak voice.

Focusing on death and the hope of paradise, Brother Davis concludes his prayer:

> Now Lord Jesus,
> > for we know that the road is rough and rocky down here.
>
> But just help us,
> > Lord Jesus.
>
> For afterwhile,
> > Lord Jesus,
> > > we won't have to come to this building no more.
>
> We'll be where we can praise Your name,
> > Lord Jesus.
>
> Where everyday will be Sunday and the Sabbath will have no end.
> And when we, too,
> > Lord Jesus,
> > > must quit the walks of this life,
>
> We're asking that,
> > if You will,
> > > Lord Jesus,
>
> to give us a place in Your Kingdom,
> > where we can praise Your name forever.
> > Amen.

Following this final prayer, the deacons are ready to sing a more lively spiritual. Simon's brother, Deacon Sims, likes to end the Devotion with one of his favorite songs, "Wade in the Water," adding lots of hand clapping to mark the closing sobriety of Devotion:

> Wade in the water,
> Wade in the water, children.
> Wade in the water,
> God's gonna trouble the water.

Musicians scramble to reach their instruments, knowing that in a few minutes they will be called upon to play.

"See that host all dressed in white," bellows big young Deacon Milton, president of the male chorus.

Pastor Pearson enters the sanctuary with his guest and assistant preachers following in his wake, signaling that the Devotion is about to draw to a close.

"The leader looks like the Israelite," the stout deacon continues.

Taking their seats in thronelike chairs, the preachers survey the congregation, some with smiles, others with blank stares.

"See that band all dressed in red," Deacon Milton's voice grows with excitement, "Looks like the band that Moses led."

The alternation of song and prayer may stop on its own, indicating to the pastor and his guests in his study that Devotion has ended and the Service may now begin. Church members say that Devotion is so indispensable to a spiritual preparation for the Service that to start without one would be hard to imagine. In her thirties and one of the best soloists in the choir, Sister Rosie Sims observes, "I've been a Baptist all of my life, so I've never been in a church service where we didn't have a Devotion."

The Service begins when the deacon presiding over Devotion, that is, the one initiating the first lined hymn, announces the end of this part of worship. He says, "This concludes our Devotion. The Service is now in the hands of the Pastor." The ushers guarding the entrance now pull open the doors to the sanctuary so that the choir can march up the center aisle. Dressed in long maroon and white robes that swoop with each movement, the Young Adult Choir enters rocking and swaying to "Oh Happy Day," as piano, organ, drum, and electric bass guitar beat out the marching rhythm. The first and only gospel song to appear on the top popular music charts in the late 1960s, "Oh Happy Day" breaks the more somber mood created by the lined hymns and prayers. The song gets the Service off to an exciting start.

Once the choir is installed in the choir stand, the youngest of the assistant preachers, Pastor Washington, who is barely in his twenties, announces a congregational hymn. From the pulpit, he instructs the congregation to turn to hymn number 94, "Jesus Keep Me Near the Cross." Although every pew has a few hymnals in its book rack, none of the congregation needs one for this well-known camp meeting song, composed by Fanny Crosby near the turn of this century. The congregational singing drawing to an end, a preacher other than the pastor will read a passage from the big Bible lying on the lectern, then offer an altar prayer after congregational members have gathered around the pulpit. With arms extended above the heads of his listeners, he begins to extemporize:

> Father, I stretch my hand to Thee,
> No other help I know.
> If Thou withdraw Thyself from me,
> Oh whither shall I go?
> Our Heavenly Father, we bow before You to give You thanks for all
>   night lyin' down last night.

As his voice rises with sing-song cadences, in a soft background supported by piano and organ, the choir and congregation together sing "Thank You Lord." The pastor continues:

We thank Thee, our Heavenly Father, early this morning.
For waking us up, Oh Heavenly Father, clothed in our right mind.
Oh God, we thank Thee for food.
We thank Thee for raiment and shelter.
We ask Thee, Oh Heavenly Father, to bless our homes and families.

Moved by this eloquence, Deacon Sims cries out, "Yeah! That's right!" while Sister Pearson, slowly nodding her head, merely utters "Yes, yes. Sho' nuff." Tears, whether of joy or sorrow, start rolling down the cheeks of several faces, as the speaker continues:

Oh Heavenly Father, we ask You to go by the hospitals and the nursin' homes.
Lord, touch the sick and the afflicted.
You knows our hearts.
And You knows our heart desires.

As the prayer turns into a chant and grows louder, Brother Davis stiffens, then shouts, "Thank you, Jesus!" He shoots up a hand that catches in the ceiling fan, and droplets of blood sprinkle the white blades. As the prayer continues, all four deacons and ushers, alarmed at the sight, rush to his side to carry him out. Aware of no pain nor of anyone surrounding and lifting him, Brother Davis has gone into trance. His shouts continue as the sanctuary doors close behind him.

The rising waves of the preacher's cadences now fall for a last time as he draws his prayer to an end with "I ask these things in Jesus' name. Amen." After the congregation moves back to their pews, the church announcements are made. Following the emotional tension of the altar prayer the congregation has regained composure. After the announcements, the ushers and deacons conduct the collections of monies in two different offerings. During the second offering, the choir sings a fast gospel song, "Get Right Church," in order to expedite the collection of tithes and other contributions as the congregation marches up to the communion table to drop their money into either of two brass plates. While the sopranos and altos imitate the "toot! toot!" of a train whistle, the young tenors sing, "I'm goin' home on the morning train," and, "back up train and get your load." The curious train sounds recall an earlier period in this century when imitations of trains in secular and sacred black music voiced hope of traveling north by rail to find jobs in an escape from Southern racial oppression.

Having given their offering, the congregation now awaits the choir singing with anticipation. The bass guitar sounds a few deep chords and pauses. The pause is pregnant. The guitarist repeats the phrase slowly, this time eliciting "Alright!" and "Put your soul in it!" from the congregation, noticeably from Deacon Sims, who yells encouragement. Now piano and organ join the guitar in counterpoint. First, the sopranos begin the chorus of the old spiritual "I Am Determined to Follow Jesus." Hands begin to clap in polyrhythms. Now the bass voices join those of the women. What emerges is a syncopated three-part fugue—instruments, sopranos, and basses in succession—causing the congregation to stir. When the choir reaches the refrain for the fourth time, they hum instead of sing the chorus. Their Oo's prompt a smiling Deacon Simon to holler, "Ain't no harm in moanin', children! That way the devil don't know whatcha talkin' about." During slavery, the "devil" was clearly the white overseer. Black field hands would surreptitiously hum songs calling for a secret meeting or escape whenever he was present (Campbell 1989: 175; Harding 1981: 196).

Their second selection, "His Eye Is on the Sparrow," is also an old song, and it too is slow. In an earlier arrangement it was a favorite of gospel singers Ethel Waters and Mahalia Jackson during the 1930s. The major modern change is the introduction of an underlying *habañera* rhythm, a widely dispersed feature of Afro-American music in the Western Hemisphere (Roberts 1974: 51–56).

"Take your time," Pastor Pearson says, turning around in his high-backed chair to address the choir. "Make it pretty, now." Not until their third selection does the choir show its virtuosity in a fast, contemporary song. The snare drum and organ begin, followed by piano, until the choir joins in singing the song's title, "I'll Be with You, That's What He Said." The third time they reach the refrain the repetition of the words, "Said it, that settles it," adds to the musical tension created by the instruments. Piano and organ have become as percussive as drum and cymbals. One soprano swoons in a faint, while surrounding choir members try to prop her up.

Their attempts are useless in the face of the continuing music. Another singer begins to shriek, jumping up and down, tearing the constraining robe off her shoulders. Closing her eyes while singing the refrain, soloist JoCarole Bradshaw can no longer hold herself back from the descending Holy Spirit. Concerned that her jerking movements are moving her precariously close to the edge of the dais, the ushers hurry to prevent her from tripping and falling. Sister Rosie, vigorously tapping her stiletto heels against the floor, yells out, "Let her go! She can't hurt herself in the Spirit."

With the instruments' pulsations, shouting spreads from the choir to the congregation. Several members to stand up and wave their uplifted palms, a joy that usually precedes trance.

Several members, seemingly on the verge of convulsions, are restrained by the ushers, who grab their arms. Their torsos and feet move backwards and forwards synchronously with the first motions of holy dance. While one usher fans the face of a convulsive member, another removes a pair of eyeglasses that may get broken in the frenzy.

"Let Him have His way!" someone says, referring to the free movement of the Holy Spirit among the congregation. The ushers and fellow members who come to the aid of another, however, are cautious of the contagious nature of shouting.

"When an individual get happy, you can feel it yourself . . . if it's real," Sister Pearson observes. She adds, as a word of warning: "You might go and put yo' hands on 'em to help, but the next thing you know, if you don't be careful, you might end up with It before it's over with."

As choir members help carry their unconscious fellows out of the choir stall into the reviving air outside, the upheaval finally dies down. Waving cardboard fans bearing colorful lithographs of Christ, Martin Luther King, Jr., or Mahalia Jackson, the congregation settles down for the continuation of the service. A congregant, not yet calmed, sporadically shouts, "Hallelujah! Thank you Jesus!" The pastor, rising slowly from his high-backed chair, comes to the pulpit. The ritual has reached its focal point: the sermon. In a reassuring, calm voice that contrasts with the preceding shouting, Pastor Pearson requests that the congregation sing "Must Jesus Bear the Cross Alone?" —composed in the seventeenth century—as he lines out the verses from the pulpit.

The singing is not a cappella—piano, bass, and organ support the congregation's voices, while Sister Millie Moore, a virtuoso soloist in the Senior Choir, takes over the lining that Pastor Pearson began. When the singing ends, the musicians continue to play, creating an instrumental dialogue among themselves; the organ and piano imitate the antiphony between pastor and congregation. The piano, with its lighter sound, calls out the line, while Sister Jackson pumps the organ's

pedals to answer in a heavy bass. Sister Pearson fans herself and nods
her head to the beauty of it all, quietly saying, "Yes. Yes."

Acknowledging that the choir sang well, Pastor reminds his hearers
that the "word of God," that is, the sermon, is the most important part
of worship. Tugging at the ends of his walrus moustache, he begins in
a barely audible voice, pausing noticeably between words as he speaks:

> We want to talk this morning
> About these things that may help the Christian
> who know God's way.
> "Love not the world neither the things that are in the world."

"Alright!" interjects Sister Jackson, voicing her agreement from her
organ bench. Other members only offer a subdued, "Um hum." In fif-
teen minutes, Pastor reaches the climax of his sermon. At one point,
he swirls around behind the pulpit and suddenly drops to one knee to
recreate a praying but betrayed Christ in the Garden of Gesthemane
on the eve of the crucifixion. His voice and language style change
dramatically. No longer spoken in slow sentences, his words now come
in gasps of breath, each gasp ending with an audible expulsion of air.
Gone is the flowery seventeenth-century English of Devotion prayers:
a vernacular Black English gradually replaces it. Pounding the lectern
at the end of each line with one hand, while cupping his left ear with
the other, Rev. Pearson listens for the response to each line:

> You'll have to work—
> "Amen"
> To make the church great—
> "Yeah!"
> If you want the church new—
> "That's alright! That's alright!"
> It won't grow no more than you 'llow it to grow—
> "Yeah!"
> Ah!
> "Amen"
> Can I get a witness?
> "Oh yes!"
> Jesus—
> "Yes?"
> Said to the little boy—
> "Yes, Lord!"
> I have need of a bowl of fishes—

"Yeah!"
I have need of five loaves of bread—
"That's alright! That's alright!"
Raise in here to be—
"Yes?"
You see

Each declaration from the audience grows more melodic. Sister Jackson answers each time, "That's alright! That's alright!" as other members in their responses seek the musical key that Pastor Pearson has been hovering around. The antiphonal rhythm between preacher and congregation has settled into a predictable pattern that allows the preacher to begin chanting his lines. Dashing from one end of the dais to the other, pointing his index finger at his hearers, and, as piano and organ imitate his speech melody, Pastor continues, taking us to the events surrounding the sermon on the mount:

> Jesus knew what he was gon' do—
> "Yes!"
> The little boy, he know what he was gon' do—
> "Oh Yes!"
> But Jesus knew about the five thousand people—
> "Amen!"
> And they had traveled a long way with him—
> "Yeah!"
> And they don't know what it's all about—
> "Sho' you right!"
> I caint let these people go back—
> "Yes!"
> Because they came a long way—
> "Yes!"
> I have to set out and feed these people—
> "Put yo' soul in it!"

Sister Rosie's stilettoes pound the floor more vehemently than ever, while cries of "Preach!" and "Alright! Tell it!" go up. Gradually the sermon draws to an end. Pastor Pearson returns to prosaic speech: "I hope you got a lesson out of our brief message this mornin'."

Without leaving the pulpit, Pastor starts singing the chorus of "Old Ship of Zion." Not waiting for him to complete the first few words, the congregation joins him in somber unison. Sister Odessa's soprano soars like a wail above the rest to sing the verses that tell of a refuge that only a secure ship like Zion provides on a rough sea. "Ain't no danger in the water," they sing, "Get on board, get on board." "Why?" cries Pastor Pearson. "She has landed many thousands," his audience responds in song. Sister Rosie, whose stilettoes can speed up no more, dashes from her pew. Her broad grin erupting into that peculiar holy laugh, "Ah ha ha!" she bounds for the sanctuary's doors. While the ushers follow her as she leaves the church in apparent trance, the older women, like Sister Pearson and her companion, Sister Reese, stoically continue the verses about the old steady ship called Zion.

"It will take you safely over," Sister Reese begins the next verse. While ships in the storm get tossed and sometimes sink, Zion perseveres, just as the two women have persevered through innumerable difficulties and impossible situations. Zion is the indomitable church that brings them back every Sunday morning to reaffirm their faith. They will persevere. That is why Sister Pearson quietly utters, "Yes, yes," and Sister Reese holds up one waving arm and sighs, "Yes, Lord!" as the verses of "Old Ship of Zion" unfold once more.

During the singing, Pastor Pearson "opens the doors to the church" by extending an invitation to anyone present to join the congregation or become a candidate for baptism. The deacons open two folding chairs before the pulpit so that new members and candidates can sit facing the congregation. The deacons then add their names to the church roll. The choir along with instruments welcomes the newcomers with a rousing "I'm So Glad Jesus Lifted Me," which expresses the congregation's joy at having embraced new members and candidates. Expected to deliver a short speech, each new member testifies why she or he wants to join the congregation or be baptized. Having said so much, the pastor and the board of deacons, hugging each new member, offer them the "right hand of fellowship." Their handshake is a welcome into the church. Thereupon, Pastor Pearson, figuring on warm weather, announces a date for the outdoor baptism in the nearby Colorado River. After the clergy and lay officers have extended this welcome, the entire congregation marches in front of the new members to shake hands and greet them. Finally, the pastor says a short benedictory prayer and the ritual is over.

In review, we note that the relatively somber mood of Devotion yields to the Service, whose rhythmic songs and sermon bring down the Holy Spirit. Through their combined artistry, singers, musicians, and preacher arouse emotion so that the Holy Spirit can enter the sanctuary by manifesting through individual congregational members. Shouting is dependent on the singing preceding the sermon. Sister Rosie comments, "The choir can kill the church service or they can help it. They can sing with no feelings . . . no clapping. If your choir is not in the Spirit when they're singing, the members out there are not gonna get It."

Likewise, the sermon owes much of its emotional quality to the rhythm and tune of the preaching. In turn, the rhythm and tune of the sermon depend on verbal repetition and audience response, which launch the preacher's words onto a new level of expression. When shouting results, members at St. John Progressive are fond of saying, "Don't give me no religion I can't feel." If Sister Pearson believes that the Holy Spirit spreads contagiously throughout the congregation, Brother Davis in a key statement explains how the Spirit enters in the first place: "You invite the Holy Spirit to come in. . . . That's why people shout." Sister Rosie explains her ecstatic behavior when she says, "I shout when the Holy Spirit comes on me. . . . I feel so joyous. I can't sit down." The satisfaction that the experience entails, according to Sister Edna McLennan—a fellow musician—is like "a burden has been lifted."

The eleven-thirty worship service is not the only one in which a somber Devotion precedes a more exuberant Service. On any given Sunday, this binary structure undergirds not only the ritual called "morning worship," described above, but also "appreciations," in which church musicians, pastor, or any members are recognized; "annuals," in which any church organization marks an anniversary other than the pastor's and church's; "anniversaries," which mark only those of the pastor and church; "musicals," where choirs from several churches present their songs; "homecomings," when members living far apart reconvene at the church; and "prayer meetings," set for Wednesday night for the teaching of Scripture. Certain Sundays are set aside for the men, women, or youth to conduct the entire worship service, including the praying, preaching, and singing. These special Sundays are called Men's, Women's, and Young Adults' days, respectively. The only rituals that do not exhibit this binary structure are rites of passage such as baptisms, weddings, and funerals, which have their own distinctive structures.

A typical Sunday may be spent in a series of programs and services, taking place within a fifty-mile radius or more. When morning worship closes at one-thirty, congregational members stand in front of the church for nearly a half hour exchanging embraces and news. When the pastor announces an afternoon event, such as a fellow pastor's anniversary out of town, members try to find out where the other pastor's church is located and how the congregation will get there. Usually a convoy of cars is decided upon and a rendezvous time set, allowing a half hour for members to hurry to lunch, usually at a fast-food establishment.

When the members reconvene, the convoy takes off a few minutes after the time agreed upon because of late arrivals. "Are we gonna party all the way?" Sister Jackson wants to know, climbing into the front seat of Sister Whitaker's car. Taking the hint, Sister Whitaker turns off the radio, which was tuned in to the popular rhythm and blues station.

"Keep your mind on things not of this world. Wasn't that Pastor's text this morning? We don't need no backsliding, now," Sister Jackson continues laughingly. Her humor conceals the seriousness of her evangelical nature. Sister Whitaker turns the wheel as the convoy leaves the asphalt parking lot, making its way to Solid Rock Baptist Church near Webberville.

She peers into the back seat. "By the way, Brother Davis, you certainly did shout this morning! The Holy Ghost was sho' nuff on you!"

"Not meanin' to cut you short, Sister Jackson," Brother Davis adds softly, "But if the Good Lord's blessed you like He's blessed me, then you've got something to shout about." The glassy new skyscrapers of the Austin skyline begin to fade into the background.

"I know that's right!" Sister Whitaker adds with zest as she follows the car ahead of her along a very lonesome stretch of highway. Winged Liberty atop the State Capitol, built by slave labor, dips below the horizon, and the ride out into the country becomes the most relaxing time of this late fall day (Takaki 1979: 123). Vistas of cows grazing next to sky-blue ponds and horses gamboling in the warm sun are enough to put the viewer to sleep.

"What are we going to sing this afternoon, Sister Jackson?" Sister Whitaker wants to know. "I thought I'd do 'Throw Out the Lifeline.'"

"Well, that's just fine. Of course Sister Millie will want to sing something. Probably 'Jesus Will Work It Out.' And that's fine too. I think the Seniors and the Young Adults oughta combine choirs and sing those old gospel numbers everyone knows." Thus the afternoon's musical repertoire is fixed on the road to Webberville.

Reaching its destination after only one wrong turn, the convoy pulls up to a wooden structure that sits at the edge of a grove of pecan trees.

St. John's members wander inside. Solid Rock Baptist has slightly peeling paint and creaking floorboards. Older members of both congregations are well acquainted with each other. Younger members try to recall just who this congregation is. Looking about the strange building, the musicians first test the instruments, listening to hear if they are in tune. Other members gaze at the potbellied wood stove standing in the middle of the room, wondering if it will push out enough heat when afternoon shadows fall. Everyone comments on how beautifully decorated are the chairs for the honored pastor and his wife. On this occasion celebrating his anniversary as pastor, the couple will face the congregation in seats lined with colorful streamers and papier-mâché flowers. Next, having surmised who the deacons, clergy, and host musicians are, St. John's members find their seats next to one another and wait for the deacon to call out the first line.

Before one of Solid Rock's deacons begins to line a hymn, Sister Sally and several other mothers go to round up their children in time for Devotion. Shaking her head, Sister Rosie comments as if delivering an omen, "If the young people were allowed to . . . take over the church, we would lose Devotion. They think Devotion is a waste of time."

After the service, food is customarily served in the fellowship hall behind the sanctuary. The meal consists of barbecued chicken, potato salad, pinto beans, red-colored punch with a single ice cube in it, and a slice of vanilla cake. St. John's members have to eat their fare quickly though, since they must attend another service—this time a musical— which they are sponsoring back in Austin.

Why the black folk church should have so many types of services is less baffling when one considers the historical role the black church has played for African-Americans. Long deprived of any other institutions for their social, economic, and political expression, black Americans during slavery and afterwards controlled the church with minimal white interference. Throughout its 250-year-history in North America, the church provided the only meeting ground for issues affecting the black community. Always excluded from mainstream society, it became the legal and extralegal court, settling disputes, making judgments, and censuring behavior when necessary (Creel 1988: 278–79). Zora Neale Hurston was aware of this role when she wrote of the black Baptist church: "You see de church punishes fuh things de law don't chastise fuh, and if iss so bad 'til de law handle it, de

church is bound tuh" (Hurston [1934] 1971: 242). It was a school for
learning the ABCs as well as manners and religious doctrine, an initiation into mystical secrets, as well as an indoctrination into adulthood (Creel 1988: 281, 288). It was a mutual aid and burial society. It
was a theater for the performing arts. The myriad programs the church
now sponsors are only a fraction of those carried on during the days of
Reconstruction and Jim Crow.

The Afro-Baptist Church

St. John Progressive Baptist exemplifies all the characteristics of
the "black folk church." I would rather use the shorter term "Afro-
Baptist" (although members at St. John Progressive never themselves
use it) because it is rich with cultural significance. This term refers to
a working-class black Baptist church that interprets biblical Scripture
found in the King James Version as God's unalterable word to humankind. In this literalist sense, Afro-Baptists are popularly thought to be
fundamentalists. Like black Pentecostals, who are also fundamentalist,
Afro-Baptists regard the occurrence of trance in the ritual as focal.
Afro-Baptists, however, belong to a church that is historically older
than the black Pentecostal movement. Founded before the American
Revolution, the Afro-Baptist church predates the Pentecostal church by
a century and a half, the latter being an urban twentieth-century revitalization phenomenon. Although black Pentecostal groups draw many of
their number from Baptist ranks, their insistence on moral and physical
purity as well as glossolalia ("speaking in tongues") as the sign
of spiritual conversion—of "being saved"—differ from black Baptist tradition. The Pentecostal ritual structure also differs from the binary pattern found in Afro-Baptist ritual (McIntyre 1976: 13–15; Paris 1982: 54).

Depending largely on the socioeconomic status of its members and
clergy, black Baptist churches differ greatly from each other in terms
of ritual expectations and behavior exhibited during the ritual. Black
middle-class Baptists who have attended college or have achieved some
material success tend to follow mainstream American values. These
church members elect a preacher who, like themselves—or as they
would like to think of themselves—is educated, the preacher with at
least some seminary training. The middle-class black Baptist ritual
differs little if at all from its white counterpart in terms of preaching

style, amount of music used for worship, and musical style heard in that worship. Above all, the middle-class black Baptist church is not fundamentalist in terms of a literal view of the Scriptures, but, like its white counterpart, insists upon a figurative, rational interpretation. The biographer of Martin Luther King, Jr. reports that the young man, newly graduated from his theological studies at Boston University and assuming a pastorship in Alabama, had this reaction: "Though a small church, [it] counted mostly middle-class folk among its membership, and it had a long tradition of an educated ministry, which King liked" (Oates 1982: 48). Little, if any, of the activity such as the constant call-and-response between preacher and congregation or sound of handclapping to rhythmic music that characterizes black working-class Baptist congregations occurs in the middle-class black Baptist ritual. Ecstatic "shouting" is absent among middle-class congregants. Indeed, if such activity should occur in a bourgeois church, the congregation would demonstrably frown upon it.

The Afro-Baptist church is historically separate from other black working-class fundamentalist churches, such as the Primitive Baptists, with whom they often join in fellowship worship services. Although the specific details of their separation are historically clouded, more is known about the white Primitive Baptists who splintered off from other separatist Baptist sects in the mid-eighteenth century just before the American Revolutionary War. Choosing to follow one Shubel Stearns, an itinerant Baptist preacher of pre-Revolutionary fame, a few white Baptists separated from the orthodox Calvinist doctrine of salvation only for a select, particular few (Sobel 1979: 84–86). They incorporated Stearns's innovation of washing each other's feet during worship rituals. During the two-hundred-year span from the 1770s to the present, some blacks were obviously converted to the Primitive Baptist Church. In today's Primitive Baptist worship services musical instrumentation may be used—albeit sparingly—but it is not encouraged. The distinctive melodic and staccato rhythmic phrasing of Primitive Baptist lined hymns is foreign to the Afro-Baptist experience.

The Afro-Baptists with whom I worshipped are Missionary Baptists whose church history, like that of the Primitive Baptists, predates the American Revolution. The Missionary movement influenced a large number of blacks throughout the entire history of North American slavery. Because eighteenth- and nineteenth-century slave owners allowed blacks converted by a Missionary clergy relative freedom and control of their worship rites, the first black Baptist converts were able to import some African forms of worship into their new Christian faith. Owing to this religious permissiveness on behalf of a plantocracy that initially attached little significance to their slaves' religious behavior, one scholar correctly states that "the Black Church, as the most important institution in the Black community, is the chief reservoir of Africanisms that have survived in the West" (Walker 1979: 19).

Because African cultural forms were allowed to continue initially among bondsmen converted to the Baptist sect, the term "Afro-Baptist," again, more aptly captures the cultural essence of the church represented mostly by the descendants of enslaved Africans than does any other designation. In sum, this term denotes that church that (1) is in the full social and economic control of African Americans, or as another scholar observes, "it is the one institution under the full ownership and operation of the Black community" (Wright 1976: 1); (2) has members and clergy who are predominantly working-class; (3) has clergy that are not seminary-trained but who are "called" to preach through some visionary or dream experience; (4) reaches back historically to the mid-eighteenth century, when the influx of Africans into North America reached its peak; (5) literally interprets Scripture rather than allowing a rational, intellectual view; (6) has remained through slavery to the present the chief social and political center in the black community. It became the major outlet for collective emotional and physical expression during a time when such expression was strictly circumscribed. A great part of that expression comes from the crucial place given to music and preaching in the Afro-Baptist church, quite unlike its counterpart in middle-class Baptist congregations. One commentator writes, "As music was central to West African culture, so is music central to the historic Black religious experience . . . the dominance of worship time—singing versus preaching—could very well be a tossup in almost any Black worship experience" (Walker 1979: 22).

Whereas Afro-Baptists prefer their music rhythmic for emotional expression, black middle-class Baptists are imitative of music that is "considered the 'best' in white church life" (Walker 1979: 24). Just as musical style is one of those psychological expressions to which Afro-Baptists give vent, the style of preaching also stems from that same black psyche. There is no better testimony to the power of the black preaching style than Martin Luther King's discovery of how to use the pulpit:

King learned to appreciate the southern Negro church as never before. Here in their church—the only place that was truly their own—black people could feel free of the white man, free of Jim Crow, free of everything. Here they could be spiritually reborn and emotionally uplifted, exhorting their preacher as he in turn exhorted them, both engaging in a call-and-response dialogue that went back to their African ancestry. (Oates 1982: 57)

Ritual Frames

Why an ecstatic Service should always be preceded by a lugubrious, archaic Devotion in Afro-Baptist tradition is puzzling. The enigma begins to unravel, however, when the observer considers both Devotion and Service as two distinct metaphoric frames. These ritual frames are the metaphoric paradigms that join to produce the ritual syntax, or structure. Within the Afro-Baptist ritual structure there are two such adjoining frames. In a sense, "frame" is like an event that is a bound segment of activity or behavior (Lawless 1982: 201). According to anthropologist James Fernandez, however, "frame" moves beyond its usual meaning of parameter of action to include a bound event that assumes affective value through the vehicle of metaphoric expression.

Believing like pioneering anthropologist Franz Boas that metaphor becomes the basis of religious ritual, Fernandez states that "metaphors, not symbol, should be considered the basic analytic unit of ritual because ritual and ritual symbols spring from metaphors" (Fernandez 1973: 1367). The metaphoric frame, by uniting such disparate entities as speech, song, and gesture, create and control desired moods over its participants (Fernandez 1974: 125). Once initiated, the metaphoric frames control participants emotionally by imposing upon them metaphoric predications, that is, new identities, in the course of the ritual. Furthermore, these metaphoric frames are not static in the ritual's development but change during the course of the rite in order to achieve the emotional transformation sought by ritual participants. Thus, the metaphoric frames move up or down an affective scale, for example, between the poles of "disparagement" (association with inferior qualities) and "adornment" (association with superior qualities) during the ritual's progression (Fernandez 1974: 123). By shifting the metaphoric predication from disparagement at the ritual's beginning along a continuum of emotion until adornment is reached at the ritual's end, the participant is borne along an affective span during the rite, finally being transformed from an initially miserable state of mind to one of emotional satisfaction. The mission of metaphor in religious ritual is to effect that transformation by presenting an image of what the participant is to become in the ritual (Fernandez 1973: 1367).

As Fernandez does, the present study will use the term "frame" to refer not only to a bound sequence of events but also to the appropriate feelings that accompany those bound actions. These feelings are the direct result of a "certain and finite class of metaphoric fillers" (Fernandez 1974: 127). The contiguity of events within a frame becomes metonymically associated, that is, associated by contact, so that all events within the same frame evoke a similar emotion. The frames, therefore, become emotional paradigms containing as fillers such behavior as a specific type of speech, song style, and gesture. These fillers create the same, associational value of emotion. The ritual, itself, is a syntactical joining of different frames much like a progression of scenarios, to use Fernandez's imagery (1974: 127). As the ritual progresses, the metaphoric frames make the identity of Lord and devotee clearer as both move towards definiteness, less abstraction. The primacy of the metaphoric frame is to plan and direct that definiteness via the participant's ritual performance. Since Afro-Baptist liturgy is not written but oral, speech and song—as metaphoric fillers—become powerful tools in keeping the frames, and consequently the ritual itself, intact.

As we will see in the following chapters, the performance of song acts in conjunction with speech to define the nonclimactic and climactic aspects of the ritual frames. The interplay of speech and song operates to maintain the parameters of this folk ritual structure. Devoid of an iconography that facilitated the syncretism of African powers with Roman Catholic saints in other parts of the diaspora, Afro-Baptist tradition placed major importance on the symbols of speech and song as vehicles of an African ethos. The historical, poetic, and prosodic relationship of speech and song within the Afro-Baptist church makes it clear that no student of this church can ignore either speech or song in an analysis of its ritual. They are mutually dependent and inextricably woven together in their combined function of preserving a ritual that has survived the corrosive effects of North American slavery.

Before looking in detail at the ritual and its language and music, however, a history of this particular church, as well as a history of its speech and song, is necessary for understanding its frames, Devotion and Service. In order to understand how the frames work, we must understand their origin and the origin of their speech and song components. In the next chapter the historical development of these frames and their fillers leads us to an answer to the enigma posed above.

2

"We Free!"
History of the Afro-Baptist Church

The origins of the Afro-Baptist church lie in the antebellum South. For the sake of clear analysis, the history of this church is best seen as developing in three stages before the Civil War. The first stage begins with the European colonization of North America in the seventeenth century and ends approximately in 1750, two decades before the American Revolutionary War. The second stage begins in the mid-eighteenth century as the first waves of the Great Awakening revival reached the American colonies. The last stage begins in the second decade of the nineteenth century, after the winding down of the Second Awakening revivals, when the ominous threats of slave insurrections convinced many planters to convert their chattel en masse. This last stage concludes with the South's military defeat by the Union army and the freeing of black bondsmen after the Civil War.

Colonial North America (1650–1750)

In the second decade of the seventeenth century European religious dissenters fled their homelands to seek religious freedom from the established churches in their countries. Both Roman Catholics and Protestants joined this exodus and arrived in North America only to find themselves once again confronting each other in a theater of religious dissension against the established ecclesiastical orders that had forced them out of Europe. The Roman Catholic Church had established itself firmly in the Maryland colony; the Calvinistic Congregational

Church rooted itself as the established denomination in New England; and the Anglicans ruled elsewhere (Jackson 1943: 7–13). Fleeing Britain were Puritans, Calvinistic Presbyterians and Congregationalists, Roman Catholics, Quakers, Moravians, Deists, and Baptists—all of whom soon discovered that the Anglicans had extended their religious control to the new colonies from London. Even German, Swedish, and Finnish Lutherans, settling what is presently Pennsylvania and New Jersey, found that England soon gained political control of these colonies and extended its church into those areas. The established churches discouraged members of other denominations from exercising religious choice (Jackson 1943: 7–13).

During the time when seventeenth-century Europeans were carving out their religious niches in North America, captive Africans, from the west coast and the central interior, also arrived in North America. In 1625 the European population in Plymouth Colony, Massachusetts was 180 while that of the Virginia Colony was 1,800, bringing the total European population of the North American British colonies to 1,980 (Southern 1983: 22). A year later eleven black Angolans arrived in New Amsterdam as indentured servants whose presence accounted for the first black population statistics in the North American colonies (Southern 1983: 22). By 1649, however, Virginia counted 15,000 whites and 300 blacks in its colonial records; and by 1650 blacks were commonplace on the streets of colonial American cities. Around the time of Bacon's Rebellion in 1677, the practice of indenturing West Africans ended, and perpetual enslavement based on a perpetual state of "black-skinned heathenism" became the rule in all colonies (Breen 1987: 109–19; Fredrickson 1981: 63, 72–80; Harding 1981: 30). Slavery for life, along with rising demands for tobacco, led to a voracious increase in the African slave trade, especially from the Bantu-speaking areas of the continent (Breen 1987: 118). By 1700 the enslavement of blacks was a legal reality in all thirteen colonies (Southern 1983: 23).

The African, coming to North America as slave and not religious dissenter, was on the periphery of the religious debacle consuming the colonists. He, instead, had his own religious cosmos to adjust to the strange, hostile reality of slavery. In constructing that worldview, Africans also had to adjust to the different tribal customs of African origin that had made the crossing with them. The diverse African ethnic groups, to be sure, did not relinquish their indigenous beliefs but were able to hold on to those cosmological views that helped to maintain their sanity and sense of order in the midst of disorder around them. Theirs was a culture "built upon the shared core of African understandings of man, spirit, and the world" (Sobel 1979: 224). Allowed certain freedom in forging a new worldview from disparate African cultures, the African in North America was able to continue in some fashion his own culture and cosmology, "particularly in folk literature and religion" (Southern 1983: 22).

The chief institution that allowed Africans of various tribal backgrounds to combine and continue their religious practices in a pan-African ritual was the clandestine plantation meeting between slaves who convened at night in "secluded places—woods, gullies, ravines, and thickets" where the risk of planter interference was lessened (Raboteau 1978: 128; Fisher 1963: 67). The purpose of these secret gatherings was multifold. They were protests against slavery, curing rituals, rites of passage marking events such as marriage and death, and communal fellowship for the suffering that slavery caused (Fisher 1963: 32). These secret meetings were more than emotional support systems in that they became the principal means of transferring esoteric African knowledge to the North American colonies for the first generations of American-born African slaves. The parents of these first generations brought "the customs of secret meetings" with them during the seventeenth century (Fisher 1963: 183). The secret meeting was called in part to train black youth in the sacred knowledge still remembered from Africa. In the meetings, songs "taught to each generation of African boys and girls" instilled the esoteric sacred wisdom that also crossed the Atlantic (Fisher 1963: 10). In West African tradition, for example, secret meetings were held under the auspices of powerful political, legal, and economic units, called "secret societies," that trained males and females separately. Transferred to the Americas, the secret meeting took over the role of the society for training children at every step in life (Creel 1988: 289–90; Fisher 1963: 77).

The slave meetings began in secrecy not because the planter feared the continuation of African beliefs but because he found any prolonged slave gathering an obstacle to running an economically productive plantation. In the North, for example, African slavery took on a relatively mild form in comparison to Southern plantation slavery. In the North small groups of blacks would work in individual shops or houses. In the colonial South, however, large groups of Africans worked under more severe pressure on large isolated, autonomous plantations that

were fiefdoms unto themselves, consumed with making money. Any
gathering of slaves that detracted from productive labor was not only
discouraged but penalized harshly. One activity that was indeed coun-
terproductive to the plantation economy was the secret meeting if it
failed to keep within "reasonable bounds," that is, if it took away the
slaves' energy to work in the fields from the following morning until
sunset (Sernett 1975: 165). The energy spent in the secret meeting
definitely siphoned off energy needed to increase the planters' wealth.
Therefore, slave owners generally outlawed such meetings by punishing all slaves who liked "to stay up all night . . . or to engage in what
appeared to be African 'devil dances'" (Sobel 1979: 170). The secret
meeting became entrenched on the plantation in spite of the planters'
opposition: "It was only by taking the risk of forbidden meetings that
they could freely continue certain quasi-African traditions. . . . They
were the highpoint of communal as well as individual emotional life:
they were the scene of spirit travels" (Sobel 1979: 170).

Because enslaved Africans and their children needed to keep these
fellowship and religious meetings secret, they invented codes and practices unknown to the planter and his staff in order to convene such
gatherings. A favorite code used was usually a song, or spiritual, such
as "Steal Away to Jesus," that told of such a meeting in words of double
meaning (Fisher 1963: 66). Although planters had occasionally
oppressed the secret meetings in the early decades of the seventeenth
century, Virginia and Maryland passed laws outlawing these meetings
on any and every plantation by the end of the century. Despite these
oppressive laws, passed in 1695, "neither outlawry nor soldiery prevented the secret meeting from having hemispheric significance" (Fisher
1963: 67). The planter was usually aware of the continuation of such
meetings, so he hired poor white males who lived near his plantation
to disperse them and beat blacks who attended them. The slave avoided
this threat by holding the meetings shortly before sunrise when whites
were still sleeping. These poor whites became known as the infamous
slave patrollers, called "paddyrollers," who took delight in routing and
beating slaves caught or suspected of being at the illegal meetings:
"Many ex-slaves remembered having been beaten for praying or
attending meetings" (Sobel 1979: 224).

Peter Randolph, a former slave in Virginia who later bought his freedom, gives a vivid account of the manner in which a secret meeting
was called and the events that took place there:

Not being allowed to hold meetings on the plantation, the slaves assemble in the swamps, out of reach of the patrols. They have an understanding among themselves as to the time and place of getting together. This is often done by the first one arriving breaking boughs from the trees, and bending them in the direction of the selected spot. . . . They first ask each other how they feel, the state of their minds, etc. The male members then select a certain space, in separate groups, for their division of the meeting . . . then praying and singing all around, until they generally feel quite happy. The speaker usually commences by calling himself unworthy, and talks very slowly, until feeling the Spirit, he grows excited, and in a short time, there fall to the ground twenty or thirty men and women under its influence. . . . The slave forgets all his sufferings, except to remind others of the trials during the past week. . . . [The meeting closes as] they pass from one another, shaking hands, and bidding each other farewell. . . . As they separate, they sing a parting hymn of praise. (Randolph 1855: 68)

The "devil dances" and "spirit travels" that the planter found so distasteful and taxing on his slaves' capacity to produce were the manifestations of African possession trance that surfaced in rituals he happened to have observed. In the words of one historian, "American blacks retained the basic concept of spirit and its power, and of the soul as a participating spirit, a concept shared by most West African peoples" (Sernett 1975: 41).

In Afro-America as in West Africa, it was "a mark of distinction to be possessed by a spirit." Enslaved Africans and their descendants continued the practice and distinction of being possessed spiritually by supernatural powers (Simpson 1978: 131). In many West African cultures spiritual mediums, or adepts, brought on spirit possession by dancing and singing until they "would go into a trance . . . and transmit the divinity's commands or advice" (Sobel 1979: 228). To Euro-American colonists, African possession trance seemed ridiculous—some form of exotic lunacy. One historian records that planters thought the behavior so ludicrous that it "was not particularly upsetting as long as it siphoned off discontent that would spill over into the social or political realm" (Sernett 1975: 165). However lightly white colonists may have regarded African possession trance, the slave was serious in his expression of spiritual feeling. As Peter Randolph wrote, "Often in the religious meetings, the visitor is caused to smile and laugh out loud, at what appears to him to be amusing, if not ridiculous. But the worshipers, perspiring at every pore, were never more serious" (Randolph 1855: 106).

Although some psychologists and anthropologists have theorized that ecstatic religious behavior in African-American revivalistic sects is a substitute for real political revolutionary action, its ancient origins point to more significant functions. The early black worshippers in the colonial South brought possession trance with them on the Middle Passage from a continent where European political colonialism had not yet become as widely entrenched as possession trance itself (Lawless 1982: 87). While possession trance may be "practiced by the politically impotent," as I. M. Lewis, the sociologist, believes, the act of possession was both a sign of personal power and a distinguishing characteristic marking the humanity of the slave from the barbarity of his owner (Lawless 1982: 87).

The religious content of those colonial secret meetings was hardly Christian. During the late seventeenth and early eighteenth centuries, American colonists in the South were uninterested in, if not opposed to, converting their chattel to Christianity for several reasons. Their paramount objection to conversion was economic: white slave owners feared that Christian values would undermine the "peculiar institution" of slavery (Burnim 1980: 54–55): "The process of slave conversion was blocked by major obstacles, not the least of which was the antipathy of the colonists themselves. The economic profitability of his slaves, not their Christianization, held top priority for the American planter" (Raboteau 1978: 98).

Fearing that Christian baptism would automatically end the institution of slavery, slave owners were at first opposed to slave conversion. Individual colonies, to ensure the owners of their property, passed legislation guaranteeing that baptism of a slave did not entail his or her freedom, arguing that a black skin—as the curse of Ham—was a sign of perpetual heathenism (Fredrickson 1981: 71–80). Even with these laws binding a converted slave to chains, the planter still regarded Christian conversion an unnecessary economic burden (Raboteau 1978: 99; Southern 1983: 40).

Another major factor preventing the Africans' immediate conversion to Christianity was the religious indifference that had settled over the North American colonies, especially in the South. This indifference stemmed from a lack of time and interest among planters and city folk in learning the Anglican catechism. On the rural, isolated plantations, the Anglican Church had no regular clergy or itinerant priests who could administer the sacraments to planter families. The few missionaries complained that slaves used their one free day, Sunday, to either cultivate their own small private gardens or socialize among themselves. Furthermore, the few Anglican missionaries were so busy attending to white families that they had to ignore possible slave converts. One missionary complained to the home church in London that he had to neglect the slaves since he had "work enough from the white folk on his hands" (Raboteau 1978: 99).

Planters also complained that Africans were too "brutish" to understand the concepts of Christianity, and efforts to overcome the linguistic and cultural barriers between master and slave would not be worth the time spent in trying to instruct them in theological complexities (Burnim 1980: 54–55; Raboteau 1978: 100; Roberts 1989: 138). In addition to being a waste of time, the planters argued that conversion would make their chattel proud and lazy if the latter thought they were the moral equals of whites (Raboteau 1978: 103; Southern 1983: 40). Despite the planters' objections, the Anglican Church in London organized the Society for the Propagation of the Gospel in Foreign Parts to the Heathens (SPG) in 1701 to convert slaves and Indians in North America while providing regular instruction and churches to white colonists.

Before mid-century, the SPG was failing dismally in its efforts to win black converts while supplying the needs of white families. From the bondsmen's point of view, there was nothing to be gained by conversion: a slave did not become free by becoming Christian. Disappointed by the false hope of emancipation upon baptism, enslaved blacks adamantly rejected efforts to convert them (Roberts 1989: 138). From London's point of view, not only did the SPG lack money to carry out its intended program of building more churches in the rural South, the Anglican Church overestimated the patience of its Southern members for learning catechism: "The importance of the scriptural word . . . encouraged literacy and religious learning . . . [and] becoming Christian was seen as a process of careful nurture and slow growth" (Raboteau 1978: 120). The SPG made little impression on blacks, who were forbidden to read but had to memorize the Apostles' Creed, the Lord's Prayer, and the Ten Commandments by rote before becoming converted (Roberts 1989: 138). Africans and planters alike became bored with the efforts of the Anglican Church: "There was little church drama . . . it was a generally dull and dreary affair" (Sobel 1979: 64).

The discrepancies between African worldview and Anglican belief were probably insurmountable. Whereas the African saw all nature as "permeated by the holy," the Anglican had reduced the holy to a "moral-ethical dimension" foreign to Africa (Roberts 1989: 138–39; Sobel 1979: 58–60). The Anglican Church had rationalized the animistic "magic" out of religion. Adding to this drabness, "the absence from Christian ritual of drumming, dancing, sacrifice, and possession would have been keenly felt by most Africans" (Raboteau 1978: 127). Instead of converting to Christianity, colonial blacks rejected the Anglican Church by refusing instruction (Burnim 1980: 54–55; Sobel 1979: 41).

The SPG did make a few inroads into slave religiosity, if only on a minuscule scale by presenting the Christian cosmology to the African, who realized that his indigenous beliefs and those of his captors were not completely incompatible. Both religious systems were monotheistic, believing in a supreme being. From the African perspective, both appeared to accept a pantheon of deities: the Holy Trinity and Satan for Anglicans and various divinities in diverse olympiads for West Africans (Mbiti 1969: 36, 76; Raboteau 1978: 127; Wallace 1966: 190; Zahan 1979: 3–5). Both believed in an afterlife and worshipped their spiritual powers with prayer and adoration (Raboteau 1978: 127). By being the first Christian church to present its dogma to the enslaved African, the Anglican Church paved the way for more successful proselytization of the bondsman in North America. By the mid-eighteenth century, however, slaves on the Southern plantations looked to their secluded meeting for religious strength, much as their African ancestors had regarded initiation rites, in which "the initiates must leave the community to fast and suffer as a symbol of their deaths; later they return in joy, reborn" (Sobel 1979: 15).

The Revival Periods (1750–1822)

In England at the beginning of the eighteenth century a religious storm was brewing that blew ashore in New England in 1738 with the arrival of the Reverend George Whitefield (Pipes 1951: 60; Raboteau 1978: 128; Sobel 1979: 102–4). Whitefield, a powerfully loud speaker who used dramatic gestures to arouse and strike fear in his audience, preached without a prepared manuscript. Traveling up and down the seaboard of the American colonies, Whitefield electrified his hearers with his whining voice because, as he explained, "the Christian world was in a dead sleep and . . . nothing but a loud voice can awaken them out of it" (Pipes 1951: 61). The age of revival thus became known as the Great Awakening, which spelled the end of Anglican complacency, Anglican control of the colonies, the SPG, and, eventually, England's rule over the North American colonies themselves (see Alho 1976: 51). Although the early colonial religious dissenters were only loosely allied, if at all, this Great Awakening united them against the established order of religious denominations.

The Great Awakening "raged intermittently throughout a long generation before the Revolutionary War and another generation after" (Jackson 1943: 11). Whitefield's dramatic oratory sparked a host of other preachers who traveled the seaboard circuit preaching their "fire and brimstone" warnings to colonists to awaken from their stupor. Jonathan Edwards became famous as an Awakening preacher in New England; Samuel Davies and Whitefield preached in both North and South; Shubel Stearns, the founder of the foot-washing Primitive Baptists, preached mainly in North Carolina; and the Tennent brothers preached in New Jersey and Pennsylvania.

These preachers held revivals wherever they traveled, and they renamed their converts, as well as themselves, "New Lighters." With a philosophy radically opposed to Anglican elitism in religion, the New Lighters succeeded in bringing upon themselves the opprobrium and censure of the established order wherever they went. Harvard and Yale colleges condemned the "ravings" of Whitefield, whom they called a "barbarian"; and various colonial governments enacted laws to prosecute and persecute New Light evangelists (Jackson 1943: 12–13). The religious elitism that the New Lighters attacked was the Calvinist doctrine of double predestination, the cornerstone of many established churches. This doctrine held that only a small number of elite Christians were saved from damnation. Everyone else, despite efforts to the contrary, was hopelessly doomed to burn in hell. The New Lighters preferred the doctrine of Arminianism, which preached an egalitarian paradise where salvation was available to all humankind alike, regardless of class, color of skin, or status as free individual or slave. The New Lighters angered Anglicans by insisting on "believer's" rather than infant baptism. Using emotionalism to draw a crowd, these preachers called for sobriety, condemned alcoholic beverages along with fancy clothes, gambling, dancing, and cursing—that is, everything associated with the wealthy and planter classes. As one historian states, "Practically everything these evangelists did was highly offensive to instituted religion (Jackson 1943: 11)."

Before the Revolutionary War, these Arminian or separatist Presbyterians, Methodists, and Baptists split from their established churches and in a united effort invaded the South, recruiting poor whites and slaves to their ranks. Their hearers swooned under revival tents as the preachers "came to God with noise and celebration, inviting the masses and being joined by them" (Sobel 1979: 83–84). These revivals, which became known as camp meetings, were important for three reasons. The first was that they provided struggling whites with a religious outlet for their economic frustration and political impotence in the face of the power of the planters, who bought up fertile farmland, leaving poorer whites either landless or dependent upon sandy soil (Owsley [1949] 1982: 34). The second phenomenon is that these same poor whites, who formed the ranks of the slave patrols, began to welcome blacks, slave and free, to their camp meetings. The third phenomenon is that blacks and whites together were converted to this new brand of emotional Christianity by becoming overwhelmed by the Holy Spirit. Catechism and dogma were no longer requirements for Christian conversion. A direct conversion experience, that is, a trancelike vision of the divine which forced one to behave bizarrely, was the only proof of conversion as a New Lighter (Bruce 1974: 50–51; Raboteau 1978: 128; Sobel 1979: 84).

The New Lighters "welcomed blacks to revival meetings, for blacks clearly helped to build the emotional excitement and bring down the spirit" (Sobel 1979: 98). Oftentimes, blacks outnumbered whites at these revivals (Southern 1983: 83–84). If whites were amazed by the vigorous trance behavior of blacks in attendance, blacks were no less amazed by the fainting, groaning, and barking of whites undergoing trance (Bruce 1974: 52). For the first time since they had been in North America, Africans and their descendants witnessed religious behavior in whites that was somewhat similar to their own. However, major differences in trance behavior, which the revivalists called "shouting," existed between black and white revivalists:

> The ecstatic "shouts" of blacks . . . were not unknown to whites. Davenport [white] and his followers were known for their screamings, crying, swooning, and fits. . . . At revivals, white shouts became the norm. . . . There was clearly a white shout, although it was occa-

sionally called the "singing exercise" . . . in which the sound issued
entirely from the breast, and not the nose or throat . . . it is likely
that American whites developed their attenuated form, which had
European roots under the unconscious influence of black practices.
The black form of the shout is far more ritualized and . . . is clearly
an African form which was brought to America and penetrated by
Christian meaning. (Sobel 1979: 140)

Other differences existed between whites and blacks who shouted
at revivals. For whites who wanted to join the New Lighter fold, the
requisite experience of trance was a traumatic encounter that one had to
bear only once, since this trauma need not ever be repeated as proof of
one's devotion to New Light Arminianism. Whites generally feared the
awesome requirement of experiencing trance and were glad when the
experience was over. To blacks, however, shouting was a welcomed
experience that could be repeated as often as the believer attended a revival meeting. George Eaton Simpson, an ethnologist of Afro-American
religious rituals in the western hemisphere, describes the difference
between black and white trance behavior at the revivals in this manner:

The minister condemned the wickedness of his hearers and portrayed
Hell in vivid terms. Listeners felt guilty and were afraid; they wept,
shouted, prayed, fell on the ground, shook in every joint, barked like
dogs, and burst into a "holy laugh." The leaders of Neo-African
ancestral and revivalist cults . . . do not frighten their followers into
a state of possession. It is a mark of distinction to be possessed by
a spirit. (Simpson 1965: 109)

Another distinction between white and black forms of trance exhibi-
tion was the spasmodic muscular jerking in the neck and shoulders
of African-American revivalists, which was absent in the movements
of their mostly Scotch-Irish counterparts at these brush arbor meetings
(Simpson 1965: 110).

The effect of the Great Awakening revivals upon enslaved blacks
was that these gatherings brought Christian doctrine, although heretical to the established denominations, within their hearing and allowed
some blacks to preach to white and black crowds (Raboteau 1978: 150).
In fact, the Reverend Francis Asbury, the outspoken abolitionist preacher
who was also a Methodist bishop, often turned his pulpit over to his
assistant, Black Harry, who had an uncanny ability to win black and
white converts (Raboteau 1978: 148). The various New Light sects

brought enslaved blacks to conversion in large numbers because their doctrine espoused the abolition of slavery and an egalitarianism that appealed to slaves humiliated and demeaned by the "peculiar institution." Uneducated blacks could assume the responsibility of preaching since New Lighters condemned the intellectual elitist notion that preachers must be trained and educated. Instead, the New Lighters insisted that their preachers must be "called" by God and not trained by men (Jackson 1943: 29).

Although separatist—that is, New Light Presbyterian, Lutheran, Methodist, and Baptist—sects vied for supremacy at the revivals, the Baptists had the greatest influence on the slave and won most black converts. The attractions of the Baptist sect were many. One significant attraction that it held was its incorporation of magical power into church doctrine, which the Anglican Church had replaced with a rational-ethical approach. According to Baptist fanaticism, the mystical body of Christ enabled a convert to heal and prophesy (Sobel 1979: 82).

An even more powerful attraction of the Baptist sect for blacks was the rite of total immersion baptism—the candidate was submerged in water instead of merely sprinkled. Total immersion closely resembled African water rites. Blacks "were responding to this ritual as an initiation rite . . . that the Methodists could not provide" (Roberts 1974: 166; Sobel 1979: 130).

The most significant attraction of the Baptists was that its churches were governed by the autonomous body of each congregation, who did not have to submit to any jurisdictive hierarchy. Presbyterians, Lutherans, and Methodists were governed by an overseeing authority that could appoint preachers to specific congregations, or, likewise, remove clergy of whom the authority did not approve. Baptist congregations governed themselves. Even black congregations had a certain freedom from white intervention when they began to surface during and shortly after the Revolutionary War: "Independent black churches were members of white associations and yet functional with much self-determination" (Sobel 1979: 128-29). White control over these black Baptist churches was only nominal: "[T]he Baptist associations [white] were technically no more than mutual aid societies" (Sobel 1979: 128–29).

The single most important outgrowth of the Great Awakening was that blacks who had been converted at the revivals formed their own independent congregations, thereby beginning the political, social, and economic autonomy of the Afro-Baptist church.

The first Afro-Baptist church to organize was pastored by David George, a slave who inherited his small church in Silver Bluff, South Carolina from a white preacher named Palmer. His first congregants were eight slaves from the Galphin plantation (Raboteau 1978: 139). This church was founded with George as its leader in 1774, a year before the war of independence from Britain. Another black pioneer preacher was George Liele, a former slave who founded the Yama Craw Baptist Church near Savannah, Georgia just before the British Army reached Georgia. Andrew Bryan, a black disciple of Liele, founded the First African Baptist Church in Savannah in 1788. He was later imprisoned for doing so and his congregation received floggings at the hands of neighboring whites (Harding 1981: 44). In the North, black members of white Baptist congregations separated and formed their own churches since whites continued to segregate and humiliate them. In 1808 Thomas Paul organized the Abyssinian Baptist Church in New York City, while in that same year the First African Baptist Church was founded in Philadelphia (Southern 1983: 72). In Petersburg, Virginia black members left the white First Baptist Church and formed their own congregation between 1788 and 1809, calling their new church Gillfield Baptist Church (Raboteau 1978: 139).

W.E.B. DuBois questioned the Christianity of these first Afro-Baptist congregations. In his 1903 essay, "The Negro Church," he wrote, "It was not at first by any means a Christian Church, but a mere adaptation of those heathen rites which we roughly designate by the term Obe [sic] Worship, or 'Voodooism'" (Pipes 1951: 55). In spite of their Christian veneer, the first Afro-Baptist congregants retained many of the African characteristics of worship that their forebears had imported with them. One writer remarks that "the great bulk of the slaves were scarcely touched by Christianity, their religious practices being vastly more African than Christian" (Stuckey 1987: 37). In fact, so alive were congregants' identification with distinct regions and tribes in Africa that Denmark Vesey was able to organize his famous slave insurrection in the early nineteenth century around the tribal groups in the church that he pastored. He grouped Angolas, Ibos, and native-born blacks under appropriate leaders (Sobel 1979: 36).

The Second Revival period saw a deeper Christian penetration into slave religion. In 1799 the Great Awakening moved across the Appalachians to the western frontier of the new United States: the territories of western Pennsylvania and New York, and Ohio in the North;

Kentucky, Tennessee, and Alabama in the South. The poor white settlers, mostly of Scotch-Irish descent, took the revivals with them as they were gradually uprooted by the encroaching planter class and rich Northern land speculators and forced into unsettled western territories and the public domain (Bruce 1974: 13; Jackson 79; Owsley [1949] 1982: 34–36). Kentucky became the center for outdoor revival meetings that drew much larger crowds than the Great Awakening revivals on the seaboard had done. Caravans of revivalists journeyed great distances in covered wagons or on foot to attend these meetings, which were great social events as well as a religious experience. The revival scene was one of contradictions: whites and blacks alike, traveling for miles, would engage in horse racing, gambling, drinking, and fighting at religious carnivals whose purpose was to ban such activity. For slaves, the large camp meetings were occasions to see relatives who had been sold to other plantations and separated from family members. The revival meeting was a joyous once-a-year event that was anticipated with great excitement.

At the first western revival, which met in 1801 at Cane Ridge, Kentucky, 3,000 whites and blacks convened under the shade of trees as they drew their covered wagons in a circle to form the boundary of the campsite. They shouted, barked, and jerked with an enthusiasm never matched at an East Coast revival. An observer relates that the large crowd collapsed for hours during the preachings, paralyzed with emotion. Some of the followers ran off into the surrounding woods shouting in an agony of spiritual despair (Jackson 1943: 81). The evangelical force of these camp meetings was directed at converting the whole frontier to New Light plainfolk doctrine—the rudiments of a manifest destiny: the frontier must be "saved." By drawing everyone into their philosophy, the converts hoped to ensure social stability in a wild, chaotic frontier where lawlessness was the rule (Bruce 1974: 50). Religious, ecstatic conversion—whether in the form of fainting, jerking, barking, or screaming—was taken as proof that the participant wanted to belong to a self-controlled, socially stable group that shunned the socially disruptive activities of gambling, fighting, and getting drunk.

Because these camp meetings always convened in an orchard where overhanging brush or tree boughs provided maximum shade during the warm months, the western revival meetings became known as "brush arbors" (Jackson 1943: 79). Although the New Light Presbyterians had initiated the first brush arbor, the Baptists and Methodists quickly gained control and dominated the meetings. The bombastic, anti-intellectual preachings and shouting proved distasteful to even New Light Presbyterians, who were socially closer to the plantocracy. Because of their elitist leanings, the Presbyterians withdrew from the frenzied camp meetings, where black and white converts writhed with religious fervor (Bruce 1974: 51).

The western revivals differed from the earlier Great Awakening gatherings not only in level of emotional intensity but also in their attitude toward slaves. Whereas the earlier revivals were not racially segregated in the South, the western camp meeting required blacks to sit behind the pulpit while whites faced the preacher. As the Baptist and Methodist heretics became more accepted into planter society, their iconoclasm gave way to a more conformist ideology. The former separatist sects became major southern denominations that eventually supplanted the Anglican Church as the ruling denominations in the antebellum South. Many of the converts who had attacked the peculiar institution were now planters themselves and supported the enslavement of blacks (Burnim 1980: 56; Bruce 1974: 54–55; Sobel 1979: 84–86). By 1840, when the brush arbors had all but disappeared, the separatist Baptists and Methodists had rejoined the orthodox denominations from which they had split before the Revolution.

The revivals exposed blacks in greater numbers to elements of Christian worship, which they took back to the slave quarters. One such element was camp meeting terminology. For example, "saint," was used to refer to a New Lighter; "sinner," to a nonmember of the New Light congregation; "mourner," to a guilt-stricken sinner; and "backslider," to a member who returned to the world of sin. This same terminology has survived among today's Afro-Baptists, as well as other fundamentalist churches. Another element that blacks were exposed to was the bombastic sermon delivered by an uneducated preacher who condemned sinners to eternal hellfire. So impressive were these sermons that many blacks became famous preachers who preached to both white and black audiences. Among them were George Liele, Andrew Bryan, Black Harry, John Jasper, Peter Randolph, and Joe Willis, a former slave who was the first Protestant to preach a sermon in the Louisiana Territory outside of New Orleans (Sobel 1979: 193).

Blacks also heard the songs of the plainfolk describing the beauties of the afterlife—their hope following an earthly existence that was harsh and unfair. The religious songs of the camp meetings stressed a desire to leave this sinful world where no justice for the oppressed could be found. Both slaves and indigent whites felt the planter's oppression. It was not until the mid-1800s that the plainfolks' resentment towards the planter would also include his black chattel (Takaki 1971: 114–16). Although poor whites always had the conflicting hope that they would someday become planters—many rich slave owners had begun in this way—black revivalists found this proposition hopelessly remote (Bruce 1974: 102; Takaki 1971: 62).

The most important element that blacks retrieved from the brush arbor was the order of the worship service, that is, the ritual structure of the camp meeting. On the second day of the meeting, all the people who had sojourned to this clearing in the woods would gather on the main ground. The congregation would begin the ritual by singing a spiritual in unison, then one of the preachers would pray. After the initiatory prayer, one of the lesser preachers would deliver a lesson, followed by testimonials from individuals in the congregation. The main sermon came after these testimonials. The ritual would close with hymn singing after the sermon. A summary of this ritual order follows:

1. opening spiritual by congregation;
2. prayer by lesser preacher;
3. lesson by lesser preacher;
4. testimonials from congregation;
5. sermon by main preacher;
6. closing hymn-singing by congregation.

As a result of conversion, more independent black churches, mostly Afro-Baptist, sprang up throughout the South, where the largest Afro-Baptist congregations were to be found. By the end of the second period of the Revivals in 1822, thirty-seven Afro-Baptist churches existed in the United States, most of them in the South (Sobel 1979: 187–88). The end of this period coincided with three terrifying domestic slave uprisings, and a successful slave revolt in Haiti, whose repercussions threatened the autonomy and very existence of black churches in the South (Harding 1981: 94–100; Takaki 1979: 121). As one historian writes, "The Vesey revolt of 1822 . . . put all black religious expression into question" (Sobel 1979: 187–88). Because of the Vesey, Turner, and Prosser attempts at rebellion, all of which were blamed on the black church, almost every Afro-Baptist church had the choice of either becoming a part of a white church that would supervise its activities or dissolving itself. Terror of black rebellion running deep, most slave states legislated against black preaching. Mississippi's statute, passed after the Turner insurrection in 1831, stipulated: "It is unlawful for any slave, free Negro, or mulatto to preach the gospel upon pain of receiving thirty-nine lashes upon the naked back of the . . . preacher" (Harding 1981: 102).

In order to survive, the Afro-Baptist church became "invisible"; that is, it often attached itself to a larger white congregation. This subservient status, however, was usually fictitious. White preachers and their congregations were too preoccupied with their own church problems to interfere with the affairs of Afro-Baptists. The white supervisors "therefore often disregarded them [Afro-Baptists], while others sincerely sought to protect black churches by reducing their visibility. Still others saw black churches with one eye and denied their existence with the other" (Sobel 1979: 187). Since many Afro-Baptist churches did not keep records and had to conceal their existence from restrictive southern laws, the early nineteenth-century Afro-Baptist church in the South was "a 'hidden institution' that could not be revealed" (Sobel 1979: 187).

Most slaves seldom attended a brush harbor or church. Secret gatherings, however, were still flourishing on plantations: "Secret meetings were in the ascendancy among American Negroes during the first half of the nineteenth century" (Fisher 1963: 73). The masses of plantation slaves flocked to their own secret meetings, which they called "hush harbors," patterning the name on the white camp revival. As the black name implies, these convocations were highly clandestine and not approved by the planter (Raboteau 1978: 215). The content of the hush harbors had changed since Africans first arrived in North America. No longer able to recall the African lore and cultural wisdom, third, fourth, and fifth generations of Africans born in the United States "were too far scattered . . . to retain much of their language, myths, and traditions, or to keep alive their African culture" (Pipes 1951: 63).

Bits of Christian doctrine and ritual that slaves had gathered from the camp meetings and tales of Christian practices that seeped down to the slave masses became the new legends and traditions of the hush harbors:

> [T]he slave welcomed Christianity (especially of the Methodists and the Baptists), for to these Africans, cut off from their country and

their former tribesmen, it gave a historical tradition, a literature, and
a background all at once. . . . And from this somewhat grim Protes-
tantism of the eighteenth and nineteenth centuries the Negro's religion of the present day derives. (Pipes 1951: 63)

The slaves' acceptance of a fragmented Christian doctrine and ritual
practice, however, did not totally displace African custom, which still
formed a cultural substratum during the whole history of the secret
meeting. One historian reports that "black Christianity was to use many
of these African forms, especially those once involved in the communal celebrations of initiations and death, investing them with new meaning and purpose" (Sobel 1979:74). The events in the black secret meeting began with focus on African initiation and ritual events, which were
conducted in a furtive, ad hoc manner to avoid planter detection. By
the early nineteenth century, the plantation hush harbor had evolved
into an amalgam of African initiation practices and camp meeting
Christianity.

The Missionary Movement (1822–1865)

With the decline of revival fervor and the rise of slave insurrections,
southern white preachers, spearheaded by Charles Colcock Jones and
Charles Cotesworth Pinckney, launched an ambitious effort directed
towards planters to Christianize their slaves. Jones, a wealthy Georgia
slave owner, knew that most slaves on the plantation had missed the
camp meeting revivals and the Christian doctrines that they espoused
(Fisher 1963: 135; Raboteau 1978: 150). He argued that slaves who
embraced Christianity would make more obedient servants less ready
to rebel, while the effort to convert them would justify the peculiar
institution in the face of the abolitionists. This effort would substantiate planters' claims that they were interested in the salvation of the
slaves' souls. Ensuring the institution of slavery while assuaging guilt,
the planter along with the missionary began constructing sheds on the
plantations where slaves could learn to worship the Christian God.
Located at the beginning of the principal "street," or main thorough-
fare through the quarters, these plantation shanties became known as
"praise houses," where itinerant white clergy from the Baptist, Methodist, and Presbyterian churches would preach to a slaveowner's prop-

erty (Creel 1988: 277). The missionary's duty was strictly to justify slavery to the slave by using biblical examples of the rightfulness of submission. Ephesians 6:5, a favorite biblical verse of the missionary, directs: "Servants, be obedient to them that are your masters according to the flesh, with fear and trembling, in singleness of your heart, as unto Christ" (Raboteau 1978: 151).

This missionary outreach to slaves affected black religion more deeply than either revival period had done. No longer did blacks have to travel long distances to a camp meeting (if their master so allowed). The preacher now came to them, slaves, to teach the rudiments of Christian dogma and to perform Christian ritual before their eyes. Of course a member of the planter's family was usually present at these praise house meetings to make sure that rebellion was not the evening's topic, even when a white clergyman was in charge.

The founders of the mission program composed several catechisms for the slave, usually written in simplified language so that the illiterate slave, according to the thinking of the white clergy, could understand its lessons and prayers. The first slave catechism, written by John Mines, was titled *The Evangelical Catechism, or a plain and easy system of the principal doctrines and duties of the Christian religion. Adapted to the use of Sabbath schools and families: with a new method of instructing those who cannot read.* The innovative method of teaching slaves, contained in Charles Colcock Jones's *Instruction for Negroes in the United States*, was to have them repeat in unison the answer to a teacher's question after the teacher, himself, supplied it (Jones 1842: 68). Another slave catechist, the Reverend Dalco of Charleston, composed an Episcopal catechism whose purpose was "to show from the Scriptures of the Old and New Testaments, that slavery is not forbidden by the Divine Law: and at the same time, to prove the necessity of giving religious instruction to our Negroes" (Jones 1842: 69).

In his manual for the instruction of slaves, Jones stipulated a ritual structure that the praise-house meeting should follow, probably because of its simplicity and general acceptance in white Protestant worship. Upon careful inspection, his outline of events for an appropriate ritual appears to be a slightly modified version of the camp meeting structure of a few decades earlier (see page 49). In all likelihood, Jones's ritual structure evolved quite effortlessly from the brush arbor ritual that spawned the major Protestant denominations in the South. His praise house ritual structure is as follows:

1. opening (hymn and prayer);
2. scripture;
3. singing (hymn);
4. sermon or lesson;
5. close (prayer and hymn).

Slaves attended the white-supervised missionary services and schools when the owner allowed. Even though whites did not always have time or interest in supervising praise house meetings (Creel 1988: 284), it is believed that slaves continued the tradition of secret gatherings.

> [L]ocal plantation churches or meeting houses were very common in the last period of slavery. . . . The fact that many reports of hidden meetings come from the same plantations where slaves were allowed to go to church . . . suggests one of the reasons for this seeming inconsistency. In part, blacks wanted secret meetings. They wanted to continue the tradition of secret societies and to preserve their privacy and proprietary interest in their own practices. They could not do this in overseer or owner-supervised meetings. (Sobel 1979: 169)

More plantation blacks came into contact with Protestant Christianity because of the plantation missionaries. With a ritual structure inherited from the camp meeting and the missionary clergy, slaves returned to their secret meetings to seek religious fulfillment that the praise house could not offer. As a direct consequence of the hush harbor, the Afro-Baptist church became, even before the Civil War, "the first institution to be controlled solely by blacks, and it has remained their most powerful institution up to the present time" (Southern 1983: 72). By the end of slavery in the United States, there were 106 independent Afro-Baptist churches in the country, most of them in the South (Sobel 1979: 187).

The Afro-Baptist Church in Texas

Before the Civil War, most Afro-Baptists and their descendants came to Texas enslaved. Although African slavery existed as early as 1816 under Spanish rule in what was to become the state of Texas, it was not a vital part of Spain's economy. When the United States's ban on the African slave trade went into effect in 1808, pirates Louis d'Aury and Jean Laffitte brought shiploads of Africans to the Texas port of Galveston, where they were illegally smuggled to the New Orleans slave block (Barr 1973: 14). Other than as profitable contraband, Spanish Texas had little use for slaves (Barr 1973: 13). In fact, Spanish Texas provided a refuge for runaway slaves and free African-Americans who wanted to escape the oppression of living in the United States (Barr 1973: 4–6, 11; Campbell 1989: 11; Siverthorne 1986: 191): "[T]he number of bondsmen in Spanish Texas was always far too small to give the institution a significant hold on the province" (Campbell 1989: 10).

Not until the coming of slave-holding Anglo settlers did African slavery grow in Texas (Barr 1973: 15). Anglo settlers in United States territories in Arkansas illegally slipped across the Mexican (Texas) border at the Red River, bringing their slaves and cattle with them into northern Texas (Campbell 1989: 12). In spite of Mexico's opposition to slavery, the Anglo colonists relied upon slavery for an increased production of sugarcane and cotton. In 1833 Stephen Austin declared that Texas must be a slave territory (Campbell 1989: 32–34). Although Texas could have prospered as a free territory, it could not have done it "in the most immediately profitable way" (Campbell 1989: 34).

Planters from slave-holding states were bringing their human chattel to Austin's land-grant. However, because of the fear that the Mexican ruler, Santa Ana, would free slaves once in Texas, few Anglo settlers who depended upon the peculiar institution came to the territory. Fear of the Mexican ruler was so great that some settlers thought that, after freeing their slaves, Santa Ana would in turn enslave them under Mexican rule. This fear coupled with the threat that Santa Ana would set Indian marauders against them led the Anglo settlers to revolt.

Their fears were not completely unfounded. In 1836 Santa Ana proclaimed enslaved blacks in Texas free as he prepared to invade the territory from the south, using runaway slaves as guerrilla fighters (Campbell 1989: 42; Harding 1981: 108). Some bondsmen escaped to Santa Ana's army. Those who refused to leave their Anglo owners found themselves in permanent servitude after the defeat of Santa Ana's troops, despite subsequent insurrections and attempts to escape (Barr 1973: 32–34; Harding 1981: 108, 162, 196–98).

From the end of the war with Mexico in 1836, known as the Texas Revolution, to the Civil War, slavery grew rapidly in Texas. No longer afraid to bring their slaves to a territory where they might be emancipated, Anglo settlers followed the example of Ashbel Smith—later a prominent statesman—who migrated from the United States and bought slaves once in Texas. Others brought their chattel with them. Thousands of African descendants and most Texas Anglos lived "east of a line extending from the Red River at approximately the 98th meridian southward to the mouth of the Nueces River on the Gulf of Mexico" (Barr 1973: 17; Campbell 1989: 2).

After Texas declared its independence from Mexico, African slavery doubled within four years, the slave population growing much faster than the white (Barr 1973: 17). By 1861, on the eve of the Civil War, the slave population had increased by 455 percent! Texas had become so dependent on slavery that in 1840 the Texas Congress adopted a law—which President Sam Houston delayed signing until 1845—demanding that all "free persons of color" leave the state (Barr 1973: 9). In 1859 Texas Justice Oran M. Roberts declared, "Negroes are, in this country, *prima facie* slaves. . . . If they are dissatisfied with their condition, and have a right to be free, our courts are open to them. . . . As long as they fail to do so, they recognize this *status* as slaves" (Campbell 1989: 112). By 1858 the few free blacks in Texas constituted such a threat to slavery by their very existence that legislators passed a law allowing them to voluntarily enslave themselves to a master for life (Campbell 1989: 113).

The increase in the African-American population was limited to three areas in Texas: the Gulf Coast along the Brazos and Colorado Rivers, east Texas, and northeast Texas. The Texan slavery empire was confined to the eastern third of the state. Some blacks in Texas managed to live beyond the fringe of slavery as illegal citizens. These were mainly the black cowboys who worked in south Texas and migrated to west Texas and into the Panhandle (Dunham and Jones 1965: 29; Jordon 1981: 143–44). Many of these cowhands had been former slaves, or had worked cattle as free men on the Texas coastal plains for slave owners (Barr 1973: 19–20). However, their numbers never became greater than 4 percent of the total cowboy workforce (Campbell 1989: 124; Jordon 1981: 74, 50, 122, 143).

Because of several factors, the African-American population of central Texas remained relatively sparse. First, Indian hostility discouraged white settlement and the importation of slaves in central and west Texas. Secondly, because central and western Texas are more arid, these areas were not conducive to cotton agriculture; and slaves could not be used as herdsmen lest they escape on horseback. Thirdly, even if cotton could have been grown on the rich black soil of central Texas, the lack of windmills, which had not yet been developed, barbed wire, and a railroad precluded the extension of fenced in, well-watered cotton fields. Fourthly, central and west Texas were too close to the Mexican border for slave owners to keep their property from escaping. During the 1840s Mexico encouraged black runaways and Indians to form militias along its border to keep Anglo settlers from advancing into Mexico and claiming more land. By 1851 three thousand slave runaways had crossed the Rio Grande (Barr 1973: 28–32). By the eve of the Civil War, central Texas contained only 12 percent of the total black population of the state, most of whom worked on small farms of twenty laborers rather than on large plantations as on the coast (Barr 1973: 19, 24; Campbell 1989: 58–64; Silverthorne 1986: 213–16).

When war broke out, Texas had almost 200,000 slaves and their numbers were growing (Campbell 1989: 213; Silverthorne 1986: 191). Unlike other regions of the Confederate South, Texas was seen as a refuge against the Union Army. Slave owners believed that here slavery was least likely to be disturbed by the events of the Civil War: the state's geographic location made it least likely to be invaded by Union troops. Neither would slaves be able to desert to the Union army. By 1862 slave owners from as far away as Tennessee, Mississippi, and Missouri were removing their human property there. Most of the white refugees, however, did not settle in central Texas, which they found too crude. Leaving their central Texas holdings, including slaves, under the auspices of an overseer, they moved to the eastern third of the state along the Brazos and Trinity Rivers (Campbell 1989: 244–45; Silverthorne 1986: 200).

With the end of the war, slavery ended even as it had begun to extend into the central and west Texas plains. While the plantocracy were few in number, they produced 90 percent of the state's cotton. They were the office holders. The white middle-class majority who owned few if any slaves supported the Confederate effort throughout the war. The slaves themselves were minimally involved in supporting the Union. Arriving in the state as property to be hidden away from Union invasion and attack, blacks in central and west Texas could not participate in the struggle for their freedom as did blacks in other parts of the South. On the remote edge of black settlement, African-Americans in Texas supplied the Union Army with only 47 soldiers compared to 98,594 black Union soldiers from other slave states (Campbell

1989: 248). Cut off from the mainstream of black activity elsewhere, African-Americans secluded in central Texas held on tenaciously—perhaps more so than in any other region—to those practices that provided their identity.

One of those practices was religious ritual. Belonging to the major Protestant denominations of their owners, bondsmen were mainly Methodists and Baptists. While the Methodists were the largest white denomination in Texas, blacks, numbering in the thousands, were overwhelmingly Baptist for reasons discussed earlier in the chapter (Campbell 1989: 171; Silverthorne 1986: 158–59). With their owners, slaves attended church, where they were made to sit in specially designated pews in the balcony or in the rear (Barr 1973: 22). Sometimes special afternoon services were held for them. As in other parts of the South, white and black plantation families traveled up to fifty miles to attend camp meeting revivals, which could last up to four days, starting on Thursday and ending on Sunday night (Silverthorne 1986: 164). Some meetings lasted ten days. Sunday night culminated in frenzy and trance—both blacks and whites were converted.

The majority of bondsmen did not attend their owners' churches or revivals. Realizing that owners intended for them to be supervised in their worship, most bondsmen reverted to the secret praise meeting, which the owner could not supervise or suppress (Campbell 1989: 170–71). While blacks in Jasper County in 1853 had their own Baptist church—Dixie Baptist built by the Reverend Richard—most bondsmen held secret meetings in the slave quarters with a spy at the door of the cabin. Hushed prayers and softly sung hymns were the rule. Sometimes, if prayers and shouting got too loud, they would pray "into the large kettles or washpots to keep the sound from being overheard by human listeners" (Silverthorne 1986: 165–66).

The ritual took the form of the ringshout. Worshippers formed a ring in the middle of the slave cabin or hush harbor thicket and moved, to singing, in a circle. These ring dances started off slow and got progressively faster until a member went into trance (Silverthorne 1986: 165–66). The meetings might last until daybreak. The singing of religious songs, however, was not restricted to formal ritual. According to Millie Ann Smith, a former slave from Rusk County, "We hummed our religious songs in the field while we was working. . . . It was our way of praying for freedom, but the white folks didn't know it" (Campbell 1989: 175).

Over a hundred years later, Sister Evelyn Reese, a member of St. John Progressive, summed up the black experience for her working-class generation in Texas:

> I worked in the fields. I chopped cotton. . . . I pulled corn. . . . We was in the field when the sun rose. And we was in it when it went down, see . . . the Lord fixed it so that we do not have to go to the cotton patch. . . . You can't help but rejoice. . . . It had to be a God that brought you out. The Lord has brought us out of bondage. You free!

3

"I Want to Be at the Meeting": A History of Afro-Baptist Speech and Hymnody

Recent studies of the origins of the black preaching style have linked it to West African forms of public declamation and recitation. One scholar of Black Vernacular English writes that in light of Negro Caribbean and Guyanese preaching styles, "one could hypothesize that the preaching style was used by Blacks [in the United States] and later spread to white culture" (Vaughn-Cooke 1972: 30). In comparing Caribbean and black North American styles of preaching, another social scientist suggests that the manner in which black preachers deliver their sermons is essentially African: "Afro-American preaching is more similar to the transplanted African religious rites found throughout the Caribbean and in Brazil" (Gumperz 1982: 189).

One of the most striking features that distinguishes Afro-American preaching from most Euro-American preaching styles is the chanted quality of the black sermon. This same quality is found in the prayers that occur in the Afro-Baptist ritual during Devotion. In fact, sermon and prayer may become so melodious as they develop that church musicians can easily accompany the preacher's and deacon's patterns of intonation on their instruments. Piano and organ can become involved in a melodic antiphony like that of the congregation echoing the melody of the sermons and prayers as they evolve. Following human intonation, the piano and organ, if played well, are said to "talk." Indeed, the highest compliment that can be given to church musicians is that they make their instruments talk.

Ethnomusicologist Gilbert Rouget's description of sub-Saharan African poetry not only distinguishes black African poetic composition from that of Europe but also offers a viable explanation of the development of the Afro-Baptist preaching and praying styles. Arguing against Roman Jakobson's assertion that "no human culture ignores verse-making," Rouget states that African poetry is without the verse-making features found throughout the rest of the world:[1] "It would appear that Africa, at least, if no other region, is an exception . . . no African text . . . has been collected, that might strictly speaking be called poetry, i.e., ruled by one of the verse-making systems (syllabic, accentual, quantitative, tonematic) mentioned by Roman Jakobson (Rouget 1966: 46).

Rouget stipulates, however, that black Africa does not lack poetic forms. These forms, however, are defined by features other than those of verse-making systems. One such poetic feature is found among the West African Fulani, who use the chain rhyme system, in which the last word in an utterance recurs as the first word of the following utterance. Rouget asserts that this technique is a widely spread genre throughout West Africa, where the prominent rhythmic quality of these utterances distinguishes them from normal speech (Rouget 1966: 46).

In Sigi, which is the secret language of the Dogon, the "breath group" is the poetic feature that distinguishes poetry from normal language. Rouget describes the breath group in this manner: "Each sentence corresponds to one inhaling of air in the lungs of the speaker who accelerates his delivery if the sentence is longer in order to pronounce it in one breath" (Rouget 1966: 47). Each breath group, which may consist of one or more sentences, is concluded by a nonsense syllable which is "added . . . for the sake of musicality and rhythm" (Rouget 1966: 47). In Dogon Sigi this final nonsense syllable is "boy." Among the Mandinka, who also use the breath-group principle as a poetic marker, the musical nonsense syllables are "o," "wo," and "ye" (Rouget 1966: 47). In Porto-Novo, Benin (formerly Dahomey) the breath group is known as "one stroke recitation." It is characteristically strophic, that is, full of recurring verses. The verses are always shouted as loudly and swiftly as possible. Rouget reports that the breath group "is probably widely spread all over Black Africa" (Rouget 1966: 50).

Another West African poetic feature is the chanted, or sung, declamation. The Dogon dynastic poems, which recount the royal history in the palace, are either sung or recited with such curious intonation that string instruments accompany their performance: "We are thus confronted with a mixture of recitation and music" (Rouget 1966: 48).

Among the Yoruba in Benin, the prayers to the *orisha*, or supernatural intercessors between mortals and God, are also chanted. Called *oriki*, these praise-poems contain sentences uttered in a monotone. After each monotonic chant, the audience replies with a melodious refrain that bursts out into "truly lyrical tones, confronting us with a remarkable case of Sprechgesang," that is, sung speech (Rouget 1966: 51). The blending of speech and song qualities also occurs among the Malinke. A *griot* recites genealogies, chanting each phrase while the audience responds with full voices, again, in a melodious refrain. The griot's monotonic chant is accompanied by only a harp lute, while the listeners' refrains are supported by all the musical instruments present (Rouget 1966: 53).

Rouget's descriptions of black African poetic features suggest links to Afro-Baptist sermonic and prayer traditions. Both speech varieties in the church are chanted using instrumental accompaniment. The sermon's lines are delivered in breath groups whose ends are marked by exclamatory syllables, for example, "wo!" or "huh!" One scholar of black preaching, Bruce Rosenberg, believed that these preachers' sermons were metrical—having a certain number of accented beats or syllables to a line—that is, displaying one of Jakobson's verse-making devices (Rosenberg 1970). Another scholar of the preaching style, however, points out that these sermons do not have a consistent definable meter (Davis 1985). The sense of recurring meter is probably a result of squeezing and elongating syllables into the durational restrictions of a breath group. Although not metrical, poetic expression in West African and Afro-Baptist traditions of declaiming share rhythmicity, based on the breath group, which distinguishes declamation from normal, conversational speech. In the next chapter we will see how the preacher uses the breath group, rhythm, and chant to shape his sermon aesthetically. The underlying sense of beauty and order, however, may be traceable to West Africa.

The Diola-Fogny of the Casamance River region in southwestern Senegal manipulate formulaic or stock phrases much as Afro-Baptist preachers and deacons do in extemporaneously composing their oral texts. Like the Malinke, the Diola-Fogny have a griot tradition in which griot troubadours recite the geneologies, bits of news, and tribal history to the accompaniment of a twenty-one-stringed instrument called the *kora*. Just as Rosenberg reports that black preachers compose their sermons with the aid of formulas, David Sapir writes that the Senegalese griots, called *jalolu*, "extemporize with ease using a huge wealth of stock phrases and metaphors that are combined and recombined in an infinite number of ways" (Sapir 1965: 2).

Among the Wolof of the Senegambia, male musicians belonging to the *nyeenyo* class of artisans sing the appropriate histories, geneologies, fables, and proverbs at social events, whether they have been invited as guests or not. These musicians, who accompany their own declamations on the *xalam*, a plucked lute consisting of four or five strings, are known as *xalamcats* (Coolen 1982: 73). West Africans living in the interior savannah plains also have a griot tradition that employs the ubiquitous harp-lute. As among the Diola-Fogny, the savannah griot "is an improvising singer, shouter, orator, whose duty is to flatter and glorify his master" (Oliver 1970: 48).

The musical characteristics of the savannah griot's speech are reminiscent of black preaching and prayer styles. The griot uses a great deal of portamento, that is, vocal embellishment of a phrase characterized by slowly gliding from one tone to another, blending the intervals between them. Like the black preacher at the end of his sermon, the griot also slips back into prosaic speech during his chanted performance (Oliver 1970: 61). The griot's audience responds with hand clapping just as an excited congregation will clap along with a preacher's or pray-er's performance in order to lend support and encourage the speaker to continue. The interaction between the griot and his respondent, who answers "*namu*," or "yes," to each of his lines, has obvious correlates in the Afro-Baptist church. The griot's use of falsetto shrieks and high, forced tones in order to be heard are all characteristics found in the black preaching style.

Linguist Charles Bird draws an interesting parallel between the black sermon and the West African Mande epic praise-poem. He divides the epic into three sections (Bird 1972: 283–89). The epic begins with the free-form proverb-praise, which is spoken rapidly with no definite rhythm and little synchronization between voice and musical instrument. In the second stage the griot develops the plot line and rhythm in a narrative mode. Speech melody and *kora* are more synchronized, and the *namu*-sayer answers each of the griot's lines with "yes man." In the final segment, the griot's speech has evolved into full song as he "marks the major events of the plot" (Bird 1972: 289–90; Jackson 1981: 216).

No comparison between griot and preacher is complete without drawing attention to the use of gesture in narrative discourse on both continents. The West African and African-American man of words relies on gesture in his oral culture to enliven, punctuate, and contextualize the meaning of his discourse, while his audience never lets him out of their sight: "The oral speaker projects in gesture the oral text on the retina of the audience like a film on a screen. . . . This is why traditional literature is an ocular . . . as [well as] an auricular literature" (Fouda 1968: 282). The Afro-Baptist preacher may whirl around behind the pulpit, dash from one side of the church to the other, or suddenly fall to his knees imitating a betrayed Christ, as we saw in the first chapter. These grand gestures, like those of his African progenitor, provide a special context in which his words will be remembered by his listeners well after the end of his performance.

Black Americans retained West African poetic features over the course of two and a half centuries by incorporating them into an Afro-American tradition in the face of the cultural onslaught of Euro-American influence. Of the ten to thirty million Africans shipped to the Western Hemisphere as slaves, less than one million had arrived in the United States by 1860 (Oliver 1970: 67). The African poetic features were passed on to successive generations of North American-born blacks, since their rapidly growing population was not significantly increased by new arrivals of West Africans after 1780.

The verbal as well as musical features the griot uses are strongest, like the griot himself, in the savannah regions, which were a focal supplier of Africans for North American slavery. In the savannah area that extends 250 miles inland from the coast, stretching from Lake Chad to include northern Nigeria, southern Niger, Benin, Togo, northern Ghana, Mali, and Upper Volta, the griots employ not only drums and ideophones—so prevalent on the Atlantic coast—to accompany their speaking but also lutes, harps, and fiddles, which are less common in the coastal rainforest (Oliver 1970: 42). The savannah griot has a history in the West African interior that predates European intrusion into the region. The earliest foreign record of the griot's existence dates back to 1353, when geographer Ibn Battuta observed him as a verbal artist in the court of Mansa Sulayman, ruler of the Kingdom of Mali, from whom all modern Manding peoples of the savannah claim to be descended. Instead of the stringed *kora*, the griot of those times accompanied himself on a xylophone as he recited the geneologies for the king.

In the epics of the first Manding king, Sunjata Keita, the griot, or *jali*, is frequently mentioned as "counselor, diplomat, master of ceremonies, praiser, and entertainer" (Knight 1984: 63). By the time of European enslavement of the West African, the jali was held in less esteem. Three hundred years after Mansa Sulayman's court, the jali was considered somewhat of a social outcast and parasite, although he enjoyed special privileges not granted to other members of his society because of his knowledge of history and his skill in retelling it (Knight 1984: 60–65). Today in West Africa his social status is low (Irvine 1989: 184).

Part of the shared tradition of the savannah cultures that supplied a significant number of North American slaves, the griot arrived in the North American colonies with the Mandinka, Malinke, Wolof, Diola-Fogny, and numerous other interior tribes to continue the West African tradition of verbal artistry that incorporated music.

The History of the Black Sermon

Ethnomusicologist Margaret McCarthy finds parallels between the Afro-American blues form and the black sermon. One parallel that harkens back to Africa is the improvisational quality of sermons and blues singing, which both depend on a repertory of stock phrases that are drawn on during an impromptu delivery (McCarthy 1976: 272). Other scholars have pointed out that the chanted formulaic sermon does not belong exclusively to an Afro-American tradition. Sociolinguist Ann Pitts, for example, describes the use of the chanted, formulaic sermon among white Kentucky preachers broadcasting in Ypsilanti, Michigan, a haven for Kentucky emigrants. She reports that these white preachers chant their sermons because "a sung or chanted text would seem to have a greater impact than one merely spoken" (Pitts 1978: 93). During the chanted sermon, the white preacher varies the intensity of his voice for emotional effect but maintains a tonic center, that is, a distinct musical key, for the entire sermon. His sermon is also reportedly formulaic (Pitts 1978: 93). Rosenberg also states that, while black preachers use the chanted metrical sermon more frequently, white preachers from the "eastern Kentucky hills" and parts of Ohio and Pennsylvania also deliver a rhythmically chanted sermon (Rosenberg 1970: 10). Rosenberg writes that when he told certain Appalachian preachers that black preachers also chanted their sermons, the white preachers were surprised to find out that the chanted sermon was not exclusively theirs (Rosenberg 1970: 10).

The Appalachian chanted sermon is partly a reflection of the merging of West African and European Protestant religious practices during the revival periods that spanned more than a century of American history. The first Africans who disembarked from the slave ships brought a chanted recitation style that they performed in their secret plantation meetings. As one ethnomusicologist reminds us, "The Black preacher in the United States emerged during the period of slavery as a panegyric or praise poet, in the tradition of his cultural predecessor, the West African griot" (Jackson 1981: 206). Whites probably first heard black chanted sermons at the camp meeting, which began and held sway in the parts of Kentucky where scholars report the existence of the white chanted sermon.

There is, however, a chanted declamatory style in Welsh tradition called the *hwyl*, used by poets and preachers to heighten the aesthetics and emotion of their words. Pitts observes that "[b]ehind the chanted sermon is a very old tradition, largely rooted in the merging of the 'antiphonal performance' style of the Negro spiritual with the evangelical prose sermon of Protestant tradition" (Pitts 1978: 89). It is no accident that the chanted sermon among whites is strongest in Appalachia pockets where both revivals and Welsh immigration were prominent features. The merging of the African and Welsh oratorical chanting traditions on the American frontier is an example of cultural exchange, in which similar traits reinforce each other. Reinforcement strengthens both traits, with the result that similar practices and ideas are the most likely to survive. According to the observations of anthropologist Melville Herskovits, "In the New World, exposure of the whites to Negro practices as well as of Negroes to European forms of worship could not but have had an influence on both groups" (Herskovits [1941] 1958: 231).

If whites inherited the chanted sermon basically from African-Americans, blacks who attended camp meetings acquired the bombastic fundamentalist content and preaching style, condemning sinners to eternal hellfire, from the white preachers whom they heard there. Camp meeting sermons and songs dwelt on the rejection of earthly pleasures and the theme of death as an escape from a harsh life, providing the hope of an afterlife that would compensate poor white people and slaves for their hardships while punishing the evildoer, whom the whites identified—at least subconsciously—with the planter as much as the gambler. Although the plainfolk never articulated their hatred of and desire to overthrow the planter class after the Virginia rebellions of the seventeenth century, their escapist doctrines expressed their dissatisfaction with the planters. Because of the planters the poor white population was constantly moving on in search of new fertile ground. When the poor whites found suitable new acreage, the planter and his land speculator would, in time, seize it.

Both slave and poor white talked and sang of worlds beyond this one, though the black bondsman had some hope of escaping to a less abstract "promised land" to the North (Bruce 1974: 98–109). One of the most frequently used symbols in camp meeting songs and sermons was the Jordan River: "[T]he one specific act that would get them to heaven: crossing the river that was death. When a dying . . . woman was asked of her condition, she could only reply that she was 'Just on this side [*sic*] Jordan'" —'My bodily affliction is great'" (Bruce 1974: 102). Widespread among African peoples was the belief that the boundary between life and death was a river, a metaphor reminiscent of the River Styx of Greek mythology. Among the African Lodagaa, for example, the soul begins its journey immediately following the funeral: "At the river it is ferried across, for a fee of twenty cowries which friends and relatives provide at the funeral" (Mbiti 1969: 158). Among the Kongo peoples, the division between the living and their ancestors is called *kalunga*, represented by water: above the water line is physical life; below, death (Stuckey 1987: 13; Thompson 1983: 189–90).

One historian of the camp meetings describes the anti-intellectual quality of the revivalist preachers, both black and white, as they exhorted the congregations to convert before it was too late. Anti-intellectualism was a distinctive and necessary attribute: "The Baptists not only did not require that their ministers be educated, but valued a lack of education as a positive ministerial attribute" (Bruce 1974: 37). Black preaching uses an anti-intellectual appeal "as a common feature, a means of identifying with the hearers, many of whom were illiterate" (Sernett 1975: 139–40).

One student of the black preaching style describes at length the characteristics of old-time black preaching (Pipes 1951: 132). A prominent feature was its reliance solely on fundamental literalism—"not the word of Greek, Latin, grammar, Moody; not a word source from anybody but God" (Pipes 1951: 87). Another characteristic shared by camp meeting and black preaching is the appeal to emotional persuasion rather than any logical argument, though one observer argues that "the new, more educated type of preaching" is replacing the old-time Negro sermon in the black church (Pipes 1951: 132). The language of the black, as well as camp meeting, sermon was traditionally the vernacular. Despite this fact, the Reverend William Hatcher, an influential white preacher in nineteenth-century Richmond, deplored the Reverend John Jasper's use of the black vernacular during his sermons: "Shades of our Anglo-Saxon Father! Did mortal lips ever gush with such torrents of horrible English. Hardly a word came out clothed in its right mind" (Pipes 1951: 133).

The use of emotional persuasion rather than logical reasoning, the use of loud falsetto chanting instead of a soft spoken delivery, and the use of the vernacular instead of educated, standard speech—all hallmarks of the brush harbor meeting—did not prevent Hatcher from appreciating Jasper's famous sermon, "De Sun Do Move," that had all of Richmond stirring well over a hundred years ago. Hatcher, who considered himself a learned man, wrote that even he was moved by Jasper's persuasive argument that the universe was geocentric in spite of scientific evidence that the earth revolved around the sun. He writes that he "found a seat in the church firmly resolved not to be taken in by Jasper's eloquence about the motion of the sun." By the end of the sermon, however, Hatcher says, "Yes, I voted that the earth was flat and had four corners, and that the sun drove his steeds from the gates of the morning over to the barns in the West, and I never asked the question for a moment as to how the team got back during the night" (Courlander 1976: 353).

Hatcher himself preserved the sermon, recording Jasper's text with pen and paper. The sermon begins:

> But 'bout de course of de sun, I have got dat. I have done ranged through de whole blessed Book and scored down de last thing de Bible has to say bout de movement of de sun. I got all dat pat and safe. And lemme say dat if I don't give it to you straight, if I gits one word crooked or wrong, you just holler out, Hold on dere, Jasper, you aint got dat straight, and I'll beg pardon . . . but my God don't lie and He aint put no lie in de Book of eternal truth. . . . (Courlander 1976: 354)

Jasper concluded by stating that scientific knowledge was faulty where biblical truth was infallible:

But I got another word for you yet. I done work over dem papers dat you sent me without date and without your name. You deals in figures and thinks you are bigger dan de archangels. Lemme see what you done say. You set yourself up to tell me how far it is from here to de sun. You think you got it down to a nice point. You say it is 3,339,002 miles from de earth to de sun. Dat's what you say. Another one say dat de distance is 12,000,000, another got it up to 27,000,000. I hears dat de great Isaac Newton worked it up to 28,000,000 and later on de philosophers give another rippin' rise to 50,000,000. De last one gets it bigger dan all de others, up to 90,000,000. Don't any of 'em agree exactly and so dey runs a guess game and de last guess is always de biggest. Now, when dese guessers can have a convention in Richmond and all agree upon de same thing, I'd be glad to hear from you again and I does hope dat by dat time you won't be ashame of your name. (Courlander 1976: 358)

The History of Prayer Speech

On January 22, 1797 Bishop Francis Asbury, an itinerant New Light Methodist preacher, reported that he had to meet with "the African people every morning between five and six o'clock at his lodging with singing, reading, exhortation and prayer, the precise ritual of secret meeting" (Fisher 1963: 75). If prayers were part of secret slave rituals, they were also heard in the shanty praise houses, where a white clergyman and one of the slave owner's family supervised the worship services (see Alho 1976: 52–55). The Reverend Charles Colcock Jones, who pioneered the plantation missionary movement, reported that the plantation was one religious "family" that replaced the individual slave family. In order that slave children learn their prayers for these supervised rites, Jones writes that "[t]he Negroes on plantations sometimes appoint one of their number, commonly the old woman who minds the children during the day, to teach them to say their prayers . . . every evening" (Jones 1842: 113).

Besides using the missionary catechism that instructed slaves how to pray to the Christian powers, black bondsmen drew their prayer texts from African prayers that resembled scriptural phrases heard in praise house sermons or lessons. For example, the Yoruba description of the supreme god as "the Mighty, Immovable Rock that never dies" was close enough to the often-heard verse from the Psalms of David, "He is a rock in a weary land," to incorporate the latter into Afro-Baptist prayer lines (Mbiti 1969: 46). Enslaved blacks also used phrases such as "crossing over Jordan" and "going to Canaanland," which they had heard in camp meeting spirituals and sermons. They of course used phrases from their own 'religious songs, which became known worldwide as Negro spirituals, a subject of the next topic in this chapter. In her analysis of a Gullah Sea Island prayer, linguist Patricia Jones-Jackson found seventeen instances where prayer lines had been paraphrased from New Testament sources but only seven instances where lines had been paraphrased from the Old Testament (Jones-Jackson unpublished manuscript). The most popular New Testament sources used by slaves for their prayers come from the books of Matthew, Romans, John, and 1 and 2 Corinthians. The most popular Old Testament sources for black prayers are Psalms and Job. Both New and Old Testament prayer text sources also happen to be those very books from which white ministers most often chose the texts of their sermons (Blassingame 1979: 86).

The following are some frequently recurring black prayer lines that paraphrase the Scriptures. "Crying to you this evening Jesus for mercy" is derived from Psalm 51, recounting David's cry, "Have mercy upon me, O God, according to Thy loving-kindness." Another frequent phrase is "the storms of life," drawn from Matthew 7:24–29, which says, "That whosoever builds his house on solid rock shall not be moved by the storms of life." The popular line, "I will go home and get my just resolve," is a paraphrase of 2 Corinthians 5:10 and Matthew 16:27. The often-heard phrases, "My soul have rest" and "There the wicked will cease from troubling and the weary will be at rest," which occur in prayers as well as spirituals, are to be found in Job 3:17 (Jones-Jackson unpublished manuscript).

Preserved in an oral rather than written tradition, Afro-Baptist prayer lines seem relatively resistant to change over time. During the 1930s, John and Alan Lomax recorded a black prayer in progress at the Darrington Prison Farm in east Texas. They recorded these introductory lines: "This evening, our Father, I come in the humblest manner I knowed" (Lomax 1947: 222). Another prayer, recorded in 1928 in Nashville, begins likewise with a statement of humility before the Almighty: "['T]is once more and again that a few of your beloved children are gathered together to call upon your holy name. We bow at your foot-stool, Master, to thank you for your spared lives" (Hughes and Bontemps 1958: 257). The same humility surfaces in prayers recorded in the 1980s:

> Master Jesus, Hear me
> Another one of your servant bow this evening, Jesus ╱
> . . . its [sic] no lower
> Could I come this evening
> Excepting my knees are down at the floor

> It is once more and again that we bow to give Thee humble
>   thanks for a yet-spared life

> My Father, we're comin' and bowin' down in the most humblest
>   way that we know how,
> Comin' as a disobedient child before their parents
>   (Jones-Jackson unpublished manuscript)

The following prayer lines evoke the feeling of life's transiency in much the same language:

(Texas, 1930s)
> I'm thankin' Thee, O Lord
> That my laying down last night
> Wasn't my cooling board
> And my cover was not my winding sheet
>   (Lomax 1947: 222)

(Tennessee, 1928)
> We thank Thee that our sleeping coach
> Was not our cooling board,
> Our cover was not our winding sheet
>   (Hughes and Bontemps 1958: 257)

(Texas, 1984)
> You saw fit for me to open my eyes, Heavenly Father
> To put my feet on the floor, Oh Heavenly Father
> The bed I laid in last night, Heavenly Father
> Was not my coolin' board

  On the feebleness of humankind, these lines emerge:

(Tennessee, 1928)
> Strengthen him where he is weak and build him up where
>   he is torn down
>   (Hughes and Bontemps 1958: 257)

(South Carolina, 1980)
>We ask you to please strengthen us
>Where we are weak
>And build us where we are tearing down
>>(Jones-Jackson unpublished manuscript)

The theme of the Crucifixion and the redemption of sin continues through the ages:

(Tennessee, 1928)
>Same God dat hung on Calvary and died,
>Dat we might have a right tuh de tree of life
>>(Hughes & Bontemps 1958: 257)

(Texas, 1984)
>But then, Father, we thank Thee for hanging out on
>Calvary's Cross one day, Oh Lord, giving us all the right
>to the Tree of Life

The conventional closing of the prayer always offers a vision of one's final hours and paradise. The black prayer tradition endures against the erosion of time, as these prayer texts demonstrate. In the following lines the River Jordan keeps its camp meeting symbolism:

(Tennessee, 1928)
>Lord, right soon in the morning, meet me down at the
>River of Jordan, bid the waters to be still
>>(Hughes and Bontemps 1958: 257)

(Texas, 1930s)
>When they all is standing in glory,
>And, Thou art satisfied at my staying here,
>O meet me at the river, I ask in Thy name
>>(Lomax, J. 1947: 227)

(Tuscaloosa, Alabama 1934)
>[T]hen, Lord, Lord make that crossin' over Jordan an easy
>one fo' me. I don't want to get bowled over by no swift
>an' splashin' stream
>>(Carmer 1934: 25)

(South Carolina, 1980)
>When, Master Jesus
>Me too got to pull off mortal
>Put on [im-]Mortality

Because then Jesus
Going down by the river of Jordan
Gonna stake my sword in the golden sand
(Jones-Jackson unpublished manuscript)

(Texas, 1984)
I'll walk on down to Jordan one day, Heavenly Father
You spoke to Jordan one day, Heavenly Father
Speak to Jordan again, Heavenly Father.
Tell Jordan to be calm, Heavenly Father
Cross my soul on over, Heavenly Father

Whereas antebellum as well as contemporary observers of black preaching comment on its exaggerated use of the black vernacular, black prayer, in contrast, is rendered in an approximation of standard but Jacobean English embodying, in Jones-Jackson's terminology, "Ciceronian, Quintelianesque" ornamentation (Jones-Jackson 1987: 77). The major source of this embellished seventeenth-century English was the plantation missionary church. Beginning with the colonial SPG efforts in South Carolina until the pre–Civil War praise houses of the plantation South, white clergy taught Protestant catechism with Bible verses, the Lord's Prayer, and the Apostles' Creed to illiterate slaves by rote (Blassingame 1979: 89). The missionary church on the plantation was, however, more than just a Bible school. For the slave, it became the principal means of learning his owner's language as well as the latter's strange religious customs. One historian draws this conclusion about the significance of the missionary movement in the South:

> Just as the school was the major institution for "Americanizing" nineteenth and twentieth century European immigrants, the church was the single most important institution for the "Americanization" of the bondsman . . . white ministers taught not only moral precepts to the slaves, they also taught them their master's language. (Blassingame 1979: 98)

Because of the linguistic distance between the slaves' speech, which might have been an American plantation Creole, and that of their masters, the missionary teachers spent a considerable amount of time just teaching slaves how to communicate in their masters' language. The missionaries' justified their efforts as attempts to aid in converting the African to Christianity. As a result of this effort, the Missionary Movement instilled standard but biblical English in the black vernacular of the last century: "Because of the lessons they learned in the churches, Biblical language would resonate in the nineteenth-century black speech and writing. This was, perhaps, the Southern church's greatest legacy to the slave" (Blassingame 1979: 98). Although black sermons may occasionally use a biblical phrase as an intermittent ornamentation, Afro-Baptist prayer primarily reflects the efforts of Bible and language teachers to impart the fundamentals of Protestant Christianity and English to the plantation slave. The archaic phrases of the Bible and the approximation of standard English found in the twentieth-century Afro-Baptist ritual are remnants of these earlier attempts to proselytize the African-American in North America.

The History of Afro-Baptist Hymnody

When the first shiploads of West Africans intended for slavery disembarked in North America in the seventeenth century, the captives brought with them "fixed songs for all life situations" (Fisher 1963: 10). In spite of popular belief that Africans left their cultural heritage behind after enslavement in the Western Hemisphere, they brought indigenous melodies, which they taught to each successive generation of enslaved youth through the medium of the plantation secret meeting (Fisher 1963: 33–34). Thus the African musical legacy, representing varied African cultural backgrounds, was able to continue in North America despite attempts to dislodge it. The common condition of slavery forced the similarities to coalesce into a cultural defense against the psychological and physical assault of the slave system: "Although the musical cultures of West Africa during the slave-trade period varied from nation to nation, the cultures shared enough features to constitute an identifiable heritage for Africans in the New World" (Southern 1983: 21–22).

African songs were used to convene secret slave meetings by becoming secret codes that slaves sang to each other while working in the fields (Fisher 1963: 66–67). These meetings were initially rites of passage for black adolescents held to teach them the mores of African adulthood. At the meetings, native African songs were the principal "vehicles for instilling the morality of the African cult" (Fisher 1963: 10). So pervasive were these West African melodies that two centuries later, during the fervor of the camp meetings, blacks who attended claimed to have heard camp meeting songs that were melodically the same as some African songs (Fisher 1963: 33–34). Peter Randolph, an Afro-Baptist preacher who had endured the horrors of slavery, recounts that most of the songs used in the slaves' secret meetings were composed by slaves themselves. He recalls one such popular song text:

> No more rain, no more snow
> No more cowskin on my back
> Glory be to God that rules on high
> (Randolph 1855: 69)

Although slaves may have begun to compose their own songs for these meetings after being in North America for several generations, the African melodies did not die but formed the musical foundation for slave and later camp revival song tunes (DuBois 1971: 30).

The Negro spiritual, which was crafted by slaves from both African and European musical sources, became the first indigenous religious music in North America besides that of the Native American. Although the precise date and place of the spiritual's origin is unknown and impossible to fix, this song form appeared in the recordings of whites approximately a century after the first cargoes of Africans arrived in the American colonies (Levine 1977: 24–26; Lovell 1972: 400–401). Folklorist Lydia Parrish surmises that the Negro spiritual had possible beginnings in Port Royal, South Carolina where the first Anglican SPG missions began proselytizing among the Sea Island slaves, using white spiritual hymns as their tool for conversion (Parrish 1942: 5). In spite of a European influence on the formation of the black spiritual, one must remember that "[W]hatever portion of the spiritual can be proved to be African or American, one fact is incontrovertible: The originators of the Negro spiritual were African in their attitudes toward religion and music" (Lovell 1972: 16).

In order to understand the creation of the spiritual, the student must review the history of Euro-American Protestant hymnody of England and colonial America. The singing of religious songs in seventeenth-century and eighteenth-century Protestant churches in North America was abysmal. This poor quality of hymnody resulted from the Anglo-American sentiment that singing was not as important as preaching in praising the Almighty, which meant that the established Protestant churches of England and its North American colonies neglected aesthetic considerations in the performance of religious songs. When the Puritans arrived in New England, they brought a Protestant tradition that held psalm singing to be the only permissible form of music for worship. Protestant psalmody was performed at an extremely slow tempo by the whole congregation without the accompaniment of musical instruments. The Puritans believed that musical instruments, as used in the Anglican church, smacked of popery, that is, Roman Catholic practice, which was one of their major reasons for leaving England and its church (Chase 1966: 7). The New England Puritans were so intent on remaining "pure" in their worship that they created their own psalmbook, the *Bay Psalm Book*, in 1640. This work gave a more literal translation of the Psalms than did the English psalmbooks. The first book printed in North America, the *Bay Psalm Book* contained only new translations of the psalms in text form without any notation of the psalms' melodies. The inclusion of tunes, however, was needless since the colonists and British alike passed down the same few tunes they had always used for the singing of psalms. Although these New England Puritans were obsessed with moral purity, they were unaware that their psalm tunes were originally lively secular melodies from Continental ale houses, royal courts, and brothels, brought to the British Isles from France and Germany (Chase 1966: 17). The original energy of these pieces was destroyed by the Puritans' fashion of singing them.

The dullness of New England Puritan singing of psalms rests on the fact that these songs were always "lined out," that is, a song leader would read aloud a verse of the song and the congregation would then sing the verse, or line, verbatim. Because the song leader was usually a church deacon, the practice of lining out, or simply lining, was also called "deaconing." The practice of lining, or deaconing, originated in a 1644 Westminster Ordinance recommending that "the minister, or some other fit person appointed by him" line the psalm for his congregation who were almost entirely illiterate (Chase 1966: 30). What had begun in England as a means of coping with illiteracy became a folk institution that British exiles brought to North America with them. In the colonies the practice of lining degenerated into a cacophony of embellishment and lack of group coordination in singing. The time spent to line a verse slowed the original lively tempo of the song, and congregants slowed it further by dragging it out with a great deal of melismatic ornamentation, that is, giving individual syllables several notes apiece. Since the church had banned the use of musical instruments, the congregants began to embellish each note as a sign of their individual musicianship (Chase 1966: 32–38). The tunes were often lost in the slow tempo, "since it is impossible for the human voice to hold a single note-syllable through two breaths" (Jackson 1943: 17).

Shortly before the arrival of George Whitefield and the Great Awakening revival in the mid-eighteenth century, new hymns appeared in the colonies to rival the old *Bay Psalm Book*. Having grown bored with the dry psalms, the colonists were enthralled with the hymns of Englishman Isaac Watts that were gaining popularity in the colonies long before his hymnal, *Hymns and Spiritual Songs*, appeared in North America. Watts's loose translations and imitations of the Psalms of David were a heretical change in Protestant hymnody in the colonies as well as in Britain. Defying the sanctity of the *Bay Psalm Book*, the Watts hymns and spiritual songs offered freedom in the creation of religious songs, although Watts still included psalms in his first hymnal. Watts, however, did not provide new tunes to accompany his new translation of the psalms (Jackson 1943: 18). Whitefield, more interested in revolutionizing the sermon's message than the way of singing religious songs, ignored the fashion of religious singing, and the same dismal melodies and languid lining practice continued after the fires of revival were aflame in the colonies.

Watts's rebellion in the creation of hymns sparked other hymnists in North America and England to show their talent for creating new religious songs. Samuel Davies, John Cennick, John Newton (a former slave ship captain who wrote "Amazing Grace"), John Wesley (the founder of Methodism), and his brother Charles began writing new hymn texts and supplying them with new British folk tunes so that the ever-expanding revivals would have fresh songs to accompany their spread (Jackson 1943: 18–23; Chase 1966: 46–52). Samuel Davies was one of the first New Light preachers to bring the Awakening southward. Armed with Watts's *Hymns and Spiritual Songs*, he introduced Christian doctrine and songs to Virginia slaves around 1750 (Chase 1966: 79; Jackson 1943: 279; Levine 1977: 21–22; Southern 1983: 41). Davies deplored the neglect "of slaves . . . who generally continue Heathens in a Christian country" (Chase 1966: 79). Although the slaves seemed uninterested in his gift of religious instruction, they relished Watts's hymns. Davies wrote the following description to John Wesley in England: "[They were] attentive to every word they heard . . . some of them covered with tears. . . . They are exceedingly delighted with

Watts' songs. . . . They have a kind of ecstatic delight in psalmody" (Chase 1966: 79).

So effective a conversion tool was Watts's hymnal that the book was a necessary item in the arsenal of every itinerant preacher who preached to slaves (Blassingame 1979: 90). The slaves delighted in singing the Protestant hymns, especially in the lined-out fashion, which Davies and other New Light preachers introduced to them (Jackson 1943: 279–82; Southern 1983: 41). The effect of these lined hymns upon the slave was so uncanny that Davies continued to write Wesley, perhaps seeking an explanation for the hymns' repeated success with black bondsmen (Roberts 1974: 161). "All the books were very acceptable," he wrote, "but none moreso, than the Psalms and Hymns, which enabled them to gratify their peculiar taste for psalmody" (Chase 1966: 80). Slaves would spend all night in Davies' kitchen singing the psalms: "[W]hen I have waked at two or three in the morning, a torrent of sacred psalmody has poured in to my chamber" (Chase 1966: 80).

Following the Revolutionary War, New Lighters from the North converted thirty-one thousand slaves to Baptist and Methodist sects. These missionaries continued to sing the Watts hymns in the old-time way, lined out as Davies had shown the slaves (Jackson 1943: 282). By the beginning of the western revivals across the Appalachians in the early 1800s, however, the old way became antiquated (Chase 1966: 183–84). The singing school tradition and the practice of notating the tunes of hymns had replaced lined-out, dirge-like psalm singing in Northern cities. Consequently the sound of the urban religious song improved. Well-trained church choirs had now become the fashion in New England and New York. Musical instruments were now permissible in church worship; and for city-dwellers the old deacon-lined song of the Puritans was a thing of the past.

The singing school, imported from European fashionable circles, was not yet known in the South or on the western frontier. Musical instruments were uncommon too because the plainfolk could not afford them. The revivalists across the Appalachians, however, did compose their own camp meeting songs using tunes from British Isle folk songs (Chase 1966: 191). Sometimes the New Lighters created their own tunes, or as blacks witnessed, the revivalists used melodies imported from Africa by the first slaves.

The texts for these camp meeting spirituals came from two sources: the Protestant hymnists and Southern folk themselves. During revival meetings, the preacher would sing a hymn verse composed by one of the noted hymnists of the day. The congregation would supply a refrain of their own making. This refrain was simple enough in text and melody that anyone hearing it for the first time could easily join in singing it. For example, the preacher would sing out one of Samuel Stennett's popular stanzas:

> On Jordan's stormy Banks I stand
> And cast a wishful eye
> To Canaan's fair and happy land
> Where my possessions lie

The people would sing in reply:

> I am bound for the promised land
> I am bound for the promised land
> O, who will come and go with me
> I am bound for the promised land
> (Bruce 1974: 90–92)

While the hymn verses made their way to the folk revivals, the folk relished their own refrains that focused on rejecting the vices and temptations of the secular world, or looking to death and the Promised Land as an escape from misery: "Relief from their situation was inextricably bound up in the hope of a world to come in another place" (Bruce 1974: 104). Favorite refrains were:

> To the land, to the land I am bound
> Where there's no more stormy clouds arising
>
> And we'll pass over Jordan
> O, come and go with me
> When we pass over Jordan
> We'll praise th'eternal three
>
> I'm on my way to Canaan
> To the new Jerusalem
> (Bruce 1974: 98–103)

These popular refrains, some of them the result of improvisation, were movable couplets or single lines that could be used as refrains for a number of different hymns: they "floated" from song to song regardless of the verses that initiated the hymn (Jackson 1943: 86). The use of these wandering, or floating, refrains increased audience participation in the singing. So greatly did black congregants appreciate camp

meeting singing that oftentimes their voices were heard for miles—
well above those of white singers (Chase 1966: 327; Levine 1977: 21).

While it was common knowledge that antebellum blacks were singing and composing songs at the camp meeting, little is known of their
songs at their secret plantation meetings. Few white observers ever
reported hearing religious singing in the slave quarters prior to the Civil
War (Chase 1966: 232). Southern whites did not believe that slave songs
of any kind merited attention. Northerners became aware of religious
slave songs during the Civil War only after an educational mission from
the North, visiting Port Royal, South Carolina, recorded and published
the Negro spirituals it encountered for the first time. This publication,
Slave Songs of the United States, was white America's first account of
the slaves' religious songs (Chase 1966: 239). Although Watts's hymns
were circulating around the slave quarters, these hymns were "too cold
and static to allow for the full expression of the slaves' religious sentiment" (Blassingame 1979: 137). They did not adequately reflect their
sense of relationship with God: "The God of the spirituals was visible
in nature, present in the conscience of man, omnipresent; He revealed
himself directly to men" (Blassingame 1979: 146).

For their own religious meetings sequestered in the brush out of the
master's hearing, slaves composed their spirituals by inserting verses
of Euro-American origin into their own African melodies (Southern
1983: 145). Although the precise date of the first spiritual's origin
is unknown—and impossible to ascertain—some musicologists date
its birth around 1760 when Davies introduced the Watts hymns to
Virginia's slaves. Folklorists Parrish and Fisher, however, place it fifty
years earlier in South Carolina (Walker 1979: 40). Regardless of the
date of its creation, the slave spiritual undoubtedly expressed the bondsmen's obsession with freedom and "desire for justice . . . upon his
betrayers" (Walker 1979: 32). Drawing principally from the Old Testament as a source, the slaves' spirituals vividly retold the sufferings of
an enslaved people living in a strange, hostile land.

The use of Old Testament imagery of oppression, however, was not
solely the possession of enslaved African Americans but has a history
as long as colonial North America. The Puritans of the Massachusetts
Bay Colony, in order to explain to themselves who they were and why
they had left Britain, often referred to themselves as "Israelites," fleeing from the "Egypt" of despotic England. They chose to remove themselves from the tyranny of the English monarch by coming to the

"Canaanland" of North America to build their City of God (Baltzell 1964: 88; Erickson 1966: 43, 49–54). As a part of the Puritan legacy and plainfolk heritage, Old Testament figures and events found their way to the camp meeting.

Not only did the spirituals function as a psychological release of emotions, they were also a "musical expression developed as the chief means of covert communication among slaves (Walker 1979: 37). One historian, for example, claims that the hero of the spiritual "Go Down Moses" is none other than Bishop Francis Asbury, the abolitionist Methodist New Light preacher who made his circuit in the prerevolutionary South advising the planter to free his chattel. Another scholar, however, sees this fictional "Moses" as Denmark Vesey, who led the Charleston slave insurrection in 1822. In either case, because slaves could not openly talk about their hope that Bishop Asbury or Vesey would succeed in ending the peculiar institution, they masked their yearnings in biblical imagery. Slaves could voice their admiration for their heroes and immortalize them in song (Fisher 1963: 40; Harding 1981: 69).

George Pullen Jackson supported the Southern school of musical scholarship that proposed in the middle of this century that the Negro spiritual was nothing more than a facsimile of the white camp meeting song. According to Jackson, the simplicity of the camp meeting refrains lent themselves to easy copy by the slaves: "[T]he simplicity of text was an important factor in opening the white man's song flood gates to the negro" (Jackson 1943: 261). These white texts, so goes the argument, were further simplified in black musical versions, illustrating "general poetic disintegration as one of its outstanding characteristics" (Jackson 1943: 261). Shown to have more of a chauvinistic motive for defending the white spiritual rather than carefully weighed evidence for his position, most of Jackson's assertions in regard to the black spiritual are dismissed today (Levine 1977: 22–25; Waterman 1943: 32–36).

Trying to defend the European origin of the black spiritual, Jackson makes curious comparisons between the spiritual and the lined hymn as sung by blacks. By contending that rhythm alone does not make the slave spiritual any more African than European, Jackson asserts, somewhat snidely, that the Negro spiritual may be less African than the rhythmless, lined Watts hymns, which he labeled "surge-songs." Although eighteenth-century New Light preachers had taught blacks

these hymns and how to line them out, writes Jackson, slaves still sang
these hymns in such a dirgelike manner that the naive hearer would
consider the singing to be exotic and alien to European experience. He
claims that

> [N]o scholar or dilettante has, to my knowledge, tried to trace [lined
> hymns] or merely their movement back to Africa. But why not? Noth-
> ing could seem to the listener at first hearing more exotic, weird,
> "African" . . . than the group singing of these endlessly drawn-out
> and filled-in songs. And the negro sang surge songs half a century
> before there was such a thing as a revival Spiritual. Why should not
> the earlier custom be more "African" than the latter? (Jackson 1943:
> 257)

Of course Jackson was well aware that all musicologists of American music knew that the lined hymn, despite its phantasmal sound, was
instilled in slave music via the British hymn tradition of lining, thus
denying any African origin. Although the argument seems to hold up
to this point, we will return to the surge song in the next chapter and
reconsider its European exclusivity.

Countering Jackson's thesis that the Negro spiritual was a melodic
copy of the Euro-American camp meeting spiritual, Mieczyslaw Kolinski
found fifty black spirituals "to have the identical formal structure
of certain West African songs (Chase 1966: 256; Lovell 1972: 400;
Roberts 1974: 168; Waterman 1943: 41–43). This finding is not surprising if one remembers that original African tunes were still heard
on early nineteenth-century plantations. So prominent was the rhythmic difference between white and black spirituals that whites gladly
invited black singers to the camp meeting so that the latter would provide the syncopated, energetic hand clapping and foot stomping, as well
as strong voices, that brought on the desired state of trance (Levine
1977: 21; Waterman 1943: 36).

The consensus among scholars of the Negro spiritual is that "while
many of the spirituals are evidently patterned after European tunes,
some without apparent distortion, they are all either altered so as to
conform, or selected for adoption because they already did conform,
to West African musical patterns" (Chase 1966: 256). Just as elements
of preaching styles and trance behavior were shared by whites and
blacks at revival meetings, the Negro spiritual is an example of cultural adaptation between European and African musical structures that
occurred at the frontier camp meeting. Conducting field work on the

Gullah Sea Islands in the 1930s, Lydia Parrish made the following
observation of Negro song types probably applicable to antebellum slave
singing:

> "[I]f Fanny Kemble [wife of a nineteenth-century Georgia planter,
> Pierce Butler] had visited Africa and heard a few of the native songs
> . . . she would not have been puzzled by those sung by her husband's
> slaves. . . . Side by side with these semi-chants you hear songs which
> show clearly the white man's influence. The oldest Negroes say that
> they shouted after . . . prayer meeting at night. Before the shouting
> began, they sang spirituals and "line out" hymns. The chances are
> that all three types were sung from the time the white man con-
> cerned himself with the religious instruction of his slaves. (Parrish
> 1942: 80)

Before the close of the Civil War, African-Americans were singing
at least three kinds of religious song: the lined hymn taught to them in
the eighteenth century; the camp meeting spiritual, learned during the
nineteenth century; and their own spiritual, a new form forged from
European and African tradition. It was the Negro spiritual, however,
that predominated in the antebellum Afro-Baptist church, which had
the "greatest number of the illiterate black masses who had no other
means to make known the longings of their hearts" (Fisher 1963: 180).

The camp meeting reached its peak around 1835, when the plantocracy was affected by its fervor (Chase 1966: 237). After the planter
class accepted the New Light teachings and spirit of the camp meetings, the Baptist and Methodist sects began to lose their heretical
approach and started to gain respectability. With their rise in acceptance among the powerful planter class, the Baptist and Methodist sects
soon ousted the Episcopal Church as the largest and most powerful
denomination in the South among whites (Bruce 1974: 54–55). As
Baptists and Methodists became part of the Southern elite, they natu-
rally turned away from their former egalitarianism and abolitionist
yearnings: they now supported slavery.

With the enticements of respectability within reach and the new rail-
roads cutting across brush arbor sites, the revivalists abandoned the
camp meeting, and the fires of conversion slowly died. By 1880 the
original excitement and unbridled singing characteristic of the brush
arbor was gone. A few songsters who remembered the fervent singing
of the camp meetings, however, tried to preserve their songs in hymnals and shape note, that is, Fasola or "sacred harp," singing conven-

tions. The most popular work was Ira Sankey's and Dwight Moody's collection of camp meeting spirituals, *Sacred Songs and Solos with Standard Hymns* (Waterman 1943: 78), which tried to capture the spirit of the antebellum revival. This effort, however, was somewhat lackluster: although these songs used harmonized parts, they were more solemn than the original camp meeting songs. The new Sankey and Moody songs called for piano and organ, a modernization strikingly absent from the brush arbor.

During Reconstruction Afro-Baptists sang these new songs, called "Sankeys," composed in varied meters. Just as many freed men and women changed their old slave names and former gloomy styles of dress, and took up new social activities, so black Baptists adopted these white-inspired songs as a symbol of their new free status (Harding 1981: 279). The antebellum Negro spiritual, while still sung in the Afro-Baptist ritual, was pushed aside as a stigma reminding blacks of their recent condition of servitude (Levine 1977: 163, 170). The new meter music, or Sankey, was an emblem of hope, "a transitional form that bridged the slavery and Reconstruction periods and persisted in evidence until the beginnings of the twentieth century" (Walker 1979: 75–78).

Disappointment came quickly, however, with broken Reconstruction promises and the passage of the repressive Black Codes, which prevented blacks from voting or owning property and forced the homeless into prison chain gang labor. A new music was called for. Charles Albert Tindley, an ex-slave Methodist preacher, realized the futility of singing white hymns as an expression of hope for black people since white America had no intention of extending the rights and privileges of citizenship to them (Maultsby 1990: 201–2). Combining the Sankey tunes with the newly emerging blues form—which in itself was a socioeconomic protest (Ellison 1989: 1–14)—Tindley directed his songs to the black masses by using "the musical and verbal language of the poor, struggling, often illiterate black Christian at the turn of the century" (Boyer 1983: 104). By the turn of the twentieth century, rural blacks began their migrations from the fields to urban centers first in the South, then in the North. Rural fieldhands moving to the city, faced with a new set of problems, did not want to hear white hymns while they were praising God. They wanted to stomp their feet and clap their hands as they had done during the hush harbor. They also needed hope that they could overcome their problems in the crowded city slums.

Tindley offered that hope, supported by a rhythmic base, when he wrote "I'll Overcome Someday," "We'll Understand It By and By," and "The Storm Is Passing Over" shortly after 1900. Incidentally, the first composition, "I'll Overcome Someday," became the standard for the civil rights movement a half century later as "We Shall Overcome." By paraphrasing biblical Scriptures and retelling Bible stories in the black vernacular, Tindley's songs captured the feelings of the urban black masses who loved to improvise their songs so freely that "[a]t times the original melody is barely discernible, and most of the original rhythmic patterns have disappeared" (Boyer 1983: 125).

Along with the new metered Sankey, the slow, long-metered lined hymn survived during Reconstruction. The lined hymn, however, was confined to the Devotion, or was saved for funerals and solemn occasions (Chase 1966: 249; Southern 1983: 447). The reason for the continued use of the lined hymn, argues more than one musicologist, is that it is a perfect case of musical syncretism: the "call-and-response pattern of African song" fits with the lining procedure inherited from seventeenth-century England (Bailey 1978: 4; Chase 1966: 249; Levine 1977: 33; Roberts 1974: 167). The reason that African retentions remained so abundantly in the black church is that "[t]he doctrines of Negro churches were, of course, superficially Christian, but in truth they were the traditional beliefs of the secret meeting" (Fisher 1963: 187).

After World War I, black migration to the North, especially to Chicago's Southside and New York City's Harlem, was much greater than the post-emancipation rush to Southern cities. Railroad lines, exiting from the South's cottonfields, led to these Northern urban enclaves, where employment and living conditions looked promising. Urban disappointments in the form of expanding ghettos and race riots met the sharecropper families as they settled. Black sacred music now required a different, more urban sound: it demanded a "driving beat . . . supported by forceful voices singing in harmony" (Sapp 1976: 110).

Although the poor black immigrant was accustomed to rhythmic religious music, the sacred music of the black middle class was strictly imitative of the white metered hymns. Upon arrival in Northern cities, black immigrants found that these middle-class black churches did not welcome them but were embarrassed by their ecstatic antics. The Southern sharecroppers discovered that the music in these churches was too static for the type of worship to which they were accustomed.

During Prohibition, Thomas A. Dorsey, the son of an Atlanta Afro-Baptist preacher, was playing piano under the names "Georgia Tom" and "Barrel House Tom" in Southern "tent shows" for blues singers Ma Rainey and Tampa Red (Bontemps 1958: 314–17; Hughes and Meltzer 1967: 84; Levine 1977: 181–83). After attempting to combine his blues singing with a career of composing sacred songs, Dorsey finally quit the blues circuit in 1929 and became a full-time gospel song writer. The result of his decision was that, "Five or six years later, observers . . . noticed that Negro churches, particularly the storefront congregations, the Sanctified groups and the shouting Baptists, were swaying and jumping as never before. Mighty rhythms rocked the churches" (Bontemps 1958: 313). Dorsey admitted that Tindley's compositions had a great influence on him. In addition to including piano in his songs, Dorsey organized the first black gospel choir and insisted on harmony in the singing. During his prolific career, he published over 1,000 songs, both religious and secular (Southern 1983: 451–53). His two best-known sacred compositions are "Peace in the Valley" and "Precious Lord," the first favored by white congregations, the second, an Afro-Baptist standard. Combining elements of ragtime and blues, Dorsey provided the African-American immigrants with a new urban gospel music that supported them psychologically and spiritually during the Depression.

The Wall Street crash was the least of disappointments to confront black Americans after World War I, although it hit them the hardest. Booker T. Washington's death deprived African-Americans of what many saw as both a powerful negotiator with the white power structure and a heroic figure. The Ku Klux Klan terrorized the South and harassed black soldiers returning from the war. In 1919 the "Red Summer" of race riots flowed bloodily across the nation's cities in one of the most violent years of racial conflicts. The promise of the Harlem Renaissance failed to turn America's attention to the plight of her black masses. It became clear to African-Americans that the United States intended to maintain the status quo—to keep them segregated and powerless, second-class citizens in a closed society (Walker 1979: 104–5). Since the Sankey songs were inextricably associated with the oppressor, poor blacks in the cities turned to the rhythmic, bluesy gospel "Dorseys" to express their frustrations and hope.

Secular and sacred styles merged in the new gospel music. Discussing the success of her brother's songs, Dorsey's sister explains that "people got tired of the hymn, found it boring. Musicians . . . brought the swinging, hard rhythms of the blues first to the hymns" (Sapp 1976: 113). Blues songster T-Bone Walker admitted that the first time he heard a boogie-woogie piano was the first time that he went to church (Levine 1977: 108).

One of the first soloists to sing Dorsey's songs was Mahalia Jackson, who went with him to Chicago's Southside streetcorners to peddle his sheet music (Goreau 1975: 56). Recently arrived in Chicago from New Orleans, the sixteen-year-old Jackson was like many Southern immigrants: she wanted to hear rocking rhythms in her church music. The wealthier Northern black churches were so ashamed of the rural blacks' ecstatic worship that their doors remained almost entirely closed to them. When Jackson and Dorsey performed one of his new songs before the rich black congregation of Zoar Street Baptist, "she let loose—sang of and to the Lord with her whole heart, being and body as she'd been accustomed—Halie [Mahalia] got her next major shock. The pastor rose in wrath. Blasphemous! Get that twisting and that jazz out of his church!" (Goreau 1975: 55).

Jackson was one of the first gospel singers to charge admission to her audience. Black religious music gradually became a commercial enterprise. During the 1930s, gospel music produced other professional singers, including Clara Ward, Roberta Martin, and Rosetta Tharpe. Through the success of Mahalia Jackson's Carnegie Hall recitals, numerous television appearances, and a private audience with the emperor of Japan at the Imperial Palace, black gospel music gained national and world attention; it became and continues to be a major facet in America's music industry.

After World War II two opposite trends in gospel music were popular: the a cappella quartet and expanded musical instrumentation. Beginning at the turn of the century, the quartet tradition reached its zenith in the 1940s with male and female singing groups. Although the development of that gospel genre is beyond the scope of this discussion, it still attracts audiences and produces young groups that seem to be making a resurgence today. The male gospel quartets, which relied on a cappella voice harmony, were the forerunners of the popular male singing groups like Motown's Temptations and The Four Tops (for a fuller discussion of the gospel quartet tradition, see Jackson 1988: 33–96).

Alongside the development of a cappella quartet singing, gospel instrumentation expanded from piano and organ to include a full orchestra for the most elaborate performances. No musical beat was to be left unsounded: all melodic gaps were to be filled with rhythmic chords or passing tones. Key changes for variety became standard. Improvisation on the singer's part was required and expected (Southern 1983: 462–64). While the established, rich black Baptist churches opposed gospel singing before World War II, the major national organization of black Baptist churches, the National Baptist Convention, endorsed gospel music in the 1950s by making Dorsey the director of its own gospel choir (Southern 1983: 471).

Black gospel music's influence on black secular music was tremendous. Almost all the successful black popular singers during the 1960s and 1970s were former gospel singers. If Tindley and Dorsey borrowed heavily from the secular music of their times, Sam Cooke, Wilson Pickett, Billy Preston, Dionne Warwick, and Aretha Franklin—all originally gospel singers—returned the loan to secular music in the form of "rhythm-and-blues" (Franklin 1982: 30; Heilbut 1985: passim).

A key figure in the latter half of the twentieth century in incorporating secular styles and tunes into gospel is the Reverend James Cleveland, whose bluesy gospel singing style is directly descended from Dorsey and influenced by Jackson. Continuing the early gospel sound into the 1970s, Cleveland introduced an innovation in black gospel singing that will probably continue into the next century: the use of a massive number of voices. Hardly a state, city, or large social organization with a substantial African-American population lacks a mass choir that it sends to the annual Gospel Music Workshop of America, which Cleveland founded in 1969 (Heilbut 1985: 8).

The musical exchange between sacred and secular styles has been continual throughout African-American history throughout the Western Hemisphere (Roberts 1974: 77–78). When an interviewer questioned Mahalia about her debt to jazz for her gospel rhythm, she replied: "Baby, don't you know the Devil stole the beat from the Lord" (Goreau 1975: 150)? Her summary of rhythm-and-blues' debt to Dorsey is equally succinct: "All this mess you hear calling itself soul ain't nothing but warmed over gospel" (Goreau 1975: 155).

The recent advent of black contemporary gospel reflects the return of a secular genre into the sacred. The secular music belongs to "progressive" or "urban" jazz. Some of the changes that are developing in the sacred music are the use of traditionally nonharmonic tones and chords, more syncopated rhythms, more complex chordal progressions than the previous I-IV-V-I one of the blues form, the use of bongo and conga drums, and the inclusion of electronic synthesized keyboard instruments (Franklin 1982: 32; Roberts 1974: 180). One contemporary scholar of the black church is worried that the religious function of the new sacred music has been lost, since the new music seems to be designed primarily for entertainment and the contemporary church musician must always keep abreast of new songs, which are constantly being replaced by newer ones, unlike the relatively stable earlier spiritual and gospel songs (Franklin 1982: 33–34). In chapter 5, we will look at the musical cycle to see how the ritual accommodates new musical material with the old so that relatively few songs are completely displaced, casting a new light on the stability of the spiritual and gospel songs.

A gospel song that remains in the contemporary Afro-Baptist ritual and is still a favorite at St. John Progressive is sung by Brother Leroy Davis, and is called "I Want To Be at the Meeting." It rarely fails to stir excitement, if not shouting, though the text reminds the hearer of a much earlier time—the period of revival and the camp meeting.

Chorus:
> I want to be at the meeting.
> I want to be at the meeting.
> I want to be at the meeting,
> When all the saints get home.
> After separation of the right from the wrong.
> I want to be at that meeting around the throne.

Verse:
> After separation of the right from the wrong
> I want to be at the meeting when all the saints go
>   marching home.
> I'll talk with God the Father.
> I'll talk with Christ the Son.
> And then we'll have a meeting around God's throne.

[Chorus]
Verse:
> When I get to heaven, I'll meet my mother there.
> She'll say, "God Almighty, here comes my child.

He must have gotten here by prayer."
I'll talk with God the Father.
I'm gonna talk with Christ the Son.
And then we'll have a meeting around God's throne.

[Chorus]
Verse:

> When I get to Jordan,
> I'll cross Jordan like a man.
> Unbuckle my sword right off my side
> And stick it in the golden sand.
> I'll talk to God the Father
> I'll talk to Christ the Son.
> And then we'll have a meeting around the throne.

In the context of the rampant materialism of contemporary society, it is remarkable that this song, with its otherworldly theme, should cause such a stir in today's Afro-Baptist church. If one remembers, however, that enslaved African-Americans who attended camp meetings were usually not allowed to articulate the joy of being there except in surreptitious song, this meeting was indeed a wondrous event where slave families broken by sale could be reunited once a year. Is it possible that this gospel song is a legacy of those meetings, coming down to us with the jubilation that bondsmen must have felt while singing it over a century ago? Of course those in bondage planning escape could sing of a joyous meeting of family and friends across, not the Jordan, but the Ohio River, which marked the boundary of the slave states. In either case, black people have captured the essence of hope and rejoicing in songs that can still be heard in their second ritual frame today.

Another song that is slow to change within Afro-Baptist tradition is the lined hymn. This form has survived the oppression of slavery, Reconstruction, two world wars, and the era of the 1960s civil rights movement. The original melodies of the Watts hymns have long disappeared. One student of the black lined hymn believes that "the relationship between tune and text in the black tradition has not been fully explored and known" (Bailey 1978: 5). Lined hymns with different texts use the same, undifferentiated melody (Tallmadge 1961: 99). The contemporary rhythm of the lined hymn is almost imperceptible: "There is a beat to the long-meter, however, it is obscured by slow tempo and elaborate embellishment" (Bailey 1978: 6). Far from dying out completely, the long-metered lined hymn is still sung in wealthy black churches in urban Mississippi by both young and old congregants (Bailey 1978: 9). In central Texas, too, Afro-Baptists cling to the lined hymn for use in Devotion. On the other hand, except for a small number of white Primitive Baptists in pockets of Appalachia who still line their old hymns,

> white congregations . . . no longer practice [lining] regularly. . . . Lining out is very common, however, among black Primitive Baptists [because of the] fortuitous compatibility of the alternation of lining out and singing, which is of European origin, and the call-and-response . . . structure of much African and Afro-American music. [Sutton 1982: 2–3, 16].

The history of the lined hymn among white Protestants spans more than three centuries, from 1644 in England to the latter half of the nineteenth century in the United States. Afro-Baptists, however, continue to line their hymns a full century after the last vestiges of the practice have disappeared from mainstream churches (Tallmadge 1961: 95). Afro-Baptist retentions of archaic eighteenth- and nineteenth-century speech and song suggest a mysterious ongoing imitation of early American Protestant practice. The next chapter investigates the reason for these apparent linguistic and musical imitations. We will see that the lined hymn is more than merely a compatible accommodation of European and African song patterns. We will also accept George Pullen Jackson's challenge—extended in 1943 to "scholars and dilettantes"—to substantiate the African origin of long-metered lining in the black tradition.

Note

1. Rouget is unaware of the widespread lack of Jakobson's "universal" poetic features in cultures outside Africa. See Sherzer and Wicks 1982: 150).

4

"Kabiesile Shango!"
A Cross-Cultural Comparison
of Ritual Frames

According to some students of the Afro-Baptist church, the plaintive-
ness created by the archaic prayers and hymns during Devotion is a
legacy of slavery that has lingered into the modern era as an expression of economic hardship (Wiley and Wiley 1984: 7). Following this
line of thought, the plaintive sound, full of wailing and moaning, is
part of a rhetoric of despair that finds expression in religious ritual:
"For working-class Blacks the plaintive sound is necessary; it is con-
soling; it provides catharsis; and communicatively, it links the past with
a present culture still groping for a respected place in the American
environment" (Wiley and Wiley 1984: 9). Prayer, then, becomes an
expression of sorrow, taking the form of pleading instead of praise.
The lined hymns merely reflect this despair.

Another interpretation of Devotion holds that the retentions of antiquated prayer speech and hymn singing that appear to be African-
American imitations of early Euro-American Protestant practices can
only be explained sufficiently as religious custom inherited from
Africa. Aside from any impressions that Afro-Baptists are historically
despondent, this alternative view explains the plaintive sound as a
result of cultural reinterpretation. Despite the trauma experienced by
members of African families and communities who were forcibly separated, transported Africans were able to hold on to some of their traditional customs in the Western Hemisphere. The mixing of different
tribal peoples did not necessarily cause all African beliefs and prac-

tices to become confounded and uprooted in the way that slave dealers and slave owners had calculated.

Religion was one of those especially tenacious traditions that enabled Africans to maintain their sanity and sense of control in a strange, hostile land. Instead of being forgotten and laid aside, deities and supernatural powers "were carried in the memories of enslaved Africans across the Atlantic. To be sure, they underwent a sea change" (Raboteau 1978: 16). However, "much remained of . . . the vitality and durability of African religious perspectives. And it should be emphasized that it is the continuation of perspective that is significant, more so than the fact that the cults of particular African gods . . . have been transmitted to the New World" (Raboteau 1978: 16).

A cross-cultural comparison of eight African-derived rituals in the Western Hemisphere illustrates the durability of an African perspective that continues into the present century, although the specific deities and cosmologies have changed. One surviving African perspective relating to religious ritual reveals a pattern of two distinct paradigms that combine to produce a ritual syntax, or structure, common to all eight rituals reviewed here. These paradigms could be seen as "mood" frames, group behavioral events that are metaphorically associated with each other, as we have already discussed in the first chapter.

The two frames contain on the one hand, European-derived practices, and, on the other, African-derived practices. The European-derived frame always precedes the African-derived frame where possession trance chiefly occurs. In fact, the focus of the second frame is possession trance; and, although this type of trance is not endemic to all the African continent, the possession of devotees by spirits is widespread in the savannah region, the west coast, and central Africa—the geographic homeland of most black people in the Western Hemisphere (Simpson 1970: 94). It is therefore not surprising that some form of trance, whether possession or not, should exist in black religious practice in the Americas. If trance were not found in the Western Hemisphere, that phenomenon could not be so readily explained.

The North American Ringshout

The ringshout of North America is a form of African-derived ritual that was a common form of black worship on the Southern plantation and as far north as Baltimore (Stuckey 1987: 138). While the plantation missionaries were intent upon erasing African worship practices, enslaved blacks secretly continued their religious rituals in the plantation hush harbors. During these clandestine religious meetings, worshippers performed the ringshout, an event combining dance and song where participants would shuffle their feet in a counterclockwise circle. The song leader would call aloud the verse of a song, inviting the ring members to join in echoing the same verse in a chorus.

Actually a group of three to eight singers off to the side of the ring would supply the most vigorous singing, pounding the floor with broomsticks as a makeshift drum (Creel 1988: 298; Marks 1982: 310; Roberts 1974: 162–63). As ring members moved in their circle, the call-and-response singing would increase in loudness and tempo until some of the ring members became possessed by the Holy Spirit (Creel 1988: 298; Raboteau 1978: 70; Roberts 1974: 163). According to one historian, this particular form of dance worship shows "close parallels between the style of dancing observed in African and Caribbean cult worship" (Raboteau 1978: 70).

Those parallels, like the counterclockwise circle in which participants never lift their feet from the ground, are seen in the funeral ring dance among the Ekoi people of southern Nigeria. The West African Ibo, Yoruba, and Ibibio folk also perform the counterclockwise shuffle so that a "wave-like ripple . . . runs down the muscles of back and along arms to the finger-tips. Every part of the body dances, not only the limbs" (Stuckey 1987: 11). Among the Bakongo of central Africa, the ring dance, like that of the Ekoi, was performed at funerals in order to connect the living with their ancestors. The West African Mende and Temne also performed the counterclockwise dance for religious purposes, in particular to celebrate marriage (Stuckey 1987: 11–13).

One of the first accounts of the ringshout in North America is H. G. Spaulding's description of one that took place in the antebellum South. Writing for a Northern chronicle, *Continental Monthly*, in 1863, he reported that during the Civil War ringshouts also took place after regular praise house worship services. After this conventional gathering had concluded,

> Three or four [people], standing still, clapping their hands and beating time with their feet, commence singing in unison . . . while the

> others walk round in a ring, in single file, joining also in the song.
> . . . Soon those in the ring leave off their singing, the others keeping
> it up the while with increased vigor, and strike into the shout step.
> . . . (Spaulding [1863] 1969: 4–5)

The result of this increased vigor was "shouting," that is, some form
of trance, "a simple outburst and manifestation of religious fervor"
(Spaulding 1969: 4–5). Enslaved African-Americans were so filled with
the Holy Spirit by the climax of the ring's excitement that they could
thereby forget the never-ending torments of their slavery (Blassingame
1979: 145).

Another vivid depiction of the ringshout (Allen [1865] in Sobel 1979:
141–42) describes the site of the performance, its opening, and the
customary singing at one of these performances:

> The true "shout" takes place on Sundays . . . either in the praise
> house or in some cabin in which a regular religious meeting has
> been held. For some time [before the ring is formed] one can hear
> . . . the vociferous exhortation or prayer of the presiding elder or
> the brother who has a gift that way . . . and at regular intervals one
> hears the elder "deaconing" a hymnbook hymn, which is sung two
> lines at a time, and whose wailing cadences, born on the night air,
> are indescribably melancholy.

This melancholy lined, or "deaconed," hymn singing gives way to a
more lively event:

> But the benches are pushed back to the wall when the formal meet-
> ing is over, and old and young, men and women . . . all stand up in
> the middle of the floor, and when the "sperchil" is struck up, begin
> first walking and . . . shuffling round . . . in a ring . . . the progres-
> sion is mainly due to a jerking hitching motion, which agitates the
> shouter, and soon brings out streams of perspiration.

Whereas the preceding hymns, which the worshippers called "sperchils,"
were sung by the whole congregation before the ring was formed,
a band of singers off to the side provided the jubilee songs, called
"runnin' sperchils," that led to trance (Allen 1967: 78).

> Sometimes they dance silently, sometimes the song itself is also sung
> by the dancers. But more frequently a band, composed of some of
> the best singers, stand at the side of the room to "base" the others,
> singing the body of the song and clapping their hands together or on
> the knees. (Raboteau 1978: 70–71)

Frederick Douglas, born into slavery, and W.E.B. DuBois, writing in *Souls of Black Folk*, have been the most eminent voices to call the Negro spiritual the "sorrow songs" of the slave experience. Descriptions by Spaulding and others of the vigorous singing of spirituals during the ringshout, however, indicate a jubilation rather than pathos in the black slave song, at least as the ringshout progresses. Lydia Parrish reported that, on the Gullah Sea Islands off the coast of Georgia and South Carolina, worshippers began their ringshouts with slowly lined hymns that later gave way to more ecstatic singing just before the shouting began (Parrish 1942: 80). According to one musicologist, the ringshout gathering "divided itself into two groups, shouter (that is, dancers) and singers," while the "dancers participated in the singing according to how they felt" (Southern 1983: 169). This division into singers and dancers will become an important point to remember in the development of this chapter's discussion of musical performance and ritual in a cross-cultural perspective.

Before the Civil War remnants of the ringshout were ubiquitous throughout the plantation South, especially in Virginia, Alabama, and Georgia (Sobel 1979: 140-42). On the Gullah Islands the ringshout found an enduring role in Afro-Protestant—namely Methodist and Baptist—ritual. The following description of a ringshout occurring on the Georgia mainland in 1927 suggests that the practice so common on the Sea Islands could also be found inland after the Civil War:

> It [the ringshout] was regularly permitted in all churches . . . but not as a part of the service. After that had closed, the wooden benches were pushed back and the centre of the floor was cleared to give room for the circle of shouters. This was done regularly on two fixed occasions—Christmas Eve and the last day of the old year. . . .
> (Gordon 1972: 447)

Held on the occasion of a Baptist or Methodist worship service, the ringshout could only take place after benediction (Creel 1988: 298).

The ringshout obviously continued as an African-American religious ritual form after emancipation. In 1934 folklorists John and Alan Lomax observed ringshouts in Louisiana, Texas, and Georgia, as well as in the Bahamas, where many Sea Islanders were taken as slaves of owners loyal to the British cause during the American Revolutionary War (Raboteau 1978: 70). Ringshouts still occur on the Delmarva Peninsula, where "praying bands" perform the ring dance after the conventional Methodist ritual has ended (David 1988).

After services in a Frankford, Delaware Methodist church, praying band members, whose average age is sixty, change from formal attire to less restrictive clothing. Men take off their neckties, starched shirts, and suit jackets and replace them with a loose-fitting shirt made of coarse, burlap-like material. They leave the top button unfastened. Women put on a white apron; the reason for this is unknown, but it is reminiscent of the practice of Gullah female "seekers," who wear a white band around their foreheads during the winter period of their spiritual initiation into the band of ringshouters (Creel 1988: 287; David 1988: 2–3). Because the pews in the modern church are anchored to the floor, ring members can no longer push them back out of the way as they form the circle (David 1988: 2). After a deacon has prayed one of the ornate prayers similar to Afro-Baptist tradition, the ring leader calls band members to the rail in front of the altar. Men stand behind the rail, closer to the altar, while women gather in front of it, closer to the congregation (David 1988: 2). At this point, the leader will begin to line out a hymn—usually of eighteenth-century vintage—that the band members answer in a slow, almost dragging tempo (David 1988: 4). The lines are so distorted that many younger congregants admit that they do not understand the hymn texts.

As the hymn progresses, the tempo gradually speeds up and the tonic key rises by the interval of a half step, creating the effect of the hymn's rising off the ground. By raising the key with each new musical phrase, the hymn ends on a much higher tonic center than the one on which it began. When the hymn is concluded, another member prays and another hymn is lined. In order to encourage the band members and congregation to sing enthusiastically, the ring leader, calling the best singers to the front of the congregation,

> gets the singers to "pitch up" the hymn and to increase its tempo; as they catch on, the singers clap their hands and stamp their feet to keep time. By the time the bands reach the final line of the hymn, they are singing in a tight unison, with individual singers providing her or his own melodic embellishments to the tune. . . . While singing out the hymn, the worshippers' embellishments become more exaggerated until they are no longer adorning the tune, but are shouting. (David 1988: 4)

This alternation between prayer and hymn continues until a praying member becomes so emotionally affected by his or her own prayer that he or she begins to shriek, tears visibly running down the prayer's face. Moved by the sincerity of the prayer, band members now begin singing without lining. The new song is a black folk spiritual, beginning slowly but progressing to a quickening pace so that the members begin to rock, first from side to side, then back and forth on their heels. Referred to by some members as "prancing," the energetic movement resembles a horse's gallop. While prancing, members march counterclockwise around the mourner's bench then eventually around the sanctuary, constantly repeating the verse "Goodbye. Goodbye. I ain't got long to stay here" (David 1988: 5–6). This act of marching around the congregation is similar to the practice in some black churches during the 1940s, where "[if] ring shouts were not practiced, marching round the church often was . . . as a semi-dancing march to an intensely rhythmic spiritual" (Roberts 1974: 163).

The Frankford, Delaware band members return to the rail after the march around the church, increasing the intensity and tempo of their spiritual until the Holy Spirit takes hold of one or more of them: "When He arrives, He makes His presence audible as a hissing sound that runs from person to person. To the band members, this hissing sound is the same as the "rushing wind" with which the Spirit came onto the apostles on the Pentecost" (David 1988: 6–7).

The modern restriction imposed by the immovable pews in no way diminishes the excitement that black worshippers feel. In the 1920s Newbill Puckett, the folklorist, described ringshouts in which "before the service there is a long period of singing, tapping of feet on the floor, and rhythmic swaying of the body. This seems in itself to produce a sort of hypnotic effect" (Puckett 1926: 531). This initial languor eventually gave way to what the observer called "some native African dance" (Puckett 1926: 532). Today's ringshout on the eastern Chesapeake shore has undergone some changes since that time but nevertheless exhibits a structural division into two frames: a Euro-American beginning and an Afro-American finish. The first frame contains slow, surge-like singing in unison by the congregation, free of trance. The second frame contains faster songs provided by a group of singers who perform off to the side while the dancers enter trance.

The Jamaican Revivalists

The revivalist groups in Jamaica also manifest a two-frame ritual structure. The Pukkumina and Zion religions of the twentieth century grew out of the Great Revival that swept Jamaica in 1860. This revival was a combination of *myalism*, a belief system of African origin, and the fervor of the National Baptist Movement, which George Liele, the former slave from Georgia who founded the Yama Craw Baptist Church near Savannah, brought to the island. Confined mostly to the eastern parishes of the island, especially the poorer sections of the capital, Kingston, the larger and more active revivalist groups attract mainly women followers (Moore 1979: 293). In fact, women may become spiritual leaders, called "shepherds," in either the Pukkumina or Zion groups or "bands" (Moore 1979: 294).

Both groups draw members from among lower-income groups, primarily fishermen, port workers, and household servants. Partly because of the social stigma of poverty, the Jamaican middle class shuns the revivalist bands. The greater stigma, however, is the fact that both Pukkumina and Zion bands oppose orthodox Christianity, represented by the established denominations on the island. In the eyes of the middle class, the revivalists are polytheistic because they make appeals to spirits (Seaga 1969: 1–6). Although most revivalist rituals are open to the public, members conduct clandestine gatherings for the most serious spiritual endeavors, such as curing and death rites (Moore 1979: 293; Seaga 1969: 6). A gathering of revivalists includes "both members who 'have the spirit,' that is, have experienced possession by a spirit, and those who have never. During the meetings, many of those who 'have the spirit' are 'possessed by supernatural powers'" (Seaga 1969: 7).

Differences between Pukkumina and Zion followers center on the nature of possession and of the possessing spirits, although the structure of their rituals is quite similar. Both bands seek the aid of possessing spirits, but the Zionists are closer to European Christian doctrine. The rituals of the Zionist bands begin with "speeches, Bible-reading, praying and the singing of choruses . . . accompanied by drumming" (Seaga 1969: 10). These "choruses" are songs taken, rhythmically unaltered, from the Sankey and Moody hymnal; members do not add syncopation to the original meter (Lewin 1968: 54). During hymns and prayers, the congregation "begins a mild *trumping* and *laboring*," that is, audible breathing and a rocking back and forth on their heels (Moore 1979: 304). The initial drumming stops as trumping and the pounding of feet begin to supply the percussion.

At this point, praying, reading, and hymn singing come to an end. The shepherd then organizes only those followers adept in becoming possessed into a ring formation, while he or she starts groaning rhythmically in order to change the beat of the earlier hymns. Thus, the first verse of a hymn like, "Hold My Hands Again Lord," may begin as written, sung in monophonic melody, that is, with no harmony. The second verse, however, is transformed by heavy, fast polyrhythmic breathing in which the singers also hum, hiss, and inhale audibly (Murray 1961: ATL 1524). In "Steal Away" the singers use lip vibrations, clapping, whistling, and grunts to change the melody and rhythm (Murray 1961: ATL 1524 [Archives of Traditional Music]). Thus, the hymns' former tempos are altered when ring members begin contrapuntal groaning and trumping in answer to the shepherd's groans (Lewin 1968: 54).

Possession trance for Zionists happens gradually as ring members clap their hands, stamp their feet, and continue trumping to the drummer's polyrhythms. When they stop bowing to and fro and move from side to side they have become possessed. At this point, members begin to "talk in tongues," a phenomenon known as glossolalia. The shepherd interprets this speech for the gathering, for only the shepherd can understand the groans and glossolalia. The possessing powers are usually "heavenly" spirits—namely, biblical characters who are benevolent: the Holy Trinity, the Holy Ghost, archangels, Old Testament prophets, New Testament disciples, evangelists—and ancestors (Moore 1979: 304–5; Seaga 1969: 10–13). Both types of revivalist groups call on these powers through possessed ring members in order to heal or rectify wrongs done to band members and their friends.

The Pukkumina ritual opens similarly to the Zionist one, though no drumming occurs (Seaga 1969: 10). After the leader organizes the ring, members begin moving in a counterclockwise circle around the altar to the accompaniment of hand clapping, foot stomping, and the clanging of cymbals and a bell (Lewin 1968: 7; Moore 1979: 304; Seaga 1969: 8–10). Pukkumina possession, unlike that of Zionists, is sudden, signaled by a ring member whose leg stiffens in a paralytic shock while he or she continuously stomps the normal leg on the ground. Suddenly the possessed person falls forward and remains motionless for a minute. The member returns to activity by breathing rapidly and audibly, while barking and imitating the sounds of a clanging bell (Seaga 1969: 7). The possessed communicates his or her message from the world of the supernatural in glossolalic song instead of speech (Seaga 1969: 8–10). Instead of benevolent biblical characters, the possessing powers are "earthbound" and "ground" spirits. For Pukkumina followers the earthbound powers include fallen angels, biblical prophets, and apostles, while the ground spirits, also called *zombis*, include ancestors (Moore 1979: 294).

Pukkumina followers do not call upon these powers to enact evil but believe that fallen angels and ancestral dead are less abstract and thus more efficacious than the Christian Trinity. The earthbound and ground spirits are more like the African intermediary powers who offer quicker and more effective results to their followers by addressing God on behalf of band members or bestowing blessings that are within their power to grant. Followers "consider all supernatural forces as capable of good and evil. They quote the Mosaic law: 'an eye for an eye, and a tooth for a tooth' . . . revenge therefore can be just and good, as well as evil and wrong" (Seaga 1969: 13).

The bell ringing and trumping that help ring members to become possessed are accompanied by singing from band members who do not get possessed. Those "in the spirit" do not sing; songs leading to and sustaining trance are provided for them. The commonality in Zionist and Pukkumina ritual frames is that both groups, in their first frame, use Bible reading and unimprovised group singing of Sankey hymns— a reflection of Euro-American influence. Their second frame, however, reveals a sharply contrasting African influence in which vocal improvisation, polyrhythmic percussion involving trumping and laboring, as well as hand clapping and foot stomping, alter the brief riffs or hymn melody beyond recognition. The ritual music in frame two accompanies African-derived trance with Africanized singing, especially among the Pukkumina members, who change the triple-metered Sankey hymns into quadruple and duple meters (Lewin 1968: 7). In neither group does possession trance occur in the first frame. Only in frame two do band members become possessed. Most important to remember is the fact that the possessed members do not sing—this is done for them by the nonpossessed.

The St. Vincent Shakers

On the island of St. Vincent, a former West Indian colony of Great Britain, Shakerism continues as a religious practice derived, like the North American ringshout and Jamaican Revivalist bands, from Judaeo-Christian concepts. Like the revivalists, the St. Vincent Shakers are probably socially and economically stigmatized, since most members are reportedly dark skinned and poor (Simpson 1978: 122). In light of this stigma, Shakers are probably more akin, culturally, to Africa than Europe. As an amalgam of European Christianity and African religious belief, "Shakerism appears to be a blend of a Methodist base; some elements borrowed from Anglicanism, Catholicism; some modified African religious traits. . . . An outstanding feature . . . is the mild states of dissociation" (Simpson 1978: 121–22).

The Shaker ritual begins with hymn singing, consecrating the four corners of the sanctuary with holy water, and the reciting of prayers. "The members of the congregation . . . recite the Apostles' Creed, kneel, repeat the General Confession, the Lord's Prayer, and another prayer, stand and sing the Gloria Patri again" (Simpson 1978: 121–22). Trance, in the form of trembling—which act gives the group its name—rarely occurs during this Christian-derived portion of the ritual. That must wait until the ritual opening has ended and the sermon begins. After the preacher finishes his sermon, he begins singing and congregational members enter into their shaking trance. The attitude toward trance is similar to that found at the nineteenth-century camp meeting; "[a] successful spiritual journey . . . admits the sojourner into the Shaker elite" (Simpson 1978: 121–22).

A contrasting St. Vincentian ritual is that of the Streams of Power. Beginning with fast, loud singing accompanied by instrumentation, the Streams of Power followers open their ritual with hand clapping and the stomping of feet. After this initial section, congregants enter into glossolalic trance without the use of musical instruments or percussive song. Then follows the sermon and benediction, which involve no trance behavior, only the singing of European-derived hymns. The ritual structure of the Streams of Power differs markedly from that of the Shakers because the former group was founded in Holland in 1952 as an outgrowth of European spiritualism and later imported to the island (for a discussion of Euro-American spiritualism, see Goodman

1988: 27–37). The Streams of Power attracts few followers; its "meetings are shorter, simple, and less ritualized than Shaker services" (Simpson 1978: 123).

The Trinidad Spiritual Baptists

Like the revivalist bands in Jamaica, the Spiritual Baptist Church in Trinidad has an unclear and somewhat confusing origin. In one version its first members were Shaker immigrants from St. Vincent who combined their practices with those of the London Baptists, who in turn, were descendants of North American Afro-Baptist soldiers whom the British took to Moruga, Trinidad after their defeat in the War of 1812 (Houk 1986: 31; Parks 1986: 23; M. Williams 1985: 23–25). The Spiritual Baptist Church had a wide appeal to the masses of poor at the turn of the century. The established Christian denominations, which were rapidly losing members and money, convinced the Trinidadian government to outlaw the church as a public disturbance in the Shouters Prohibition Ordinance in 1917. Accused of shouting too loud, they were branded in legal documents as "Shouter" Baptists, a derision they detest but which outsiders, especially American scholars, have used nevertheless to refer to them (for example, see Herskovits [1941] 1958: 223).

During the years of legal persecution (1917 to 1951), its membership grew considerably in number so that today there are approximately 275 Spiritual Baptist churches all over Trinidad, while emigrants established Spiritual Baptist congregations in Venezuela, Guyana, and New York City (Houk 1986: 33; Parks 1986: 26; Williams 1985: 38–39). The congregations still tend to be poor and their clergy not educated formally in seminaries, while their church buildings are always located outside the limits of any town as a reminder of three decades of persecution (Williams 1985: 28).

Their ritual "has a subdued opening, the singing of the Sankeys giving forth a heavy, doleful, dragging effect" (Herskovits 1964: 213). Other observers of the ritual have described it as beginning with loud bell ringing, the lighting of candles at the four corners of the sanctuary, and the pouring of holy water into these corners to purify the sanctuary, while the leader with his or her shepherd's staff starts reading from the Bible (Houk 1986: 41–44; Parks 1981: 50–54; Simpson

1960: ATL 4806 [Folkways Records]). During this opening segment of the ritual, which may last from one to two hours, the congregation recites in unison the Twenty-third Psalm, Gloria Patri, Hail Mary, and Apostles' Creed.

In Oropouche, a hamlet on the southern end of the island, this recitation takes place before an altar engraved with the Star of David. The sanctuary walls are decorated with colorful chromolithographs of the Hindu gods Vishnu and Krishna and gilded Hebraic letters (Glazier 1983: 41; Houk 1986: 41–44; Parks 1981: 50–54). Interspersed with the recitations are lined, somber Anglican hymns, such as, "The Church Is One Foundation," and Sankey hymns for which the song leader rapidly calls out each verse (Pitts 1990: 89–176–F [Archives of Traditional Music]; Williams 1985: 60; Waterman 1943: 118). Not needing hymnals, the congregation responds to several hymns in succession without omitting a stanza, the singing being quite slow. Noting the dragging tempo, one ethnologist wrote that these "slow, unemotional hymns [are] said to keep the Holy Ghost from manifesting Himself before the building is clean" (Glazier 1983: 42).

The second frame begins, like the North American ringshout, with emotional prayers offered at the center pole of the church and incessant bell ringing to call forth the Holy Spirit (Parks 1981: 145–50). The more emotional the prayers become the more likely a member of the congregation is to go into trance. When this happens, the song leader ceases lining hymns for the congregation and a percussive singing ensues. Using hand clapping, rattles, a bongo drum, and "'doption," that is, audible gasping, the choir of women dressed in white to the side of the altar transforms the Sankey songs to accompany the praying and trance that explode concurrently. One song favorite here, as among Afro-Baptists, is Fanny Crosby's "Pass Me Not, O Gentle Savior" or "Amazing Grace" (Pitts 1990: 89–176–F [Archives of Traditional Music]; Simpson 1960: ATL 4806). Another is "What A Mighty God We Serve" in which the verses have been replaced with the rhythmic syllables, "ram ma bam," sung in counterpoint over a staccatoed *habañera* meter.

This type of musical transformation led the Herskovitses to ponder the use of the Sankey: "What is baffling is . . . the acceptance by the folk . . . of the hymns just as the Whites sing them. . . . But just as the essential rites of the cult are carried on beneath an overlay of conventionalized decorum, so these 'Sankeys' also mask more vigorous forms"

(Herskovits and Herskovits 1964: 120). After a couple of verses, the white-composed hymn changes so as to produce trance: "[T]he singers, continuing the melody, began to change their rhythm, introducing handclapping as the tempo became faster, until the hymn was transformed into a swing idiom which in the proper setting would result in the spirit possession" (Herskovits and Herskovits 1964: 120).

Trance may take the form of short jerks and tremors or may last several minutes causing the possessed to dance in the Spirit, swirling about and shouting "Hello!" as a greeting to the Holy Ghost that has descended upon the member (Williams 1985: 47). During trance, the possessed may also speak in tongues, mixing his or her speech with Chinese, Hindu, or African words (Parks 1981: 107). Finally spent, the trance ends with the possessed collapsing onto the floor, completely exhausted but euphoric (Williams 1985: 47).

Similar to the member of the Jamaican revivalist and St. Vincent Shaker groups, the Spiritual Baptists in Trinidad belong to the working class mostly, and many are aware of their African heritage (Simpson 1978: 117). Unlike the Jamaican bands, however, the Spiritual Baptists did not develop under a strong revival movement. Still, their ritual structure resembles that of the Jamaican revivalists and others we have discussed in that the first ritual frame depends upon European speech and song forms, while the second uses Africanized improvisation that becomes polyrhythmic over a constant base line, or ostinato, leading to possessionlike trance.

Jamaican Kumina

The two metaphoric frames described above are also to be found in rituals not derived from a Judaeo-Christian theology. For example, in the Jamaican Kumina religion the ritual frames surface. Located mostly in eastern Jamaica like the revivalist groups, the Kumina religion is presumably of Dahomean origin (Logan 1982: 86). Only one identifiable West African power, however, remains in the Kumina pantheon—the Yoruba god of thunder, Shango. Along with this deity, earth, sky, and ancestral powers called zombis possess members who, like the revivalists, form a ring to bring on possession trance through singing and drumming (Lewin 1968: 54; Moore 1979: 295; Raboteau 1978: 17; Simpson 1978: 99–100; Logan 1982: 86).

The Kumina ritual begins with the singing of *bailo*, or *bilah*, songs whose texts are in standard Jamaican English using few Creole features (Lewin 1968: 54; Moore 1979: 298; Logan 1982: 86). When the bilah songs come to an end, frame two begins with *kbanda* drum rhythms in 6/8 time, invoking Oto, the sky god. As the members circle in the ring, the kbanda polyrhythms introduce a possessing zombi (Moore 1979: 298). The chief drummer receives eight years of training before he is allowed to play for these gatherings, and drummers may also act as dancers in the ring who become possessed (Lewin 1968: 54; Moore 1979: 297; Logan 1982: 86). In case one of the four drummers becomes possessed while playing, many backup musicians are on hand to play the kbanda while he dances in such a patterned choreography that observers know which power is possessing him (Moore 1979: 299–302; Nagashima 1984: 68). Meanwhile, the kbanda "keeps up a steady beat while the 'playing cast'—only one is usually played at a time—uses whichever rhythm is needed to charm the particular spirit being invoked" (Lewin 1968: 54).

The use of African ostinato to form the rhythmic base, or meter, while another instrument embellishes the beat contrapuntally, is a feature of Kumina trance music. The same contrapuntal variation occurs in the Jamaican revivalist, St. Vincentian Shaker, and Trinidadian Spiritual Baptist songs during the moments leading up to possession and during trance: the improvising rhythmic "instruments" in these cases are usually the members' voices, hands, and feet.

In the Kumina second frame bilah songs give way to *myal* or "country" songs sung in an archaic Kikongo (Cassidy 1961: 237–38, 243; Moore 1979: 298; Logan 1982: 86). These Bantu songs are reserved for the most powerful possessions. Ethnomusicologist Olive Lewin describes this ritual Kikongo as having "a large number of genuinely Congolese words . . . which are usually sung to appease or entertain the possessing spirits (Lewin 1968: 54). While kbanda and myal songs invoke and amuse the spirits, the encircling ring members communicate with the summoned spirits using Kikongo, unlike their fellow revivalists who speak in tongues with their possessing powers (Lewin 1968: 54). In the Kumina first frame a European language, English, provides the language of the songs "when there is not much spirit possession" (Lewin 1968: 54). In frame two, however, an African language replaces English as the medium for addressing the powers. Members sing songs in Kikongo that "are taught by the spirits only to those they possess" (Lewin 1968: 468).

Jamaican Convince

The Jamaican Convince religion is another belief system involving ancestors and a ritual structure that displays the binary frame pattern. Almost extinct, Convince followers are called "Bongo men," descendants of slave maroons who escaped to the Blue Mountains (Raboteau 1978: 16–17; Logan 1982: 87). Unlike the Kumina who still recognize the Yoruba Shango, Bongo men have forgotten the names of the West African powers, yet they still venerate the old African ancestors who are thought to be more powerful than the more recent dead (Raboteau 1978: 16–17).

The Convince ritual usually begins at dusk with slow, congregational singing of Christian hymns, led but not lined by a song leader (Murray 1961: ATL 1524). Mixed with hymn singing are a few prayers and Bible reading. After this opening, called "prayer meeting," the Bongo men, who are adepts in spirit possession, join the crowd, signalling to them that the possession rites are about to begin. Wellwishers among the crowd invoke possession among the Bongo men by singing well-known, popular hymns instead of the more esoteric hymns sung in the previous prayer meeting. When a Bongo man finally becomes possessed by an ancestral spirit, he "calls for hymns . . . as he dances. . . . The dancing and spirit possessions . . . may continue for two days or longer" (Simpson 1978: 101–2).

Like songs in the second frame of the other rituals, the singing in Convince rituals supporting possession trance involves polyrhythmic hand clapping, contrapuntal voices, and faster tempos than the first frame songs (Murray 1961: ATL 1524). Unlike the songs in the first frame, these second frame melodies are popular with the audience. Spirit possession does not occur in the first frame but must wait until the Bongo men enter trance in frame two. Just as in the revivalist bands, the Convince devotees who become possessed do not sing during trance. A group of singers off to the sides sing the favorite songs requested by the entranced Bongo men.

Orisha in Trinidad

The binary ritual frames also surface in more African-derived religions in the Caribbean, suggesting that the dichotomous frames are not simply a result of Christian/African syncretism. The Orisha religion in

Trinidad combines elements of the Roman Catholic, Anglican, and Spiritual Baptist ritual with Yoruba religion. Supposedly the religion developed on the island in the nineteenth century when West African descendants, namely, the Yoruba, and black immigrants from other Caribbean islands "combined traditional tribal beliefs and practices with elements of Catholicism" (Simpson 1978: 73). Because of this strong Yoruba influence, the major Yoruba powers, called *orisha*, still remain in the Trinidadian pantheon (compare with Murphy 1988: 42–43). Followers of the religion still recognize Eshu/Elegba, the West African trickster; Ogun, the god of iron and war; Yemanja, the ocean divinity and power over fertility; Shango, the god of thunder and lightning; Obatala, the creator of humankind; Oya, the guardian of the dead; Oshun, the coquettish deity, and Shakpana, the power over contagious diseases (Raboteau 1978: 21; Simpson 1965: 120; Simpson 1970: 38). Originally this religion is referred to in the literature as "Shango" worship, but followers are quick to point out that Shango is just one *orisha* among several that are recognized (Glazier 1983: 133; Herskovits [1941] 1958: 221; Simpson 1965: passim). Though appearing in separate physical manifestations when possessing a devotee, Orisha followers think of each orisha as both a fragment of and intermediary with the supreme god, which they call Olodumare (Mbiti 1969: 29–32, 76). Orisha rituals usually take the form of four-day celebrations, called "feasts," three to four times a year. Drumming to the orisha occurs at night under a covered dance area called the *palais*, with a roof commonly made of galvanized tin or thatch (Houk 1986: 76; Simpson 1965: 114–15). Beginning at night, the ritual of thanksgiving to the orisha opens with a two-hour "prayer meeting" in which "[h]alf an hour or so before the ceremony starts, the early arrivals hum and sing sporadically and watch the drummers tune the drums and beat a few practice rhythms" (Simpson 1970: 37). When the rest of the congregation arrives, the prayer meeting formally begins. As in a Spiritual Baptist opening, lighted candles are placed on the ground in each corner of the consecrated area along with libations of holy water. The congregation begins to pray in unison. This first prayer, known to all as "the gathering," is usually the Our Father, Hail Mary, or Apostles' Creed. After the opening prayer, one of the prominent guests will offer a more esoteric prayer. Because of its unfamiliarity to the crowd, he will have to line out the verses, which congregants repeat. Examples are prayers to St. Michael, St. Francis, St. George, or the Blessed Martin (Houk

1986: 76–84; Simpson 1965: 42; Simpson 1970: 38; Simpson 1978: 76). It is not uncommon for the prayer meeting to take place away from the palais, usually at a Spiritual Baptist church under the auspices of a Baptist clergyman; the singing consists of the same lined hymns and songs heard in the Spiritual Baptist opening frame (Glazier 1983: 133; Herskovits and Herskovits 1939: ATL 5306-5312 [Archives of Traditional Music]).

Familiar and lined prayers alternate until usually three of each prayer is offered. After the beginning frame has run its two-hour course, several minutes to several hours or even an entire day may elapse before the second frame begins (Glazier 1983: 133). The *amombah*, or Orisha priest, now takes charge by dismissing "Eshu, who is identified with Satan . . . before the other powers can be summoned" (Simpson 1970: 38). Having dismissed the trickster by overturning a calabash of water and ashes dedicated to him, the drummers begin a battery of rhythms for, first, Ogun and, afterwards, for the other powers (Glazier 1983: 134; Houk 1986: 79–80; Simpson 1965: 42–43). The loud drumming breaks the stillness of night in Matura, a rural settlement in the northeast corner of Trinidad. The drums signal that the somber first frame has ended and the African second frame will continue well into the next day with Ogun and St. George possessing several gathered followers. Instead of Catholic and Spiritual Baptist litanies and songs, this second frame begins with percussive drumming and repetitive choral refrains (Simpson: ATL 4806). Whereas the Roman Catholic prayers in the first frame are in French, the formal addresses, as well as the songs to the orisha, are a mixed-speech of liturgical Yoruba, Trinidadian French Creole, and possibly nonsense syllables (Glazier 1983: 135; Simpson 1970: 38).

Spirit possession begins as devotees to the different orisha march, first, clockwise around the palais, and then change the direction of the circular march (Glazier 1983: 135; Houk 1986: 80). As the drummers increase the tempos of the favorite rhythms of the orisha and other spirits, the devotee becomes possessed—the supernatural powers are believed to descend directly from the sky into his or her head. At this point devotees seized by the thunder power will shout, "Kabiesile Shango!" in liturgical Yoruba, welcoming the possessing orisha Shango into their heads (Murphy 1988: 98). A mild convulsion in the devotee then occurs, a sign that he or she has been an obedient, "respectable" servant of the possessing power. On the other hand, a violent seizure during possession means that the follower has been "filthy," or "wrong doing" (Simpson 1970: 26–28). Regardless of the form of possession, devotees cannot relate what occurred to them during it: trance is unconscious and unrelatable (Simpson 1970: 26–28).

Followers of Orisha also believe that lesser spirits precede the strong possessing powers. These less potent spirits, called *reres*, occasionally seize devotees during the second frame to announce the demands of the major powers, which will soon make their appearance. The reres are thus messengers for the principal divinities, and they manifest themselves in a light form of dissociation in which the devotee engages in playful or childlike behavior either before or after the principal orisha has arrived through the devotee's head. These less powerful reres are subservient to the major powers: "If a *rere* is manifesting on a person and powers are manifesting on others, the *rere* will not come into the *palais*" (Simpson 1970: 26–28). Like the major divinities, the reres will manifest themselves only during the second frame. Neither powerful nor lighter states of dissociation will occur in the first ritual Orisha frame.

Haitian Vodun

Although Haiti's Code Noir of 1685 insisted that all slaves be baptized Roman Catholic and instructed in catechism, Haiti's clergy complained by 1692 that Africans on the island were disguising "ancient idolatrous cult" superstition with Christian practices (Raboteau 1978: 25). At that time, the culturally dominant ethnic group of Africans in Haiti were the West African Fon, although Yoruba, Congo Mayombe, Ibo, Bambara, and Mahi—just to name a few African peoples—were present in the formation of Haiti's enslaved population (Simpson 1978: 58–59).

Between 1730 and 1790 the indigenous religious rituals involving dance and drumming, called "Vodun," developed out of a combination of African cosmologies, with that of the Fon from the present-day Republic of Benin dominating the belief system. The focal Vodun ritual, like that of Trinidad Orisha, is the annual feast of thanksgiving, or *mange sec*, to appease the African and indigenous supernatural powers, called *loa* (Deren 1953: 209). Although there are several different Vodun rituals derived from several different African ethnic groups in

Haiti, the ritual structure discussed here is the calendrical Rada ritual practiced by Fon and Yoruba descendants living in the center of the island near Port-au-Prince.

An overview of this ritual, which is probably one of the most researched and documented of rituals in the Caribbean, shows that it begins with the sketching of *veve*. Veve are the elaborate sacred drawings and designs made with maize flour on the floor of the dance hut, called *peristyle*, where the drumming and dancing to the loa will take place (Métraux [1959] 1972: 163–66, see especially 164; Thompson 1983: 188–91). The Vodun priest, or *houngan*, draws the veve by pouring the flour through the palm of his hand, then placing food offerings to the loa at certain crossroads near the peristyle and *hounfor*, the name of the sacred hut where the altar and holy paraphernalia are kept. The loa are thought to be drawn to the veve crucigrams. The houngan is usually assisted by his helpers, called *hounsis* (Métraux [1959] 1972: 62–78). Dressed all in white, the hounsis gather at the hounfor in casual conversation before the ritual gets underway, much in the same way as Orisha followers gather before a ritual in Trinidad.

After these preliminary preparations, the ritual actually begins much like Trinidad Orisha worship, with Roman Catholic litanies delivered in French (Denning and Rudolph 1979: 56; Lomax 1951: ATL 5382 [Archives of Traditional Music]). No drumming occurs during these preliminary events, although the drummers have arrived at the peristyle by this time. After the prayers have ended, the salute to the various loa and trance possession of devotees takes place, accompanied by drums and the hounsis' twirling and pirouetting before important guests (Métraux [1959] 1972: 159). After the loa have been presented their sacrifices and the hounsis have relayed their messages to the mortal listeners, the ritual draws to a close (Simpson 1978: 58–59).

A more detailed account of this calendrical ritual shows that after sacred veve are drawn, the houngan blesses the hounfor and peristyle with libations of water from a jug that he passes to each visitor and hounsi so that they may do the same. Each participant pours the sacred water so that it trickles toward the *poteau-mitan*, or center pole, down which the loa will enter the dance area and possess their devotees (Métraux [1959] 1972: 77–78). Having finished the libations, the hounsis form a line and march around the peristyle saluting distinguished visitors and their houngans with multicolored flags, representing each loa, bound to long poles (Hurston [1938] 1990: 148; Métraux

[1959] 1972: 160–61; see Thompson 1983: 184–88). This formal salutation functions as a means of resolving possible resentment and jealous competition that a meeting such as this may inspire where various religious leaders and their followers gather. The flag bearers acknowledge each visiting houngan while giving the highest authority to the host priest.

After this salutary march the Roman Catholic litanies begin. The Rada rituals pay homage primarily to the West African divinities of the Fon and Yoruba, with those of the former being the more numerous and important. The Kongo, Ibo, and Angolan powers form another Haitian pantheon, called Petro. The Petro powers, unlike their gentler West African counterparts in Rada, are thought to work quick, powerful, and often brutal results that can be violent (Hurston [1938] 1990: 116; Métraux [1959] 1972: 117–19; Thompson 1983: 179–84). For example, the amorous Rada goddess of fertility, Erzulie, who seduces young men, in Petro turns into an old, vicious red-eyed hag whom followers find it difficult to look upon (Hurston [1938] 1990: 123; Métraux [1959] 1972: 110–12). Although most Haitian rituals are given for Rada powers, Petro divinities may intrude upon them. Wanting more powerful allies, some houngans even summon the Petro loa during a Rada ritual; however, the Petro powers can only be called and appeased after the Rada divinities have arrived and departed.

The Roman Catholic litanies that begin the rituals form what is called the *action de grâce*. This opening frame in the Vodun rites consists of two orthodox Roman Catholic prayers, three Our Fathers, three Hail Marys, and a concluding Priere Guinée, or "African Prayer" (Deren 1953: 208). All of these prayers, with the exception of the last, are lined in Haitian French and Latin with the hounsis responding as a chorus while other participants finger their rosaries (Lomax 1951: ATL 5382). In central Haiti the action de grâce may last an hour, while in the southern region of the island it may take two to three hours to complete (Herskovits 1937: 157). In a ritual spanning a few days, however, the action de grâce may last an entire afternoon (Deren 1953: 208). No matter how long this opening section may take, these prayers are "entirely derived from the litany of the Church, and must always precede any vodun ceremony" (Herskovits 1937: 157). To ignore the required prayers would be blasphemous, while to fulfill them is to be blessed: "One arrived . . . as a secular individual; after such salutations the person . . . is no longer that at all" (Deren 1953: 206).

While the houngan may have charge over the loa, the *prêt savanne*, or "bush priest," presides over the desultory action de grâce. He is indispensable because he alone knows the litany (Herskovits 1937: 272). The pioneering anthropologist in Afro-American culture Melville J. Herskovits believed that the bush priest's role is indispensable because he invokes the blessing of the Christian high god towards the African loa who will surface later in the ritual. We will discuss as part of the interpretation of these various rituals the role of the prêt savanne who, like the entire action de grâce, is more than an acquiescence to European tradition or a schizophrenic religious response.

To begin with, the significance of the bush priest lies in "his ability to bring to the Vodoun service elements of a competing system which the houngan, operating within the framework of African tradition, does not provide" (Courlander 1960: 17). The role of the bush priest "became defined after the slave revolts of 1791," when he began as a pseudo-clergyman preaching in the bush without official church permission (Courlander 1960: 17). In the modern Vodun ritual he leads the hymn singing and lined, esoteric prayers preceding the African frame. The action de grâce is characteristically solemn, with slowly lined chants and genuflections accompanying the litany of prayers. When the Roman Catholic prayers end, the Priere Guinée is addressed to the loa and is chanted in the same monotonic fashion as the preceding European prayers. Seated along benches under the roof of the peristyle, the hounsis show little emotion during the action de grâce. They remain motionless, heads bowed in prayer, while they hypnotically reply to the endless chorus of the prêt savanne's incantations. From time to time a devotee will fall from the bench to kiss the ground upon hearing her loa's name called as the Priere Guinée unfolds. One devotee describes the tedium of the action de grâce, that is, the opening ritual frame, in this way:

> [T]he regular alternation between the voice of the priest . . . and the answering chorus . . . gives to the whole a sense of endurance rather than a celebration or even invocation. . . . It is an ordeal of discipline, not an offering of ecstasy but the more demanding offering of almost unbearable ennui. (Deren 1953: 208)

The clanging of the *asson* bell and sudden battery of drums, which followers call the *batterie maconnique*, awaken the worshippers from their stupor, announcing that the second frame has just begun (Lomax

1951: ATL 5382). Upon hearing the Haitian drums for the first time, one drummer remarked how purely African the rhythms had remained, despite having been uprooted from their source for centuries (Chernoff 1979: 74–86). The Haitian battery of drums is much like the battery in Trinidad Orisha, which signals the African frame of worship. In Haiti the battery opens the doors to the loa world by first summoning and dismissing Eshu-Elegba, trickster god of the crossroads. The order of drum rhythms that organize the sacred dancing of hounsis follows this usual sequence: the Yanvalou of Fon origin, the Mahi, and the various Nago rhythms of the Yoruba. If the Petro divinities are being recognized, their rhythms will follow those of the Rada gods. The Ibo and Kongo drumbeats follow those of the Petro, if the former powers are invoked at all during a Rada ceremony. In both Haiti and Africa the specific drumbeats replicate the tones and rhythm of spoken language; thus the drums "talk" to the loa (Roberts 1974: 7).

The expertise of the drummers in summoning the loa gives these musicians control over possession trance: they can properly call the loa to come and seize a certain devotee, or they can dismiss a possessing power by not providing the rhythms needed to sustain trance. Because the drummer is, "in a sense, hired for his expertness, it is to his own interest to be familiar with as many of these different beats as possible" (Deren 1953: 234). The loa who "mount" the heads of their devotees may speak to the gathering, giving certain followers advice or warnings. Other divinities, like Erzulie or Ghede, may prefer merely to dance and sing through their human vehicle. A crippled woman may dance limberly for the goddess of fertility, Erzulie, during possession without damaging herself; yet, on awakening, she may be in critical condition (Deren 1953: 230–31).

The loa are attracted to the peristyle by not only the drumbeats but also a ritual language that the loa alone understand fully. This ritual language, called *langage*, magnetizes divine attention, drawing the loa down through the poteau-mitan in to the heads of the hounsis. While the three drums (*maman*, *second*, and *petit*) call the loa, the houngan's use of langage with its form of chanted praise draws the divinities down from the sky and out of the waters to enter the ritual (Welch 1977: 343). Each chant has its own rhythm that the various loa recognize; and each chant tells the gathering which *loa* is being summoned (Rigaud 1953: 119–31). Although the total repertoire of chanted praise phrases is unknown to any one houngan, each chant gives directions to the loa to perform certain actions. For example, "Legba, open the door!" or, as the choir of hounsis chant in Creole, "*Papa-Legba, l'uvri bayè pu mwê pasé*," directs the trickster to remove any obstacle that may hinder the ritual's progress (Hurston [1938] 1990: 148; Metraux [1959] 1972: 101).

Langage is a mixed speech drawn from as many as six hundred African languages (Rigaud 1953: 259; Welch 1977: 343). Although Fon words dominate the vocabulary of langage, Wolof, Mandinka, Quimbara, Bambara, Ibo, Mahi, and Kikongo were prevalent in the early formation of this secret ritual speech. In modern times the exact meanings of the African words and phrases are being lost, resulting in a diminishing ability to call upon the loa. Many houngans know how to speak langage, but few understand what they are actually saying (Rigaud 1953: 259).

Since the meanings of langage are mostly lost, Haitian Creole is now replacing the phrases of the African mixed speech. No longer do separate Vodun groups have their own type of langage as in colonial times, when Ibo descendants living in the southwestern region of Haiti developed an Ibo langage for their rituals, or the Yoruba in the north spoke a Nago langage to the orisha. No longer do the Mondongo in Leogane have their own Bantu langage. Modern langage is a degeneration of African languages that contains a few recondite terms and stock phrases, Haitian Creole, and words borrowed from Spanish, French, and Arabic (Rigaud 1953: 347).

As we have seen, the first ritual frame in Haitian Vodun contains slow, a cappella chanting alternating with Roman Catholic prayers that are often lined, as in the first frame in Trinidad Orisha. Like the Orisha ritual, Vodun uses no drumming during this initial frame. Not until the second frame do we hear a dramatic outburst of drumming from musicians hired for the occasion. The drums summon the African powers in an African-derived language, while using African-derived rhythms and choreography to call the spirits. Possession trance is a vital event in this second frame:

> [I]t is by such manifestations that the divinities . . . make known their instructions and desires and exercise their authority, this phenomenon is basic to Voudoun . . . and is normal both to the religion and to the Haitians. In fact, the Haitian would find it abnormal if it should suddenly cease to occur. (Deren 1953: 16)

Ritual Frames in the Initiation Process

Among these geographically dispersed rituals in the northern Western Hemisphere there is a commonality: a binary frame structure. In the first frame European-derived songs that are usually slowly lined and sung a cappella dominate the repertory. Alternating with the singing are prayers in a European language, albeit archaic Latin, which together create a somber mood. In the second frame African chants and/or black folk song provides the repertory. The singing and music making here are always percussive and faster than those of the preceding frame. Second frame music is danceable, which is an important factor during trance. The speech used in this frame, like the songs, is African or a black vernacular, or a combination. Both song and speech in the second frame lead to the moment of trance, unlike the preceding lugubrious frame, in which no trance occurs or is discouraged. A select group of musicians or singers provide the needed music that will send devotees and followers into trance in the second frame, while the singing in frame one is in unison.

Why Afro-American religious rituals in the diaspora should juxtapose European- and African-derived frames is answerable only if one understands such a juxtaposition as rooted in African initiation and possession trance practices. According to the studies and writings of anthropologists Arnold van Gennep and Victor Turner, all initiations are rites of passage, which, in themselves are transitions between states. That is, initiations are the enactment of becoming something different (Turner 1965: 338; van Gennep [1903] 1960: 80–81). These rites of passage involve three stages: separation of the initiates from their social group who consider them "dead"; transition, or margin, in which the initiates are suspended in limbo, stripped of their former social status and occasionally beaten or drugged so that their past social attachments are broken; and regeneration, in which the initiates are returned to their social group as newly fashioned people who, now having a new status, are ready to serve a different function in society following their initiatory ordeal.

In addition to being fed special foods and intoxicating drugs during the first stages of initiation, the initiates, or novices, are taught the secret wisdom of their culture, which will make them "adults" or spiritual mediums or mold them to other specific roles. Among the Congolese secret societies that van Gennep studied and among Turner's Ndembu, one of the vehicles for transmitting this arcane knowledge is the use of anomalous secret language, usually in the form of riddles (Turner 1965: 343; van Gennep [1903] 1960: 80–81). This secret language is unlike that used in ordinary conversation or in the rituals where possession trance takes place. The goal of the transitional initiation is to recreate the person through instruction in arcane, sacred knowledge, which is "felt to change the inmost nature" of the novice (Turner 1965: 343). Surrounding the metamorphosis of the novice, language and music—two basic communicative codes—take on a "strangeness," or *étrangement*, not experienced outside the transformational rites of passage.

The initiation of spiritual mediums is highly important in Brazilian Candomblé and Vodun, which both have roots in Dahomey (now the Republic of Benin). Centered in the northeastern state of Bahia and around its capital Salvador, which was the chief point of entry for African slaves in sixteenth-century Brazil, Candomblé is essentially a retention of the religious practices of Fon (called *Gege*) and Yoruba (called *Nago*) (Raboteau 1978: 18). Relying on possession trance as the major communicative link with the supernatural world, followers of Candomblé prepare certain members through initiation for the role of spiritual mediums, or adepts. This preparation, known as *hospediera das divinidades*, may last from six months to a year.

The novices who are to become adepts are separated from the general population after having shown qualities marking them as possible mediums—such as epileptic seizures, migraine headaches, or a tendency to swoon at religious rituals. Separation takes the form of being sequestered as a group in a *camarinha*, or small windowless hut that was commonly used for housing enslaved Africans (Oliviera 1973: 32). Forbidden to converse with anyone except the cult leader or his usually female assistant, the *mãe pequena*—or "little mother," the novices are bound by ropes at the ankles to prevent escape, although this act is merely symbolic of their separation from the society at large.

The novices are thereupon subjected to a series of deprivations of pleasures they may have always taken for granted. They must be sexually chaste during this period. Their heads are completely shaved; and they must sleep on the hard earthen floor on straw pallets. Their daily diet consists of grains, porridge, and leaves, while they must submit to herbal baths to cleanse the scarifications inflicted by the spiritual leader's knife (Oliviera 1973: 34–36). The wounds are sacred to the divinities that the novices will later serve. During the ordeals of head shaving, scarification, and bathing, the mãe pequena leads the novices in a soft, slow chant whose text is a cabalistic variety of Nago, that is, sacred Yoruba. The mãe pequena lines out the verses of the chant to the novices who repeat them in unison in a low voice, clapping their hands all the while. During animal sacrifices consecrated to the deities who will later possess them, the novices again echo in unison the lined Nago chants. One observer of these initiation rites was astounded at the way an otherwise barbarous event was transformed into something beautiful because of the ephemeral sound of the chanting (Oliviera 1973: 34–35).

The Candomblé initiation chants, along with their texts, have nothing to do with invoking the Gege-Nago divinities through possession trance. The aim of these chants is to sustain a sense of passivity and listlessness within the novices so that the secret cult knowledge, especially that relating to the nature of their particular divinities, can be more easily and thoroughly instilled. At least four different chants comprise the Candomblé initiation repertory: the *cantiga saída de Ião*, chanted during the novices' first exit from the hut to meet their public; the *cantiga para catalação do Ião*, which accompanies the head-shaving ceremony; the *cantiga para o manhanga*, the bathing chant, which begins at three in the morning; and the *ingolosi* chant performed twice daily, once in the morning and once before retiring for the night (Oliviera 1973: 54–62; Rouget 1980: 86). These chants, which are built melodically on five notes and sung a cappella, are always lined by the mãe pequena or spiritual leader. The chants allow the novices, who are considered "dead," an opportunity to vocalize, since spoken communication is forbidden during this initial stage of initiation.

Although sufficient data are lacking on the musicality of the Candomblé secret chants (mainly because they are secret), ethnomusicologist Gilbert Rouget, interested in the relationship of music to trance, wagers that the Bahian Candomblé ingolosi and initiation chants among the Dahomean vodunsi are musically similar, and not only because many Bahians trace their ancestry to old Dahomey (Rouget 1980: 86). Sometimes taking years to complete, initiation into the mysteries is strikingly the same throughout black Africa; for example, "The schema of initiation appears with remarkable similarity among the most diverse peoples . . . separated by the immensity of central and eastern Africa" (Zahan 1979: 60).

Just as Candomblé novices are considered "filthy" and "dead" during the first weeks of initiation, Dahomean—or Benin—novices in Vodun are also the "filthy dead" until they are gradually reborn by way of the rite of passage into spirit mediumship. The *kore* secret society of the Bambara in Mali is a good example of the initiation cycle. Initiates are symbolically "killed" in seclusion with lethargizing drugs. The divinities then "eat" their secular souls as the candidates lie "entombed." After their spiritual death, the neophytes pass through a fetal period where they are bathed, fed, spanked, and talked to like infants before returning to the social world (Zahan 1979: 63–64).

In Benin the novices' rebirth is marked by several different exits from seclusion into the secular world to allow the novices to display what they have learned in initiation. During each exit, the novices are led out in single file while the religious leader lines out the verses of an extremely long prayer, which the novices repeat in a lugubrious melody. This chanted prayer consists of seven strophes, each of which is repeated two or three times. Each strophe lasts only ten minutes, followed by long gaps of silence before being taken up again, creating by this endless, slow repetition an air of melancholy. Although the novices' tightened voices use no vibrato, each chanter embellishes the strophes melismatically on the march to the king's throne. This march marks their last exit from seclusion to accept their new status of mediums. During this last march, called the action de grâce, the novices solemnly prostrate themselves before the king to acknowledge the submission of their spiritual prowess to the service of the kingdom and society, much like the Haitian hounsis' prostration upon hearing their loa's name called during their action de grâce.

Since the novices will no longer be subjected to the rigors of initiation after this day, they now chant their prayers for the last time in their lives, for these chants belong to the secret ordeal of initiation and not the popular musical repertoire. So unlike the popular musical genres of Benin are these initiation chants that one observer, hearing them for the first time, commented that "rien n'est aussi peu 'nègre' que cette musique-la"—nothing is less "black" than that music (Rouget 1980: 99).

For the crowded parades that accompany boy novices, or *kambaja*, to their initiatory seclusion, the Diola-Fogny of southwestern Senegal chant songs especially composed for this sad departure. This initiation is primarily a puberty rite rather than religious indoctrination. The kambaja's female kin wail as the boys are taken away from them. The seclusion chants, like the Benin action de grâce chants, are lined by a song leader while the whole parade crowd responds in chorus (Sapir 1965: 5 [Folkways Records]). For the Bambara of West Africa, lined, esoteric chants based on word play and riddles accompany the novices during their kore initiation into mystical union with God (Zahan 1960: 134–35). Secluded in the bush, the novices respond to the lined *kala ni* chant on the morning of the second day, while the initiation leaders take them on a tour of their village (Zahan 1960: 324). When the ninth day arrives, the leaders parade the novices in single file into the forest and have them encircle a sacred tree, chanting the slowly lined *kore kasiw*, a combination of verses and refrains of nonsense syllables sung a cappella.

In what is today Zaire, the Bushong initiate learns esoteric wisdom, such as sex taboos, by means of riddles taught him in lined chants that novices repeat every morning, like the Brazilian follower of Candomblé, in wooded seclusion (Vansina 1955: 139–40). Among secret societies like the *nkimba* of Zaire, initiation includes the use of slowly lined chants as novices, called *inkimba*, are led off to the secluded forest "school," where initiation leaders instruct them in esoteric sacred knowledge (Torday 1906: 201–3). The Bayaka initiation into secret societies requires women novices, called *l'iwila*, to echo lines after the *mazemba*, the initiation leader, who calls them out when the novices have completed their morning bath (Plancquaert 1930: 53).

It should not come as a surprise that ethnographic description is particularly scant for African initiations. Very few ethnographers have undergone the secret rituals; and those who have are reticent to reveal their secrets. The following excerpt from an anonymous ethnomusicologist's fieldnotes reveals the common result when a researcher attempts to record secret, esoteric initiation chants and riddles. Making tape recordings among the Lobi people of northern Ghana, the researcher caught the "Bogrebili [novices] coming out of the Bogre sponsor's house, singing a song they learned there. Nobody is sure whether I ought to be taping this very touchy and secret song. I am stopped" (Hagaman 1975 #81–099–F, Archives of Traditional Music). Throughout West and Central Africa, at least, the slowly lined chant, the melancholy of initiation, and secrecy seem inextricably woven together in folk tradition.

The function of somnolent, lined singing in the religious initiations in Africa is to create an atmosphere of stupor requisite for creating an unconscious double personality in the novice. By stupefying the novice with song and occasionally with hypnotic herbal drugs usually administered through vaporous baths, the novice is made receptive to each new stimulus presented during the transitional period of initiation (Verger 1954: 338; Verger 1957: 74). This stupor acts to suppress the normal reflexes and knowledge brought by the novice to the rite of passage. According to one initiate in the religion of the Fon, the new stimulus is like electroshock—the novice will carry it beyond the initiation into the public possession trance rituals to follow: "L'initiation consiste donc en somme a lui faire acquérir un réflexe conditionne" (Verger 1957: 71). As the novices pass from their old selves to the new, they are unaware of this conditioning process. Exposed to the arcane wisdom of their culture and religion, the initiated adepts in spirit possession automatically respond to drum rhythms, chants, choreography, incense, and verbal invocations learned in the initiation cloister that will trigger the moment of trance.

During the first stages of initiation, the stupefied novices are stripped of the reasoning power or social patterning that prevents them from being reconditioned. Unable to express themselves except through grunts and moans, the novices learn the sacred wisdom that will enable them to perform their societal duty of becoming a link with the supernatural world and speakers for the gods. Transformed by the rite of passage, the novice will now have two personalities: the social self instilled since childhood in a social setting, and a sacred self that emerges in possession trance triggered as a conditioned reflex (Verger 1957: 72–73).

Among the Benin *vodunsi*, or followers of Vodun, possession trance in the ritual is brought on by the sounding of specific drum beats, played by a band of musicians for the occasion. The chanted panegyrics, called *oriki*, and specific dance steps recreating the myths associated with each divinity encourage the supernatural powers to enter the ritual. Although some scholars perceive possession trance as a manifestation of an underlying schizophrenia or tendency towards hysteria, most ethnographers would now agree that African possession trance is a socially accepted, patterned normality existing within a ritual context (Herskovits [1941] 1958: 215–17; Metraux [1959] 1972: 135–39; Simpson 1970: 29; Verger 1957: 74–78). Contrary to the Western view of possession as pathology, possession trance in Africa is a carefully conditioned and predictable behavior: "the acts of possessed persons are so stylized that the initiated can identify the god possessing a devotee by the behavior of the possessed person" (Simpson 1970: 30).

Although possession trance may allow certain behaviors to surface that would otherwise be condemned outside of the ritual, within a ritual context these acts are not only permissible but also expected. For example, childish whimpering and crawling—like that engaged in by the *rere* in Trinidad Orisha—or aggressive attacks by adults are common trance behaviors in Africa and the diaspora (Raboteau 1978: 11–12; Verger 1957: 74). These actions are not considered perverse. Furthermore, by not separating the invisible world of the dead and supernatural powers from physical existence, the African was able to communicate with them and retrieve their spiritual advice for the successful continuation of their societies (Goines 1975: 42; Verger 1969: 52). Possession draws together two worlds intrinsically separate in Western philosophy: "Pour l'africain, l'invisible est exactement aussi réel que le visible" (Falcon 1970: 151).

For the African the means of entering the supernatural world is actually inviting the supernatural power to use oneself as a host (Goodman 1988: 88). Controlling the possessing spirit is learned in the obligatory initiation period. To forego the rites of religious initiation for a medium is analogous to a man's reaching maturity without the formal rites of puberty: he does not reach social adulthood though he may be quite old biologically. Only through the acquisition of arcane knowledge gained in the rites of passage can the old man leave childhood.

Although members of many African and African-derived religions may become possessed by a spirit without the necessary initiation training, their trance is considered chaotic, without communication from the spirit world. In Bahia the untrained trance is called *santo bruto*, a violent form of possession that may be physically harmful to the possessed while imparting little usable information to those gathered. Whether in Fon, Yoruba, Hausa, or Kalibari (Efik) areas of coastal West Africa, the rigors of religious initiation are an obligation for those called upon to serve in the capacity of spiritual mediums (Field 1969: 13; Horton 1969: 23; Rouget 1980: 111). So central is the importance of possession by a major divinity and its accompanying initiation that both "were brought from parts of West Africa to the New World . . . almost unmodified," so that they still have "a prominent place in black folk religions (Simpson 1978: 17–18). Possession trance continued after the Atlantic slave trade brought people like the Boni descendants of slave maroons to Cayenne, where the possession by a *gadu* is highly prized. In the Sea Islands, Jamaica, Trinidad, and Haiti, as we have seen, possession trance is central to religious followers to the extent that "possession by a spirit is the height of religious experience" (Simpson 1970: 94). Speaking for Afro-Baptists, Brother Leroy Davis says simply, "When I shout, it makes me feel good." (The survival of religious initiation in the Western Hemisphere will be considered shortly.)

The purpose of a cappella lined chant in initiation is not mysterious. During the training period, this type of chant acts as a catalyst in disorienting the novice. Likewise, the faster, more popular music leading up to trance in the public rituals is not inexplicable either. The singing of slowly lined chants in initiation helps to induce the somnolence needed to depersonalize the novices so that they can be indoctrinated, or conditioned (Rouget 1980: 85). According to this ethnomusicological view, the novices themselves must sustain the hebetude needed for self-hypnosis by echoing verses of riddles hour after hour. The continuous alternation between verse and response becomes a drone that dulls the senses through constant repetition. No band of musicians interferes in the initiation process, which the novices and initiation leader must carry on for themselves. The novices maintain their own somnambulism by means of slow, repetitious, antiphonal chants without musical accompaniment.

Just as riddles are used in initiations to instruct novices in esoteric knowledge, as among the Ndembu, the cabalistic chants also have their pedagogical value: both initiation speech and song (chant) instruct in secret matters and therefore must remain secret. Initiation's dependence upon nonvernacular speech underscores the secrecy of this act, whereas the language of possession is more akin to ordinary speech.

Because most musicians, that is drummers, are not usually devotees but employees of the religious houses where they play, they have not experienced initiation. They consequently do not know the esoteric songs that sustain the ambience of listlessness. The drummers and other musicians can only play the more popularly known rhythms that are heard in public possession trance rituals, during which the gods speak to lineages through their mediums. So purposefully distorted are the initiation songs by their slow, hypnotic pace that the songs for the public rituals are, by default, always faster.

The use of a separate band of professional musicians during possession rituals is a product of necessity: the drummers must provide music needed to summon and dismiss the divinities while the devotees, under the direction of their gods, can no longer sing but must perform as the possessing spirit commands. If a musician becomes possessed, he cannot continue to provide music to sustain the devotee's possession. Musicianship and mediumship tend to be mutually exclusive during the public performance of ritual. In Haitian Vodun the musician's role is so important that "[i]f any of the drummers, because of . . . possession loses his beat for even a fraction of a second, the entire ensemble is thrown off and the total beat disintegrates" (Deren 1953: 235).

Survival of Initiation in the Americas

The transfer of African initiation practices to the Americas presented special problems. The deliberate and sometimes not so deliberate mixing of tribes—especially when slave owners preferred to keep together African tribes hostile to each other—and the outlawing of lengthy slave gatherings on plantations would seem to preclude intricate religious rites of passage, which usually spanned months or years in Africa (Hancock 1986: 84). In the United States, especially, planters' efforts severely suppressed retentions of African values that were perceived as inciting slave insurrection. Unlike absentee slave owners in the Caribbean, North American planters were always physically present to ensure that tribal identities were uprooted, although slave holders initially dismissed African worship as ludicrous and harmless.

Instead of surrendering their customs, however, Africans and their descendants in slavery retained much of what was African. Those pioneering ethnographers, the Herskovitses, concluded in their studies of the African diaspora that when focal cultural values are endangered and "resistance is futile, the psychological resilience afforded by the process of reinterpretation comes into play" (Herskovits and Herskovits 1964: 6). Africans in the Americas "selected, squeezed, and shaped" those features of their captor's religion that corresponded with their own African institutions, such as the obligatory initiation, so that "the African Sacred Cosmos continued to determine the pattern of selectivity, evaluation, and use of white . . . symbols (Sobel 1979: 45). One example of this cultural squeezing and refitting was what George Pullen Jackson called the "surge" song discussed at the close of the last chapter. Because of obvious historical ties to white hymnody, Jackson challenged scholars as to the hymns' African origin in spite of black people's distinctive way of slowly lining them. Although these hymns were the compositions of Euro-American hymnists, the manner of slowly lining them nasally without vibrato is certainly African. Just as the Reverend Samuel Davies was perplexed as to why colonial slaves were so enthralled with the surge hymn, these newly arrived Africans in North America were probably elated, or religiously moved beyond the Europeans' comprehension, to find a musical song style so close to their own that they had heretofore been forced to sing in secret. Not only was the surge hymn fitted to conform to African tradition, but other facets of the white man's religion as well had to change in the African's hands.

In 1807 the United States Congress outlawed the importation of Africans into the country for slaves, thereby diminishing new arrivals who could replenish the store of African esoteric knowledge needed in the secret hush harbors of the Southern plantation slave (DuBois [1896] 1969: 95). Before the turn of the nineteenth century, however, the population of African-born slaves was exceeded by second, third, and fourth generation Afro-Americans who could not remember the old African esoterica very well. While the arcane knowledge from Africa was waning, the fervent Protestant revivals were gaining popularity and spreading to the slave quarters. During the period in American history between the western frontier revivals and the Civil War, African-Americans in the United States gradually lost their African sacred knowledge to white Christian belief:

> For with the stripping of the ancestral traditions in the New World, those facets of religious organization that in Africa pertained to the tribal deities, and were conducted in cult-centers by cultheads, have . . . been transferred to the domain of the established denominations. (Herskovits and Herskovits 1964: 304)

Black people in North America had to borrow the doctrines and ritual practices, including speech and song forms, of a new, somewhat strange religion, namely, Protestant Christianity, to create the content of their reinterpreted, esoteric frame. What could have seemed more esoteric to Africans, disembarking in North America with only the knowledge of a West African creole or their own indigenous language, than to hear seventeenth-century English spoken when addressing God, taught them by a slave-holding clergy?

The clandestine plantation slave meeting was initially a maturation rite of passage, or puberty rite, in which pubescent blacks were initiated into African adulthood as long as the folklore and mores of Africa could be remembered and imparted on this side of the Atlantic. As the African sacred wisdom dimmed over time, the secret hush harbor lost its function as an African puberty rite. With the advent of the revival camp meeting coinciding with the last major influx of Africans into North America, enslaved blacks' exposure to Christian doctrine and ritual gave a new theological dimension to the secret slave meeting. Whereas the loss of African cultural wisdom made the end of puberty rites inevitable, the exchange of religious knowledge with that of a new religion was not so detrimental to the ritual of possession trance: possession by a spirit could still continue, although the esoteric knowledge that prepared one for that trance was different from the original African lore. However, the possessing spirit by the nineteenth century had changed too: the West African pantheons were disappearing in captivity, but the Christian Holy Ghost was very much alive in the camp revivals and later in the plantation praise houses.

While Africans borrowed Euro-American speech and song forms that resembled their esoteric initiation symbols—that is, the lined hymn and the biblical English taught them—bondsmen were able to continue the endangered initiation into religious union with the supernatural. Their ability to put this initiation into a ritual form, however, may seem problematic at first. This obstacle evaporates, however, when we look at the proposals of the Reverend Charles Colcock Jones, one of the major advocates of plantation missions for slaves. He almost single-handedly stipulated the ritual structure that should be followed in the praise-house meeting. A modification of the earlier camp meeting ritual structure, Jones's ritual outline was already familiar to some plantation slaves who attended the camp revivals or who knew someone who did and had brought it back to the clandestine hush harbors. According to Jones's catechism, *The Religious Instruction of the Negroes in the United States*, the praise-house ritual should take the following course (Jones 1842):

1. opening (hymn and prayer),
2. scripture,
3. singing (hymn),
4. sermon or Lesson,
5. close.

Black bondsmen quite neatly imbedded the African rites of initiation into the opening segment of the praise-house structure. By alternating lined hymn and chanted prayer until the initiation had run its course—a seemingly endless period of time if antebellum worship was anything like the Haitian action de grâce—the obligation of ritual purification could continue before congregants entered trance with the Holy Spirit. The idea of encapsulating initiation—a once-in-a-lifetime experience—into a repeatable ritual form is not farfetched. Since the nineteenth-century, anthropologist Arnold van Gennep, whose work in rites of passage is still respected, was aware that this process had a precedent in European ritual:

> It would be easy to show that the ritual of the Mass also constitutes a sequence of rites of separation, transition, and incorporation. The only theoretical distinction between initiation and the Mass is that the latter is an initiation which is *periodically* [emphasis mine] renewed, like the Hindu sacrifice of soma. . . . (van Gennep [1903] 1960: 96)

Segments 2 through 4 became the Service, or second ritual frame, with the sermon as the focal point of trance, as it was during the camp meeting revival. The singing of hymns, that is, segment 3, allowed slaves to create their own rhythmic song—especially in the secrecy of their bush meetings—using various music sources, which they accompanied with percussive hand clapping and foot stomping. One musical historian writes:

> The religious songs the Negroes learned from the missionaries were soon given the "hot" treatment . . . hand-clapping and foot-stomping in lieu of drumming, and to make consistent use of offbeat phrasing in a manner directly in line with African musical thought patterns . . . were useful in inducing "possessions." (Chase 1966: 255)

The closing segment, 5, containing a hymn and benedictory prayer, remained the same in the slave ritual. By means of imbedding, the African initiation into religious secrets found a place in what was to become the Afro-Baptist ritual structure. Now as part of the ritual where trance occurred, the obligatory African initiation could also take place as often as a religious gathering of slaves was called, especially the clandestine meeting. If only as a drastically truncated reinterpretation, the African religious rite of passage into the mysteries survived in North America.

There may be objections to this interpretation of the binary frames so far. First, one historian of the Sea Island Gullah argues that the European frame necessarily preceded the African one in which the ringshout took place because the slave owner insisted that the Christian God be served first (Creel 1988: 297–302). This explanation would account for the worshippers' singing hymns and using Bible verses for their prayers only when the slave owner was present. The descriptions from folklorists who by chance had come across a meeting in the slave quarters away from white supervision also found the same binary frame structure, as noted earlier in this chapter. It is easier to believe that black bondsmen did not enact this Euro-American frame from mere pressure from whites but had borrowed lined hymns and what must have surely seemed esoteric to their forebears disembarking from the slave ships: King James English.

Akin to this view is Melville Herskovits's opinion that the descendants of Africans in the Western Hemisphere incorporated European elements in their worship as an expression of "cultural ambivalence." That is, Africans had become so culturally confused by the bombardment of European forms that out of guilt or some other psychological need they compensated this dissonance by including the European frame in their worship. Although it is virtually impossible to refute Herskovits's perspective, the fact that the frames always proceed in one direction— from European to African—suggests that more is going on than resolving cultural ambivalence. That African-derived rituals should conform to similar characteristics in their first frames is also argument against a haphazard display of ambivalence. Why are the first frame's songs usually lined, slow, and sung a cappella? Why is listlessness a requirement for this frame from coastal South Carolina to Port-au-Prince?

In support of Herskovits's interpretation of cultural ambivalence, which is hard categorically to disprove, I remember Orisha drummers who were originally scheduled to play for the night ritual mentioned above. Because the Spiritual Baptist preceding frame was taking so long to complete, the drummers left in disgust. According to their protests, they had come to play for African powers, not to listen to Christian hymn singing and preaching. While the African forebears of these drummers might have been fully aware of the need to construct and camouflage an ad hoc initiation by using Christian symbols, their descendants have found these same symbols abhorrent, or at least useless and contrary to African worship. To these drummers, and probably to some other followers, Orisha is being compromised; and those who now find themselves enacting the first frame may be confused—with a feeling of cultural compromise rather than ambivalence—as to the reason why. Be this as it may, it is safe to conclude that the initial motivation for frame one has been lost over time, as Spiritual Baptist prayers and songs flow in earnest before the orisha are allowed to come down.

A third possible objection to the interpretation presented here is that African-derived rituals have a universal predisposition to flow from a formal, tightly structured, constraining European frame towards an emergent, less constricted expression of the African *self*. In his discussion of African-American music, one linguist convincingly argues that the Europeanized outward shell gives way to the African inner being as emotional intensity increases, which can be witnessed from black American gospel singing to the Brazilian samba (Marks 1974: 64–67). We only have to look at the ritual in the African-American Spiritual Church to see that this predisposition is not always present. Founded in 1918 as a revitalization movement with a great many of its churches in New Orleans, the Spiritual Church there is a syncretism of Roman Catholic, Protestant, and Pentecostal Christianity; American Spiritualism; and possibly Voodoo influences (Baer 1984: 17–24). The ritual may take a variety of forms, sometimes opening with slow hymn singing, which is never lined, and prayers. The ritual sometimes opens with songs of fast tempos inducing immediate states of trance. As two observers write:

> Services do not have a rigid format, but generally begin with an introductory prayer service lasting anywhere from five minutes to half an hour. . . . Some churches begin this period of gospel singing at a fairly low-keyed level, while others immediately start out at a high level of intensity. (Kaslow and Jacobs 1981: 49–50)

With censers and grills pouring forth fumes of incense while life-size statues of St. Anthony, St. Patrick, and the Infant Jesus of Prague stare into the congregation from their candle-lit altars, members of Israelite

Divine Spiritual Church in New Orleans often open their services with "Bless That Wonderful Name of Jesus," a very fast song calling on organ, piano, choir, and congregation. Depending on the level of excitement, church members, clapping their hands and beating their tambourines, sometimes begin a holy dance that leads to trance in the first few minutes of the ritual. Whether the Spiritual Church ritual begins slowly or not, it would be difficult to uphold the view that some universal psychological predisposition exists for African-derived worship in the Americas.

Not only did the institution of religious initiation undergo a transformation in North America but the nature of trance, itself, also experienced a "sea change" on this side of the Atlantic. In Africa, as in certain areas of the Americas such as Haiti, trance involves an exchange of personal identity: the social self of the devotee is displaced by the identity of the god. This loss of the social self during possession trance presents no psychological conflict, since the devotee "does not experience other than a sense of enhanced value and worth at being chosen to serve as the vehicle of an Olympian divinity" (Wallace 1966: 141).

In Africa the devotee often becomes the possessing deity. In the Afro-Baptist ritual, however, those who experience trance by shouting, or "getting happy," do not become the Holy Spirit that makes them shout. Afro-Baptists never claim that they are the Holy Spirit during trance. Instead, they admit to being "filled" with the Holy Spirit. The trance state experienced by Afro-Baptists is "inspirational" rather than "identificatory" (Rouget 1985: 26–28). In inspirational trance the congregant acts and speaks on behalf of the supernatural power without ever becoming it. Inspirational trance is common in major world religions like Islam and Judaism as well as Christianity (Rouget 1985: 26–28). By a contiguous, or metonymic, association with the Holy Spirit, Afro-Baptists jump, dance, and scream because they have become spiritually close to that spirit without assuming its identity. Sister Pearson, the church matriarch at St. John Progressive, explains her trance experience this way: "You get up on the mountain, and then you lose sight of whatever's down here below. And you gone up in the Upper Room. You ain't caring what's down here. We can do some funny things when you get carried off. All of us."

Another difference between possession trance behavior and the trance Afro-Baptists experience is that the former may last anywhere from minutes to hours to days as the medium enacts the sacred role of the

possessing deity (Métraux [1959] 1972: 123). These roles, learned in
the initiation cloister, are actually orally preserved "scripts" that retell
the myths of creation and the gods' lives. The Afro-Baptists, however,
shout for only a few minutes; and their trance, should it last for more
than that, leads to panic: the shouter may become physically ill.

On the other hand, both African and Afro-Baptist states of trance
share the nature of being unconscious or unrelatable. Although the
initial stages of going into trance may be remembered, the actual deep
trance, which Brazilian followers of Candomblé call *santo* trance, cannot be recalled (Métraux [1959] 1972: 140; Simpson 1978: 17–18;
Verger 1969: 23). Maya Deren, the Russian expatriate filmmaker who
became a follower of Haitian Vodun, describes her possession by the
loa Erzulie as only a blinding "white darkness" before lapsing into total
unconsciousness and dancing the choreography sacred to the goddess
(Deren 1953: 247–62). To Deren the denial of the social self in possession is unavoidable: "To understand that the self must leave if the
loa is to enter, is to understand that one cannot be man and god at once"
(Deren 1953: 249).

Deacon Jay Pearson, older brother to the pastor of St. John Progressive, gives this description of trance: "When people get knocked out
and don't know nothing, they've really got the Holy Spirit. When God
hit you, you can't get over it right then. When they're shouting, they
don't know nothing." Trying to recall what she did while shouting,
Sister Pearson could only remember "coming down from the mountain" where she, presumably, had been close to the Holy Spirit: "You
might . . . remember that you had a book in your hand . . . and that's
the last thing you know. You don't know what else happened. You don't
know what you're doin' when you're 'happy.'"

In spite of the major differences between the trance behavior in different regions of the diaspora, "it is a mark of distinction to be possessed by a spirit" in African-derived religious rituals (Simpson 1978:
131). As observed in Chapter 1, Afro-Baptists often proclaim: "Don't
give me no religion I can't feel." The emotional and spiritual satisfaction that the trance experience imparts explains the Afro-Baptist focus
on it. As several members stated, trance is both an uncontrollable feeling of joy and a lifting of emotional burdens.

Another quality shared by Afro-Baptists and other diaspora ritualists is that the entranced follower has always invited the major supernatural power to enter. Lesser, evil powers, which are usually restless

spirits of the recent dead, invade the human host unasked and outside of a ritual context (Goodman 1988: 89). As Brother Davis says, "You invite the Holy Spirit to come in . . . that's why people shout." Similarly, the Spiritual Baptists in Trinidad shout "Hello!" as they greet the Holy Ghost in their ritual, thereby welcoming It to take control of their minds and bodies. The Yoruba-speaking followers of Orisha extend an invitation to the god of lightning and thunder to possess them by yelling, "Kabiesile Shango!"

In seeking a link with the metaphysical in ritual, the peoples of the African diaspora continue to express the African need for contact with the supernatural world that undergirds the physical. The importance of the frames is that they lead to a proper communication with the supernatural order. Speech and song, as we have seen, are integral in shaping those two frames. In the next chapter, we will examine the Afro-Baptist ritual in terms of the binary pattern extant in other parts of the African Western Hemisphere and explore the relationship between Afro-Baptist speech/song styles and the metaphoric states of African initiation and possession trance rites.

5

"Nothing New under the Sun": The Variation of Speech and Song in the Afro-Baptist Ritual

We have seen how the linguistic switch from a European language to an African or creole language is a common signal for changing frames in several major African-derived rituals in the Americas. The problem is to determine whether or not the Afro-Baptist ritual fits this pattern of linguistic change in its ritual speech. Upon an initial, brief consideration, we know that Afro-Baptists, unlike Haitian or Trinidadian ritualists, do not have two distinct languages to mark the boundaries of their ritual frames. Lacking any form of African speech, the Afro-Baptist cannot switch from seventeenth-century English to Kikongo, as the Jamaican Kumina follower is able to do. What the Afro-Baptist has, however, is the ability to shift from an archaic and standard form of English to a vernacular variety of the same language particular to African-American speakers. This is exactly what occurs. To construct the Devotion prayers, the speakers in the first Afro-Baptist frame rely on biblical and other stock phrases, which make their speech resemble a more standardized, if not stilted, style of English. In the second frame, however, the preacher manipulates the black vernacular so that the frequency of its use increases as the emotional climax of the sermon develops. By marking the frames in this manner, the Afro-Baptist participates in a reinterpretation of African religious practice, which, as we have seen, continues in the Americas.

Musical variation, like a shift in language, is crucial in maintaining the parameters of the binary frame structure. In order to mark the boundaries of the frames, a musical cycle emerges from the ritual in which older and newer song material is constantly changing and rearranging itself while the identity of the two frames remains distinct. This cycle is a key factor in the ritual's elasticity over its two-and-a-half-century history in North America.

Before taking a closer look at the linguistic and musical data, however, a brief history of the black vernacular in North America may clear any possible confusion and contention over its very existence. Beginning with the work of linguists who study the properties of pidgin and creole languages, strong evidence emerged in the 1970s that the nonstandard speech of many working-class African-Americans grew out of an American plantation creole (Dillard 1972: 74–77). Opposed to this view were historians of English who asserted that African-American nonstandard speech was a cluster of archaic retentions from various British dialects, arriving with different waves of British immigrants from different regions of the British Isles. While both views attempt to explain the anomaly of a black vernacular, the grammatical, phonological, and lexical record gives more support to the theory that some form of North American creole formed the basis of contemporary Black Vernacular English (BVE). For example, the general absence of a copula or "linking," verb in BVE—especially before adjectives—follows the pattern of known creole languages in the Caribbean (Baugh 1984: 265; Fasold 1981: 180; Traugott 1976: 88; Trudgill 1974: 71).

The remote perfective marker *done* (as in "he done busted his lip") and an action occurring in the remote past marked by a stressed *been* (such as "she's *been* married") also point to similar markers of tense and aspect in several Caribbean creoles and not in European speech (Baugh 1983: 74–77, 80–82; Fasold 1981: 73–74; Traugott 1976: 89). This remote marker has been preserved in contemporary BVE to mean not only an action that happened long ago but still occurs. "She's *been* married," for example, glosses as "she got married a long time ago and is still married." Standard English "she's been [unstressed] married" refers only to the fact that "she at one time got married." The fact of her present state of marriage is unknown and unsolicited according to the statement.

Another similarity between the English-based creoles in the Caribbean and BVE is the need to mark an action that is habitual, that is, repetitive, and the location or existence of an object in space and time (Baugh 1983: 70–74; Fasold 1981: 181–82). In the Caribbean creoles the marker for these distinctions is the same, usually *"de."* In BVE that marker is an invariant "be," found in such expressions as "she be going to church on Sundays," meaning "she usually goes to church on Sundays," and "There he be standing on the corner," for locative purposes.

The word, or lexical, item, "steady," occurring in Jamaican Creole as "study," and in BVE only resembles the standard English "steadily" on the surface, while it actually camouflages a creole distinction meaning repeated action with the same intensity, such as "his car is smoking and he steady going." The standard English word "steadily" may refer to a gradual increase in action, whereas in the example sentence the driver of the smoking car is not increasing his speed nor slowing down: he continues at the same rate of speed (Baugh 1983: 85–89). The phonological, or sound, resemblance between creoles and BVE is apparent in the tendency of both to alternate consonants and vowels consistently in words so that a cluster of consonants does not occur (Traugott 1976: 89–90).

If, then, BVE originated primarily from an American plantation creole, where did American plantation creole in turn originate? The debate over creole origins has been as heated as that over the origins of BVE (Baugh 1983: 15–17). There are several theories as to the origin of creoles, especially in the Caribbean, ranging from "baby talk" to a genetic predisposition in all human beings to speak what resembles a creole language. A plausible explanation for the existence of the Caribbean creoles is one that Ian Hancock proposes. According to his "domestic hypothesis" (Hancock 1986) these creoles developed from a contact language, called "pidgin," formed when the first Europeans settled along the African littoral during the sixteenth century. Ignorant of each others' languages, the European explorers and their African hosts developed a pidgin for makeshift communication centering around the business of trading, using the lexicon, that is, the vocabulary, of the socially dominating European language, while its grammar was based on both a simplified form of Portuguese or that of Sabir, a nautical lingua franca already circulating around the Mediterranean as a form of communication among sailors, and a composite of simplified African grammars (Taylor 1963: 800–814).

Originally used as a lingua franca for business purposes, this Afro-Portuguese pidgin gradually became the first language of the Afro-Portuguese communities of *lancados*, whose offspring now spoke it as a creole, that is, as a more linguistically complicated form of the pidgin. Entrusted with the task of bargaining for and securing Africans as slaves for the Portuguese, who initiated the African slave trade during the sixteenth century, the lancados became the slave buyers and the keepers of the slave garrisons along the west coast of Africa (Hancock 1986: 71–103). Thrown together from numerous tribes and linguistic groups, those Africans awaiting the slave ships could not communicate with each other except through the lingua franca of the Afro-Portuguese creole that had become the language of the slave dungeons. The Dutch-, French-, and English-based, and possibly Spanish-based, creoles, as these European nations eventually joined the trade, underwent a similar development among the enslaved populations, finally finding their way to the Western Hemisphere aboard creaking vessels (for a discussion of Spanish-based creoles see Bickerton and Escalante 1970: 254–67; Lipski 1986: 409–28).

It would be totally naive, however, to think that all Africans coming to the Americas had acquired the lingua franca in the holds of slave ships. The creation of creoles had to take place to some degree on the American plantation. This situation raises the question, then, of why the various creoles in the hemisphere still resemble one another grammatically, if no historical connection, such as a common slave dungeon language, can be found. The earliest creole theory that slave holders talked a similar baby talk to their slaves cannot be supported since the linguistic simplification inherent in baby talk does not correspond across these European languages in a way that could account for linguistic similarities among the various creoles. Furthermore, it is difficult to imagine a slave holder or shipper talking to his dangerously rebellious chattel as innocent infants.

To account for these similarities, Derek Bickerton proposes an innate bioprogram in which creoles, whether formulated in West Africa or on the American plantation, represent universal properties of language shared by all human speakers, thus explaining their linguistic similarities as natural genetic coding (Bickerton 1981: 294–99). Accepting that creoles display certain universals, the question whether BVE derives from original contact languages between Europeans and

Africans or from a plantation creole remains unresolved. The debate over these origins, therefore, must remain beyond the scope of our consideration.

On the American plantation, the speech of Europeans became Africanized and creolized as black nannies taught planters' white children how to talk and black and white workers labored side by side in the fields, especially in central Texas, where large plantations were rare. This linguistic Africanization of the Southern white parallels to a degree the exchange of religious practices between Africans and Europeans in the nineteenth-century revival camp meetings (Dillard 1972: 193–202). Just as whites were exposed to creole speech, black Americans soon adopted English grammar learned in Sunday school lessons and from contact with whites from different regions of Britain. Originating on the African coast and transported to the American plantation, or created there, creole speech gradually began to approach linguistic similarity with standard English as time passed, at the same time taking on features of nonstandard white dialects of American English (Fasold 1981: 185; Traugott 1976: 93).

Today, BVE is spoken by many working-class African-Americans as the language of the home, familiarity, racial identity, and group loyalty (Baugh 1983: 55). Isolated from social contact with white speakers, many BVE speakers in the urban North and rural South retain those nonstandard BVE forms, such as habitual "be," that other dialects of American English do not have. Whether or not scholars and laymen want to recognize the uniqueness of a black vernacular dialect, its importance to the field of education has been recognized. An Ann Arbor, Michigan court, concerned that school children who spoke only BVE were not successful students, ruled in 1979 that their teachers should learn BVE in order to be aware of the miscommunication arising in the classroom (Hancock, 1993). This ruling, often referred to as the King Case or the Black English Case, in effect stated that BVE was sufficiently different from standard English to be considered a distinct dialect of American English.[1]

Turning now to the speech data from the Afro-Baptist ritual, we can assess the degree of dialect shifting from standard English to BVE that occurs as a demarcation between frames. Under investigation are eight linguistic BVE features that will serve as a measure of dialect shift. These eight features are: (1) the word-final velar stop /g/ in the suffix "-ing"; (2) negative concord; (3) copula deletion; (4) absence of a marker /s/

for third person singular verbs in the present tense; (5) absence of a plural marker for nouns; (6) absence of a possessive marker /s/; (7) absence of verbal auxiliary "have" in the present perfect tense; and (8) vowel nasalization preceding a nasal consonant. A brief description of these eight features in BVE and standard American English will clarify their significance for this study.

The variation between the presence and absence of a velar stop—that is, the sound of closure made by the tongue against the back palate resulting in /g/—in the suffix "-ing" occurs in all American dialects: the velar sound of /g/ is often not heard. Especially in ordinary conversation, sounding of the suffixal /g/ almost never occurs. When asked to read word lists containing words with the "-ing" suffix, however, speakers noticeably increase their use of /g/ (Wolfram and Fasold 1974: 142). This /g/ variable, then, is a sensitive marker for vernacular and very careful or formal speech, and it holds true for other dialects of American English as well as BVE. The second variable, negative concord, like the preceding one, is sensitive to informal and formal varieties of English. Negative concord, the use of multiple negatives within the same sentence, is a "universal non-standard feature of English grammar" and for that reason is a good indicator of the vernacular's presence (Wolfram and Fasold 1974: 162). An example of this variable is a verse from the tune, "Nobody," by Bert Williams, the black vaudeville comedian: "I ain't never got nothing from nobody, no time" (Hughes and Meltzer 1967: 69, 85).

Absence of the English copula "to be" is particularly frequent in BVE, more so than in other dialects of American English. William Labov, who has done more than any other linguist in bringing attention to BVE, found that where standard English can contract the English copula, BVE can delete it, so that "we're Americans" in the standard can become "we Americans" in the black vernacular. In a study of Southern speech in Mississippi, those pupils who were white rarely deleted the verb "to be" in narratives, while black pupils were likely to delete the copula more frequently (Trudgill 1974: 71).

Both BVE and white Appalachian speakers use the suffix /s/ for present tense verbs in a nonstandard way. Their nonstandard usage, however, differs. In Appalachian English the suffixal /s/ is added to both singular and plural subjects in the third person, so that one can say, "he eats," as well as, "they eats," but not "you eats" or "we eats." In BVE, on the other hand, the tendency is not to use the marker at all or else use it with every person for certain grammatical meanings (Wolfram and Fasold 1974: 153–54). A BVE speaker would be more likely to say "he eat" or "they eat" as well as "you eat" and "we eat." When the BVE speaker uses the /s/ marker with every person, the notion of "always," that is, habituality, is incorporated into the verb as well as /s/'s use as a narrative present marker for actions in sequence, such as "After going around the house, I climbs in through the window." In the same Mississippi study mentioned above, both white and black pupils again were found to omit the /s/ marker in present tense verbs with third person singular subjects. However, blacks omitted the /s/ much more frequently than whites; in fact it was almost always absent from their narratives. So frequent was the /s/ omission that one linguist, Peter Trudgill, concluded that the deletion of /s/ may be a creole retention in the southern United States (Trudgill 1974: 70).

The absence of the plural /s/ suffix occurs in various nonstandard dialects of English with nouns of measure, for example, five cent(s) or four mile(s). In BVE, however, the absence infrequently occurs with other nouns as well (Wolfram and Fasold 1974: 173). The absence of the possessive suffix /s/ is unstable in BVE, more frequently absent in southern than in other varieties of the dialect. This variable has not been studied in other American dialects (Wolfram and Fasold 1974: 173). The absence of the verbal auxiliary "have" in imperfect past tense constructions in BVE occurs where standard English contracts the auxiliary marker, especially since the distinction between past tense and past participle is tenuous in BVE. So, where standard English can say, "We've seen it," BVE can say, "We seen it." The absence of the imperfect auxiliary "have" means that the verb is simply in past tense. The completive aspect, signalled by auxiliary "have" in standard English, is signalled in BVE by "done" instead of "have," so that where standard English has "We have eaten them," meaning "We are finished with devouring them," BVE can have "We done ate them," having the same completive meaning (Wolfram and Fasold 1974: 159).

Nasalization of the vowel preceding a nasal consonant is characteristic of BVE, but may be found in white varieties of American English, although researchers do not identify specific national or regional varieties included in this group (Trudgill 1974: 69). We will look at the vowel /o/ that becomes nasalized before /n/ in the processual verb phrase "going to," as in "I'm going to tell you something." In white nonstandard varieties of American English, the speaker can say, "I'm gon tell you something"; in BVE the speaker can say, "I'm gon tell you something" or "I'm 'o' tell you something," in which the final nasal consonant /n/, as well as the initial consonant /g/, is deleted but the preceding vowel /o/ has become nasalized because of its original contiguity with the nasal /n/. In this study it is the nasalization of the /o/ vowel in the processual verb phrase "going to" that is investigated whether the initial /g/ is present or not in "going."

Of the eight phonological and syntactic variables to be considered in this linguistic analysis of Afro-Baptist ritual speech, only two are widely common to all varieties of American English. Except for the "-in"/"-ing" variable and that of negative concord, these variables are more characteristic of BVE than of other nonstandard English dialects in the United States. Most linguistic studies of the Afro-Baptist church, as well as other black churches, have centered on preaching style. Because the preaching, or sermonic, style is the principal speech event in the second ritual frame, BVE variables should increase in frequency during the sermon, following the pattern of frame two in other Afro-American religious rituals where a creole and/or African language surfaces. In his study of black preachers' use of the black vernacular, Richard L. Wright (1976) contrasted the frequencies of four BVE variables in five Afro-Baptist preachers' conversation with those frequencies in the emotional climax of their sermons. He based frequency on the number of times a variable actually occurred against the number of environments in which the variable could have occurred. He also based the preachers' conversational speech on the first five minutes of the preachers' sermons in which they, as a rule, state the topic or Scripture around which the sermon will evolve. Before this quotation, however, the preachers greet congregational members, exchange brief pleasantries with them, and make informal announcements regarding church functions. All of this is done in conversational style.

The sermonic climax, Wright found, developed approximately twenty minutes after the sermon's beginning. Calculating the frequencies of four BVE variables ("-in"/"-ing," negative concord, absence of third person singular /s/ in the present tense, and copula deletion), Wright found that the preachers' BVE usage was four times more frequent during their sermonic climax than during their conversational speech.

In my study, I recorded ten sermons of ten different central Texas preachers. Analyzing the sermon exactly as Wright did, I see it occurring in three stages: prosaic conversation, emotional buildup, and climax. While the buildup involves the stacking of parallel syntactic phrases, which we will see in the next chapter, and raising the intensity of the voice, the beginning of chanting signals to the listener that the climax has arrived. Reckoning frequency for eight variables as Wright did for four, I found that the preachers doubled their conversational use of BVE features over all during the climactic stage—a finding not quite as dramatic as Wright's. In stage one, the eight variables occurred in only 24 percent of their utterances, while in the climax they increased to a 50 percent frequency, as outlined in Table 1. It would seem that in central Texas, anyway, climactic sermons are twice as vernacular as normal, prosaic speech.

According to the binary frame pattern, speech during frame one should not contain as much vernacular as that of the second frame. The main speech event of this first frame is the prayer. Unlike the sermon in frame two, which inflates vernacular usage, the speech of prayer deflates the frequency of BVE variables from the level used in normal conversation. Basing conversational style on the tape-recorded conversations of ten church members who offer prayers during Devotion, I was able to arrive at this conclusion. First of all, I recorded these members' conversations, with their knowledge, at regular church meetings, choir rehearsals, after the worship service, or at my home, where several members occasionally came for social gatherings. Having recorded their conversational variety and figured BVE frequencies, I then recorded their Devotion prayers from my piano bench. On an average, these ten pray-ers

TABLE 1. Percentage of Frequency of BVE Variables in Sermons and Conversation.

	Conversational speech	*Climactic sermonic speech*
In/ing	67 (301/450)	93 (279/302)
Nasalization	54 (54/101)	39 (27/70)
Negative concord	9 (22/250)	40 (120/299)
Verbal /s/	38 (141/369)	81 (146/180)
No copula	4 (19/471)	23 (74/319)
No "have"	18 (34/191)	59 (124/211)
No poss. /s/	0	48 (29/59)
No plural /s/	3 (2/89)	17 (5/32)
Average frequency (percent)	24	50

used the eight BVE variables three and a half times more frequently in their conversations than in their prayers. Their prayer speech utilized considerably less vernacular than their conversation, as Table 2 outlines.

Since the number of speakers for both preaching and praying events is only twenty, the linguistic data should only be regarded as suggestive of a trend in language use. According to this trend, Afro-Baptists resemble Jamaican followers of Kumina who use *bailo*, or standard Jamaican English, in their first ritual frame but switch to *myal*, or Jamaican Creole, as they begin the second frame, in which trance is expected. Likewise, Afro-Baptists behave like the Haitian prêt savanne and houngan who switch languages from an approximation of standard French and Latin in their first ritual frame to Haitian Creole and langage in their second. Indeed, the dialect shifting from standard English to BVE fits the linguistic pattern that Afro-American religious rituals seem to follow. Sensitive to their own ways of speaking, as represented by these eight variables, Afro-Baptist ritualists know when to use or listen for BVE and standard English in their worship service.

If the twenty speakers are divided into gender categories, the most prominent characteristic is that all ten preachers are male. According to Afro-Baptist tradition, women are not even allowed behind the pulpit. The male clergy seem to get nervous when women even approach the area, except to dust off the big Bible when cleaning the sanctuary (for similar gender attitudes in the Pentecostal Church, see Lawless

TABLE 2. Percentage of the Frequency of BVE Variables in Prayer Speech and Conversation.

	Prayer speech	*Conversational speech*
"-in"/-"ing"	59 (244/381)	85 (510/598)
nasalization	5 (8/150)	84 (193/229)
neg. concord	26 (58/223)	61 (249/608)
no verbal /s/	34 (95/280)	73 (212/291)
cop. deletion	8 (33/411)	31 (196/632)
no aux. "have"	6 (12/ 199)	83 (224/269)
no poss. /s/	5 (4/ 88)	48 (53/110)
no plural /s/	2 (1/69)	16 (13/80)
Average frequency of BVE variables (percent)	18	60

1983: 434–59). Six of the ten who offer prayer during Devotion, how-ever, are females.[2] During the Devotion prayers, the four males used the eight BVE variables slightly more frequently than did the six females. This echoes an accepted fact in sociolinguistics, that women in post-industrial societies are more sensitive to the standard forms of language and use them more frequently than men.

If the same group of pray-ers is divided on an age axis, five of the speakers are older and five are younger than thirty-five. The church sponsors Young Adult Sundays, when church members in their teens and twenties are responsible for the entire worship service, including Devotion prayers, choir singing, and preaching. Eager to take advan-tage of these Sundays to sing the faster, more swinging songs— usually from the Pentecostal Church—the young adults look forward to these occasions. On these special Sundays, one of which I recorded for this analysis, it so happens that the younger pray-ers used the BVE variables with an average 14 percent frequency, while the older mem-bers used the variables on an average of 20 percent in their prayers. In normal conversation the younger half uses the eight BVE variables 57 percent of the time, and the older pray-ers use them with an aver-age frequency of 73 percent. Younger speakers seem to make a greater effort, or are more successful than their seniors, at reducing their ver-nacular speech during the event of prayer. Their average use of the vernacular forms in prayer is one-fourth the frequency of that of their conversations. The older speakers' average frequency in these same forms in prayer is one-third less than in their conversational speech.

Sociolinguists would most likely attribute the younger half's more frequent use of standard forms in prayer to their greater access to stan-dard mainstream speech (Baugh 1983: 6–9). Because they either attend racially integrated schools, live in integrated neighborhoods, or work alongside whites, the younger pray-ers are better speakers of the stan-dard language than older speakers, who lived under the Jim Crow racial segregation laws of earlier decades. The greater social contact between younger blacks and whites has presumably decreased the linguistic distance between the two racial groups. These data suggest that Afro-Baptists who are thirty-five or younger are better speakers of standard English in their prayers, as well as in their conversations, than older church members.

This interpretation of the data may seem to contradict the work of linguists Guy Bailey and Natalie Maynor, who concluded that vernacular speech patterns of young blacks and whites in central Texas are becoming less similar over time, mainly because of increasing social and spatial segregation of the races (Bailey and Maynor 1985). While the two groups may be separating more, the standard English younger Afro-Baptists use is not a replication of any white vernacular, but the standard variety taught in school to both whites and blacks. The linguistic constraints of the first frame force younger Afro-Baptists to employ, as it were, a contrived, learned speech, which really is not spoken outside of the classroom—except in church.

In prayer, the younger half sharply decreases its use of the black vernacular, just as the elders do. This means that the younger generation of Afro-Baptists follows—and is aware of—the traditional shifting of speech patterns needed to demarcate the binary frames. Although younger members may be less devout in their Devotion prayers than older ones, because of different social circumstances, they use language more appropriately than their elders during the first frame. Perhaps less racially segregated than the town of Bryan, where Bailey conducted his research, Austin allows greater contact between blacks and whites. Perhaps younger members at St. John Progressive, working at the fast-food chains, have more exposure to standard English than black youth in Bryan. For whatever reasons, younger church members who offer Devotion prayers are sensitive to both standard and vernacular forms and can manipulate them within a ritual context.

Analysis of BVE use among older and younger preachers suggests a pattern similar to that of the pray-ers. Because the preachers are an older group than the pray-ers, the age of fifty divides this group of speakers into halves for purposes of analysis. For the preachers as a group, the BVE frequency during the sermon's climax is twice that of the sermon's conversational beginning. The five younger preachers use the eight BVE variables more frequently (52 percent) than do the five older preachers (47 percent).

A factor other than social environment may account for the disparity between the two groups of preachers. Six of the preachers are pastors with congregations; four are associate or assistant preachers with no regular following. Three of the four preachers without congregations are under the age of fifty. Preachers without congregations, regardless of their age, increase their frequencies of the eight BVE variables 11 percent over preachers who have congregations. Richard L. Wright (1976) found that Afro-Baptist preachers increase their use of

BVE during the emotional climax of their sermons. The aim of relying more on the vernacular is a means of enhancing rapport with their audiences and raising their level of acceptance with their congregations "by putting in the mouth of God the language of the people" (Wright 1976: 72). Following Wright's line of argument, it would seem that preachers without congregations are trying harder to heighten their acceptance and rapport than their elders do.

Another interpretation of this disparity is one which Brother Leroy Davis provides. A thirty-two year old man who has preached sermons occasionally but has no congregation, Brother Davis suggests that younger preachers with no following simply preach "harder" than their established counterparts. Deprived of regular opportunities to preach, younger preachers are excited during these rare occasions and revert, as if by linguistic reflex, to the black vernacular. Emotionally charged speakers tend to use the language they know best, without having to think of grammatical rules. However one accounts for the difference between older and younger groups, the important finding is that younger preachers conform to the linguistic demands of the traditional ritual structure somewhat better than their elders. Although scholars often write of the "inevitable" demise of old-time black preaching—since younger preachers are becoming too educated and assimilated to white culture—their predictions may have been too hasty (Faulk 1983: 170; Pipes 1951: 136–39; Wright 1976: 2).

Admittedly, the ability to preach in the old-time fashion consists of more than the use of certain linguistic variables. In the next chapter we will see how one preacher transforms prosaic speech into a form of verbal artistry by developing his discourse through contextual cues. This development is closer to what earlier scholars have meant by "old-time Negro preaching." The appropriate manipulation of these BVE variables, however, is an indication that younger preachers, at least without congregations, are eager to perform and know when to shift their style of speaking.

Some Afro-Baptists, like Sister Rosie Sims, who shook her head ominously at the prospect of Devotion in the hands of the younger generation, fear that the old-time style of worship is doomed. Based on the eight variables, however, the linguistic evidence does not point to such a dire conclusion. Both younger members who offer Devotion prayers and younger preachers respond more appropriately in linguistic terms within the two frames of the Afro-Baptist ritual than older congregants. These frames must remain contrasting for the trance experience to occur. A greater facility with two dialects serves well the maintenance of the ritual's binary structure. The shift of codes is a critical contextual cue that invokes the change of mood necessary for each frame, helping to make the ritual "work." In North America, younger Afro-Baptists, who are sensitive to these oppositions and who know the contextual constraints of their ritual, continue to sustain a tradition that originated in Africa and spread with the Atlantic slave trade. The axiom "The more things change, the more they stay the same" seems apt in describing contemporary linguistic behavior in the Afro-Baptist ritual.

Whether or not the traditional ritual structure will continue is, to be sure, uncertain. It is paradoxical that younger Afro-Baptists admit boredom from time to time with the first frame but simultaneously employ the linguistic styles associated with both frames at least as well as, and perhaps better than, their elders do. This dilemma makes one wonder if the Afro-Baptist Devotion, which elders deem essential to the ritual's progression, will become a brief, perfunctory exercise, leaving the Service with no shouting. Can a tradition that has held sway for nearly three centuries survive? In order to answer that question more fully, we must look at the musical cycle that helps to separate the two frames while supplying both with energy.

The Afro-Baptist Musical Cycle

The recycling of old musical material functions as a means of keeping the two frames distinct while incorporating change.[3] In the Afro-Baptist church we see, as we do in other African-derived rituals, that only those songs that are conducive to trance are placed in the second frame. The type of music conducive to trance, however, may change from generation to generation. Songs sung in the second frame have, for lack of a better term, primary emotional "meaning" or significance for each generation of churchgoers. This significance is based partly on musical features recognized as permissible, namely, certain chord progressions, harmonies, use of ensemble or solo voices, and rhythms. Today's young Afro-Baptists at St. John prefer, for example, a greater use of augmented and diminished chords, more complicated, syncopated rhythms, and more complex chordal progressions than the earlier I-IV-V-I chords of the blues form. Contemporary sacred song in the Afro-Baptist church leaves no musical beat unsounded—that is, all accents are likely to be realized either as a chord or a passing note—while key changes for variety have become standard practice (Southern 1983: 462-64).

Emotional significance (a rather ambiguous term) is affected by generational differences: younger members are more likely to shout during choir songs or solos composed or arranged within the past ten years; older members usually shout during older songs. For example, Edwin Hawkins's "Oh Happy Day," the first gospel song to appear on the popular music charts in the 1960s, will more likely lead church members under forty to shout rather than those who are older (Heilbut 1985: 248). However, congregants younger than twenty will find Donald Vail's "I'll Be With You," recorded in the 1980s, more trance-evoking than will members in their thirties. Differences in tempo have little relevance to the hymn's ability to induce trance. Both young and old members shout to slow, moderate, and fast songs, although younger congregants seem to prefer fast songs. Of course, the act of lining—a major feature of the first frame—is a cue not to enter trance, especially when performed in the first frame.

Although each new generation of Afro-Baptists creates its new sacred songs, the older songs are not so easily forgotten. Folklorist Mellonee Burnim reminds us that

> Whereas new songs are constantly being composed and added to the literature, gospel arrangements of hymns, spirituals, early gospel and even secular songs abound; their texts have such significance that they cannot be discarded, and they are simply revived and revitalized by being fused with a more contemporary sound. (1980: 166)

Likewise, in his study of black hymnody Wyatt T. Walker found that out of 154 hymns still sung in the black church whose origins he could trace, 65 were composed between 1866 and 1930, 44 between 1801 and 1865, and 45 between 1692 and 1800 (Walker 1979: 112–18).

How can the ritual accommodate new material without eclipsing the old? This feat can only be explained if outdated songs are removed from the second frame and temporarily stored in the first, leaving the second open for new material. Beginning with the colonial black Baptist church, frame one songs contained the European-composed hymns heard today as lined Old One Hundreds. Frame two contained the black spiritual, whose origins have been discussed in Chapter 3. Probably performed in the context of the ringshout in early Afro-Baptist ritual, the spirituals were the songs responsible for "bringing down the Holy Spirit" throughout the slavery period and up until emancipation (Creel 1988: 271; Fisher 1963: 180; Stuckey 1987: 27; Walker 1979: 75–78). With freedom came the Sankeys as a symbol of hope. The outdated spiritual, with its close association with bondage, was not entirely neglected but relegated to frame one, the domain of the white hymn, where older deacons could still sing them. James and Rosamond Johnson noted this phenomenon in the 1920s:

> Immediately following Emancipation those [African-American] ranks revolted against everything connected with slavery, and among those things were the Spirituals. It became a sign of not being progressive or educated to sing them. . . . It was left for the older generation to keep them alive by singing them at prayer meetings . . . while the new choir with the organ . . . held sway on Sundays. (Johnson and Johnson 1925: 49)

Not only confined to prayer meetings, the antebellum spiritual, along with the old lined hymn, was being confined to the Devotion in Afro-Baptist worship by the turn of the twentieth century (Chase 1966: 249; Southern 1983: 447).

With the mounting savagery of lynchings, forced chain gang labor, race riots, and migration to ghettos after Reconstruction, the Sankey died with black hope. Charles Tindley and Thomas Dorsey enter black hymnody as innovators of this period, as we have already seen in Chapter 3. The new gospel music, as controversial as it seemed to older black congregants for its "boogie-woogie" sound, found a place in frame two by gradually replacing the older metered song. Since the 1960s, gospel music "has evolved . . . to encompass . . . spirituals, hymns . . . blues . . . contemporary jazz . . . soul," salsa, reggae, and disco styles (Jackson and Jones 1987: 83).

In order to support a binary frame analysis with musical data, John Henry Faulk's sound recordings made in 1940 for the Julius Rosenwald Fund are valuable. Comparing his recordings with the ones I made between 1980 and 1985, the listener can hear that not all musical material has been lost over the past forty-odd years. Some songs, namely, those of African-American composition, have been reintegrated from frame one into frame two. Both Faulk and I recorded central Texas Afro-

Baptist rituals in and around Austin, sometimes at the same church. Faulk made his recordings on glass cylinders by placing a microphone near the pulpit while he crouched underneath the church building as the service was going on. He believed that, as a white man, his physical presence during the ritual would skew the authenticity of worship. Luckily I was accepted in my role as musician, which allowed me to record rituals from my piano bench. Using recordings from sixteen different worship services, I compared these with ten different rituals that Faulk recorded. Out of a total of thirty-five songs recorded by Faulk, twenty belong to the Devotion repertoire. Eleven of these songs have disappeared from today's Devotion, most becoming lost entirely to the ritual. The eleven lost songs are: "Lord, I'll Come to Thee," "How Sweet the Name of Jesus," "That Awful Day," "I'm Not Too Mean to Serve the Lord," "Dear Lord, Yes Dear Lord," "Have You Decided Which-a Way to Go?," "You Been Changed," "I'm Not Ashamed to Own My Lord," "If I Were You," "I'll Be Waiting Up There," and "Singing Low." Only "I'll Be Singing Up There," a black composition, is performed today by the Young Adult Choir at St. John Progressive. Used as an entrance march, it has been so stylistically rearranged that only elder members who can recall the song's text know that it is an older Devotion song.

Of the remaining ten songs that have disappeared altogether, six were composed by black people, while only four are Euro-American hymns. The majority of lost material is of African-American composition, suggesting that frame one primarily supports Euro-American song material. The lost Euro-American songs are "Lord I'll Come to Thee," "How Sweet the Name of Jesus," "That Awful Day," and "I'm Not Ashamed to Own the Lord". Charles Wesley's first two stanzas of "That Awful Day," published in 1739, foretold the horror of divine rejection:

> That awful day will surely come,
> Th' appointed hour makes haste,
> When I must stand before my Judge,
> And pass the solemn test.
>
> Thou lovely chief of all my joys,
> Thou sovereign of my heart,
> How could I bear to hear thy voice
> Pronounce the sound, "Depart!"

Frederick Whitfield's "How Sweet the Name of Jesus," published in 1859, foretold the joy of salvation:

How sweet the name of Jesus sounds
In a believer's ear!
It soothes his sorrows,
   heals his wounds,
And drives away his fear.

Isaac Watts in 1709 defended his faith in this verse:

I'm not ashamed to own my Lord,
Or to defend his cause,
Maintain the honor of his word,
The glory of his cross.

Further evidence that frame one supports mainly Euro-American songs comes from the fact that there are only nine remaining songs recorded by Faulk that have not disappeared from Devotion in the 1980s. These songs are: "There Is A Fountain," "Oh, How I Love Jesus," "I Love the Lord, He Heard My Cry," "Father, I Stretch My Hand to Thee," "Must Jesus Bear the Cross Alone?," "Guide Me, O Thy Great Jehovah," "I Heard the Voice of Jesus Say," "My Latest Sun Is Sinking Fast," and "Before This Time Another Year." With the exception of "Oh, How I Love Jesus," another Frederick Whitfield composition, and "There Is A Fountain," by William Cooper, these are all lined hymns. Eight of these nine songs, including "Oh, How I Love Jesus" and "Fountain," are Euro-American works, dating at least to the last century.

According to the binary frame thesis advanced earlier, the first frame should contain only Euro-American songs, while the second contains mostly black composed songs. Why, then, are some African-American songs surfacing in frame one? The problem becomes less puzzling when one compares frame two songs in 1940 with their current position in the ritual. Since Faulk's observations some forty years ago, songs recorded in the second frame have moved to the first frame. These songs are: "Stand By Me," "We'll Understand It By and By"—both Tindley compositions—"Old Time Religion," "Lord, I Want to Be a Christian," "This Little Light of Mine," "Wade in the Water," "Couldn't Hear Nobody Pray," "I Want Jesus to Walk with Me," "Jesus Keep Me Near the Cross," "Pass Me Not," "Shine On Me," "I'll Go, Send Me," "Standing in the Need of Prayer," and "I Shall Not be Moved."

With the exception of "Jesus Keep Me Near the Cross" and "Pass Me Not," both of which are Fanny Crosby's metered Sankeys, these are black compositions. These songs have moved to frame one because the deacons who initiate Devotion like to sing them. Since the deacons are usually older members, they remember the frame two songs they used to sing in younger days in the Service and now sing between their prayers. Although Pastor Pearson occasionally admonishes them from the pulpit not to sing nonlined songs (spirituals) during Devotion, the deacons, who wield considerable power, sing their favorite songs nonetheless. Deacon Simon does not need much prodding to initiate "Everytime I Feel the Spirit," "Great Day," or "I Know the Lord Has Laid His Hand on Me" in Devotion. As a former choir member, he knows he will not hear these spirituals at all unless he sings them himself. And in his own words, these old spirituals "keep the fire burnin'!" When an old deacon dies, his favorite songs, as Faulk's data suggest, die with him, unless another deacon continues singing them.

Frame one remains the domain of the lined hymn with identical melodies that must continue if the frame, so essential in preparing the congregation for a "descent of the Spirit," is to exist. The second frame stays open-ended for new songs from each new generation of Afro-Baptists. Older songs simply get pushed into Devotion along with the lined hymn. These new additions to the first frame, however, do not lose their original tunes as the lined hymns have. The former keep their melodies and are never lined. However, dated songs that have been pushed into the first frame—still preserving their own distinct melodies—may resurface in the second frame either with their original tunes intact or with new ones.

The lined hymn should never turn up in frame two. First of all, the lined hymn has no distinct melody of its own: it belongs to a never-changing genre of sacred song. There are exceptional moments, however, when a lined hymn will appear in the second frame. This occurs just before the sermon, when the preacher may initiate a hymn by lining it himself from the pulpit while the congregation follows. What distinguishes this moment in frame two from the lined hymn singing in frame one is that now the lining is accompanied by instruments, and a virtuoso soloist may take over the duty of calling out lines to show off her skill. The musicians may even create an instrumental section just for themselves at the end of the hymn singing in which piano and organ play against each other antiphonally. In other words, what was a congregational exercise in the first frame has become a different kind of performance in the second. The lined hymn now, like other second frame songs, can lead to trance. The preacher deliberately introduces the frame one lined hymn, just before he preaches, to lend a sense of sacredness, which the antiquated hymn entails, to his sermon.

There has been another shift in the performance of the lined hymn. Occasionally the Young Adult Choir, always attuned to the recording industry, will sing the text of a lined hymn with a moderately fast, percussive tempo that is frankly danceable. Taking their cue from recorded gospel singers such as Walter Hawkins and Andre Crouch, the youth sing songs recorded by Hawkins, for example, who arranged a medley of three lined hymns ("I Love the Lord," "I Heard the Voice of Jesus Say," and "Amazing Grace") on his 1975 album *Love Alive*. These upbeat, swinging arrangements of Old One Hundreds may cause considerable uneasiness among older members, and one can now understand why. These rearrangements go against Afro-Baptist tradition. One should also know that Walter Hawkins, as well as the majority of contemporary gospel writers, are not Afro-Baptist at all but belong to the Pentecostal Church, especially the Church of God in Christ, which is a twentieth-century revitalization movement that deliberately moved away from Afro-Baptist tradition. Bringing these new ways of singing the hymn into the Afro-Baptist church only testifies to the power of the modern media.

To insure that these media do not exert too much power at St. John Progressive, however, Sister Pearson meets the choir before they make their entrance into the sanctuary to remind them that they should "clap and not snap" while performing their new "jazzy" songs. By this statement she means that hand clapping is an appropriate display of devoutness, while snapping fingers belongs to secular music making. So the boundary between the sacred and the profane is constantly negotiated among generations of Afro-Baptists.

Another ongoing process, mentioned earlier, is the cycling of songs between the two frames. Four second frame songs of the 1940s that were pushed into the first frame are now in the process of returning to frame two, the Service. "We'll Understand It By and By," "I Want Jesus to Walk with Me," "Standing in the Need of Prayer," and "Pass Me Not" are making their return with younger choir members. Rearranged in the most contemporary style, they are scarcely recognizable.

Although it is probably safe to say that most Afro-Baptists are unaware—if not completely unconcerned—that their Devotion is an encapsulated African initiation rite, almost all members at St. John

Progressive admit that it is necessary for a good Service (compare with Carter 1976). Sister Odessa Houston, with the soaring soprano, sums up this feeling when she recalls once having attended church without Devotion. According to her, worship "was dead"—that is, no one shouted. Most members, even the young ones, would agree with Deacon Jay Pearson's assessment that Devotion "gets you ready for the Service" and to begin without one is impermissible.

When asked why the a cappella singing of hymns is necessary during the first frame, most church members seem momentarily baffled. They finally answer that because their grandparents sang the old hymns without piano and organ, it helps recapture a feeling of continuity with the past. Sister Evelyn Reese, for example, states, "Hymns are very sacred. With music [accompaniment] it just don't seem right. The music takes away, and all the feelin' go out of it." Further questioning, however, may undermine this reasoning. For instance, why is it permissible to sing lined hymns with instrumental accompaniment in the second frame just before the sermon? Most members would agree that Devotion songs, if accompanied, would seem somewhat blasphemous, but they do not seem to have a clear idea why this is so.

In spite of our linguistic and musical evidence to the contrary, the Devotion may be surviving precariously. Sister JoCarole Bradshaw, the young choir director, believes that most of the teenagers think the Old One Hundreds as well as Devotion are boring: "The young people, say like me . . . I've adapted to it [lining]. It doesn't bother me . . . some old deacon come out and sing. But the young people doesn't do that kind of leading [lining]." In keeping the young people interested in traditional ritual procedure, Young Adult Sunday obviously plays an important role. While the future of Devotion is a matter that time will ultimately decide, the youth seem to be continuing Afro-Baptist tradition in spite of their apparent boredom with it. As these bored youth become adult church members embracing Devotion, they may come to value the old, whether or not it is dressed out in the newest fashion.

In examining the musical cycle, we see that what appears new has already been. Recalling the old-time singing, Sister Odessa speaks of those old days when no choir existed. The congregation supplied its own music throughout worship. How then was a distinction made between frames? According to Sister Odessa, the congregation simply sped up the tempo of the songs in the second frame, like so many ritualists in the Caribbean, and added hand clapping and foot stomping for percussion. Of course, the second frame songs were mostly black people's compositions. The choir, whether present or absent, does not exclude audience participation for the enactment of both ritual frames.

The musical cycle is the work of an ingenious choir director, like Sister JoCarole. Listening to the latest recorded gospel arrangements, she is responsible for resurrecting and rearranging the older black song that has drifted into the first frame. Because of her, the youth choir at St. John Progressive sings new arrangements of "Pass Me Not" and "We'll Understand It By and By" with all the fervor of young people discovering and presenting a song to their audience for the first time.

For the moment, the Old One Hundreds that some younger members find monotonous and antiquated seem in stable condition, since the first frame could not persist without them. As Sister Odessa says with confidence, "They'll live on. There'll always be somebody to come along and keep them alive." In a stronger vein, Sister Rosie, whose dark hue makes her statement even more poignant, believes that the old lined hymns "are today; they'll be tomorrow; they're yesterday. Like my skin is black, those songs are a part of us." Perhaps both women are right. If so, the Afro-Baptist ritual has roots that stretch across the vast waters of the Atlantic and three centuries to Africa for sustenance and survival. In their task of preserving African initiation and public trance in a different ritual structure, Afro-Baptist speech and song underscore the sobering wisdom of Solomon that "What has been will be again, what has been done will be done again; there is nothing new under the sun. Is there anything whereof it may be said, see, this is new? It hath been already of old time, which was before us. There is no remembrance of former things; neither shall there be any remembrance of things that are to come with those that shall come after" (Ecclesiastes 1: 9–11).

Notes

1. The official title of the case is *Martin Luther King Jr. Elementary School Children* v. *Ann Arbor School District Board 473 F. Supp. 1371*, in which Judge Charles Joiner ruled that the educational needs of BVE-speaking students were not being met by the current system (Hancock 1993).

2. The linguistic discussion from this point until the conclusion of the linguistic material is taken from my article, "Keep the Fire Burnin': Language and Ritual in the Afro-Baptist Church," *Journal of the American Academy of Religion* 56 (1988): 89–92. Used by permission of the American Academy of Religion.

3. The discussion from this point until the conclusion of the chapter is my article, "Like a Tree Planted by the Water: the Musical Cycle in the Black Baptist Church," *Journal of American Folklore* 104 (1991): 318–40. Used by permission of the American Folklore Society. Not for sale or further reproduction.

6

"Like a Ship":
Afro-Baptist Ritual Process

When Thomas A. Dorsey wrote "The Lord Will Make a Way Some-how," he had penned what was to become a very popular song among Afro-Baptists. Using the imagery of a ship on a stormy sea, Dorsey drew parallels between life's troubles and the worshipper's faith:

> Like a ship that's tossed and driven,
> Battered by an angry sea,
> When the storms of life are raging
> And their fury falls on me,
> I wonder what I have done
> That makes this race so hard to run,
> Then I say to my soul, take courage,
> The Lord will make a way some-how.

Found in so many hymns and sacred songs, the metaphor of the ship in Afro-Baptist thought transports the traveler from one point to another. The Afro-Baptist ritual, like a ship, also transports the worshipper along a continuum of spiritual uplifting from the moment Devotion begins until the closing benedictory prayer. How the ritual manages to do this is the subject of this chapter.

The encapsulation of the African initiation rites into the Afro-Baptist ritual structure, to be sure, involves a great loss of elements found in the African initiation of novices into the mysteries. The exercise of spiritually purging the future medium is not the aim of the Afro-Baptist Devotion. Afro-Baptists in central Texas feel that their first frame is more a preparation for the descent of the Holy Spirit than a cleansing of unholy, profane qualities. This distinction, along with the absence of ritual scarification and the learning of sacred esoteric knowledge that occur in initiation, gives a new function to the Afro-Baptist first frame. In addition to being a spiritual preparation, the first frame becomes an indispensable element in the success of the ritual.

According to anthropologist Victor Turner, whose work in initiations has been discussed in Chapter 4, ritual universally consists of three successive stages: structure, antistructure, and restructure. Drawing on Arnold van Gennep's tripartite theory of rites of passage, Turner theorized that, by passing through all three stages, ritual participants are psychologically and spiritually transformed by advancing from a lower to a higher state:

> [S]ocial life is a type of dialectal process that involves successive experience of . . . the passage from lower to higher status . . . through a limbo of statuslessness. In such a process, the opposites . . . constitute one another and are mutually indispensable. (Turner 1977: 97)

The "mutually indispensable opposites" to which Turner refers are the ritual elements of structure (and restructure) and antistructure. For Turner structure is both a social, hierarchical organization, and psychological formality of mood that supports the socioeconomic and political base of society; and it is the manifestation of this power base in religious ritual. Looking at the ritual, first, from a socially hierarchical perspective, the hierarchy consists mostly of men. In order for this hierarchy to continue, however, it must be occasionally reaffirmed and strengthened from without. Antistructure provides this confirmation of the hierarchical order by offering *communitas*, a transitory moment of social reversal and leveling. During antistructure what appears to be chaos ensues in which the social order is turned upside down or dispensed with momentarily. After this brief hiatus, however, hierarchy returns to its normal order, that is restructure, reconfirmed in its existence by its break from normality.

The fleeting moment of antistructure allows for a release of tensions engendered by the social hierarchy. Not merely a "release valve" phenomenon, the communitas of antistructure also allows for ritual participants to reassess their hierarchy, repairing faults in the normal structure if it is to continue. Turner defines this transitory communitas as "[t]he notion that there is a generic bond between men, and its related sentiment of 'humankindness'" (Turner 1977: 128). The momentary release from structural constraints quickly yields to a return to structure, which is now restrengthened: "the immediacy of communitas gives way to the mediacy of structure . . . men are released from structure into communitas only to return to structure revitalized by their experience of communitas" (Turner 1977: 129). Because communitas is spontaneous as well as brief, this transitory feeling of genuine mutuality between people has been associated with the divine and restricted to religious practice "as a charism or grace sent by the deities or ancestors" (Turner 1977: 137).

In preparing the stage for communitas, that is, antistructure, in the Afro-Baptist ritual, the juxtaposition of the two contrasting rituals frames is necessary. The first frame acts as the structural component while the second contains both antistructure and restructure. The first frame, Devotion, consists of the prayers and lined hymn singing led principally by the deacons. Only men can occupy this office that places them in financial control of the church. The deacons are responsible for counting and banking the money raised by the congregation; and they pay the musicians, custodians, and preacher. If new equipment of any kind, such as a piano, is to be bought by the church, the deacons meet to discuss and determine the purchase. If, by any chance, the congregation is dissatisfied with its pastor, it is up to the deacons to dismiss him and seek a replacement. Although all pecuniary matters are the deacons' concern and decision, the whole congregation ultimately decides by vote how the church will spend its money. The deacons have a great influence over the congregation in swaying that decision, however.

Therefore, the deacons, who initiate Devotion and announce its conclusion, are the structural echelon of the Afro-Baptist hierarchy. They sit separately from the congregation on the deacon's bench. Even their wives are given special status every first Sunday. These women, all dressed in white, sit across from their husbands on the deaconess bench near the organ. The deacons are always addressed by their title, "deacon," even off church grounds on weekdays if met on the streets. Of course, above the deacons' authority, at least in spiritual matters, is the male clergy. So it is men who are in positions to control and direct not only the church's business but its ritual also.

As the ritual progresses, however, men may lose some of this absolute control. As folklorist Elaine Lawless has shown for white Pentecostals, women who shout during worship service temporarily usurp this control from male authority (Lawless 1983: 434–59). No matter how impatiently the pastor or other preachers may wait for the shouting to cease before continuing the sermon, or despite the deacons' attempts to quiet shouters, the act of trance continues until it has run its course throughout the congregation. As Lawless sees it, Pentecostal women become catalysts for communitas, just as they are in the Afro-Baptist ritual: Women "are there in greater numbers; they sing more; they march and dance around the church with tambourines more than men do; they are more likely the ones to go into trance, jerk, fall down, speak in tongues" (Lawless 1983: 434).

In the Afro-Baptist ritual, the men who are deacons and preachers manipulate the sequence of events, but they never shout. Women, however, do. As the moment of communitas unfolds over the congregation, they seize control of the ritual in the second frame. When the shouting ends, control returns to the preacher until the benedictory prayer is given. At this point, the congregation, having experienced antistructure, reaggregates under the auspices of the church authority, namely, the pastor, before being dismissed into the secular world.

If one looks at the ritual process from a psychological rather than social perspective, communitas emerges not from a breakdown in hierarchical social control but from a collapse in tightly structured behavior. This behavioral rigidity is nothing more than a sense of formality. Reviewing what anthropologists have meant by the term "formal" in their writings, Judith Irvine finds four aspects that consistently surface in their discussions: increased code structuring, code consistency, invoking positional identities; and the emergence of a central situational focus (Irvine 1984: 214–18). Using these four aspects as criteria for formality, we can apply them to the Afro-Baptist ritual—its speech, song, and gesture—to see if one frame is not more "formal" than another. In other words, formality becomes synonymous with a feeling of constraint created by systematic organization.

In respect to language use, Devotion is much more predictable than the Service, since we will see that increased code structuring entails expected actions, or speech. Both sermon and prayer, the two representative genres of each frame, use a great deal of stock phrases as poetic and rhythmic tools. Both sermon and prayer, therefore, are more structured in their codes than ordinary conversation because of the recurrence of certain words and phrases. Prayer, however, becomes more structured than the sermon because this recurrence is more regular, or frequent, in the former speech event. Folklorist Bennison Gray distinguishes two types of verbal repetition in preaching: the formula and the convention. For him the formula is "a verbal construction that is repeated within a work," while the convention is "a verbal construction that recurs from work to work" (Gray 1971: 292).

In general the Afro-Baptist constructs his prayer from conventions and his sermons from formulas. The prayer conventions, however, occur with much more regularity than the sermon's formulas. While the preacher uses formulas to build couplets, or syntactic parallels, that seem to have rhythm, the deacon who prays uses conventions to identify his speech as "prayer," as distinct from ordinary conversation. He is now conversing with God. In neither sermon nor mundane conversation do stock phrases, which we are now calling conventions, follow upon each other with such frequency as in prayer. Regardless of who is praying, the same conventions heard in one prayer will be heard in another. Conventions become devices for announcing each stage of the prayer's development. The five developmental stages are the formal opening, proem, thanksgiving, appeals, and peroration (Jones-Jackson 1987: 80–81). Each of these stages is necessary for the prayer to begin and end; none can be omitted.

The formal opening is usually a brief excerpt from the Lord's Prayer. In the proem the pray-er approaches the Creator with humility: "O Lord, it is once more and again that I come, bowed down with my knee in some lonesome valley, head to mother dust." Thanksgiving is a list of blessings the pray-er acknowledges, as "We thank Thee for our yet-spared lives, for raiment, and clothes on our back." Often heard is "Thank you Lord for a brand new day I've never seen before." Appeals usually begin with, "Dear Lord, go into the hospital wards and soothe that scorching fever," or "Go behind those prison walls and convince some mother's son that You are the way." There is always an appeal to "heal the sick and afflicted." Continuing to make appeals, the pray-er may claim that God is "a great emancipator, and a heart-regulator; a doctor who never lost a patient; a lawyer who never lost a case." The peroration is a view of life's end, often metaphorically stated as "coming down the slippery side of the mountain" or having one's "tracks blown out by the mighty wind." As in camp meeting days, most of these conventions refer to crossing the River Jordan, beseeching it to be calm upon one's own death.

Not only do conventions establish each obligatory stage of prayer; they also compose most of the prayer itself. Sandwiched in between these conventions are spontaneous requests to the Almighty or the giving of thanks for special blessings that may have recently been received. These departures from stock phrases, however, are rare; and they afford those who pray time to compose their texts. The prayer and its manner of delivery are thus learned in an oral tradition. Contrary to the observations of one scholar in the North Carolina Piedmont, no written notes help in the delivery of an effective prayer in central Texas Devotions (Heath 1983: 209–10). To jot down certain conventions for mnemonic purposes would be tantamount to cheating before God. The sincerity of prayer is judged by its ability to flow uninterrupted from the pray-er's mouth without recourse to a recorded text.

The sermon, on the other hand, uses verbal repetition for the purpose of creating rhythm and audience feedback. Unlike the prayer, which is divided into five required stages, the sermon emerges in three optional stages: the opening, the buildup, and the climax. During the buildup, the preacher begins to use the formula, a line familiar to all hearers, to balance the synchrony between himself and his hearers who are responding to his lines. The climax, however, is not a given. For reasons known only to himself, the preacher can refuse to enter the climactic stage; or, the congregation may not be enthusiastic about his performance and refuse the encouragement of their responses, thus bringing the message to a premature end. An excited preacher may begin at the buildup, foregoing the usual introductory opening statements. Some sermons may have two or more emotional apexes, each entailing its own buildup, which makes the sermon a highly unpredictable event in terms of length, performance, and structure.

In order to see the relatively loose code structuring of the sermon, let us turn to an actual text of a sermon.[1] We will see that in the first two stages the preacher's use of language is referential, or propositional, as he alternates occasionally between rhetorical and conversational speech. During this alternation his changes in prosody, that is, speech rate, volume, and sentence length, become contextualization cues shaping the thrust of his argument. The congregation's call-and-response cries, which linguists refer to as *backchanneling cues*, are actually vocalized agreement and consent for the speaker to continue. These backchanneling cues become more regularized as the rhythm of the sermon is stepped up through stages one and two, which appear in the extract that follows. In order to follow the sermon along with prosodic changes, symbols are used to indicate prosody. These symbols are: / = short pause, // = longer pause, —> = rapid speech, [*] = preacher's line-final gasp, CAPS = vocal intensity, [!] = audience response, [******] = preacher's hummed, melodic breath group. Very long pauses are indicated in brackets.

[STAGE ONE]

Now some says/ if I'm saved, I'm not a sinner
[long pause]
But you were the sinner before you were saved, but since
→ you've been saved, you are a/
SAVED sinner.
[long pause]
By grace
[!]
because you've been saved, it doesn't mean that //
you're not gonna violate
[long pause]
the laws and the principles of our God//
He said I SAW/
the serpent had two wings/
[!]
to cover/ their feet
[!]
[long pause]
It's because it's to exercise/ the Gospel//
→ then SWIFTLY carried away
[!]
[long pause]
by the great desire.
→ As you look at the tenth chapter of Romans and the fifteenth verse, it says
→ How beautiful the feets of them that preach the gospel of peace.
How beautiful the FEETS of them/
→ preach the gospel of peace mean/
a person that is BORNED again.
[long pause]
That simplification/
that newification/
that purification
[long pause]
has fixed him so that he's converted and convinced of his conviction
that he must carry the gospel wherever he go/

→   That's what he talkin'
     [!]
→   about beauty of the FEETS of them/
→   Now there's some folks/
     really not converted/
     to carry nothing nowhere.
     [!]

                              [STAGE TWO]

→   [hovering tonality] You'd so desire to see justice brought upon them/
     [!]
     or righteousness prevail.
     [softly] Then Mark looks at that.
     BUT THE CALLS/IS TO BRING OUT UNSAVED/SINNERS. [*]
→   Converted people are to SAVE/
     [softly] Of course we sit down/ and lets go give [mumbled]
     [!]
→   and that's right here in our congregation.
     [!]
     But this is what the Word say,
     Let me go to the Word/
     [!]
     And he said unto them/
     follow me.
     This is Jesus saying to His disciples I will make you fishermen of men.
     I said this last week/
     And they straightaway left their nets/
     and followed Him/
     [!]

In the preceding passages, long pauses (shown in brackets) mark
following important information, much like underlining in written discourse. Shorter pauses (marked by slashes) operate as commas, breaking lengthy utterances into comprehensible chunks. As a contrastive
marker, rapid speech (marked by arrows in the left-hand margin) indicates background information that is not necessarily essential for the
argument's main goal. Consequently, the preacher recites Bible verses
and makes asides rapidly so as to steer the audience quickly through
this important but secondary information. In the beginning of the text
in stage one, however, "by grace you've been saved," a theme to be
developed in the sermon's course, follows a long pause for notice. The
final two lines of stage one decrease in rate to highlight the fact that

several members, despite their outward behavior, are not really converted or worthy of being evangels, another sermonic theme.

The contrast between loud and soft voice also functions as a thematic marker throughout the sermon. "Feets" and "saved sinner" are stressed vocally in stages one and two as they act as poles around which the sermon wraps its logistic development. By contextualizing his sermonic argument by varying loudness, the preacher risks his face in debate with his hearers who are responsible for assessing the logic and strength of his proposition. They, subsequently, signal their agreement audibly.

The congregation's backchanneling is asynchronous in the first stage, just as it is in ordinary conversation, wherein speaker and hearer do not yet know the direction of the argument, and therefore cannot yet integrate their interpretive skills allowing each other to proceed (Gumperz 1982: 131). Shortly after a conversation's start, however, the listener has an idea of how the speaker will manage the conversation and with what intent; thus the former's audible "uh huh"s become more rhythmic as he at least understands, if not totally agrees with, the direction of the argument. Represented in the texts by a bracketed exclamation mark [!], the congregation's backchanneling cues are initially arrhythmic and vocally weak, as the fourth line indicates, where only a few worshippers respond in the opening of the preacher's line—unlike the more rhythmic responses later, in which most of the congregation calls back "Amen" or "preach it" at the end of each of the preacher's verses. As the sermon progresses, however, these backchanneling cues become more frequent and predictable at line ends so that, by the climactic third stage, congregational response follows each of the preacher's lines.

The second sermonic stage begins with a rise in the preacher's volume and rate of speech. Rhythm between audience and speaker becomes more regular in stage two, as the backchanneling cues indicate. At this point the preacher hovers around some tonal center that seems on the verge of melody. Not until the third stage will this hovering note find a scalar value—someone in the congregation will provide it. This note is the precise one that the preacher has been intimating in stage two. In providing the note, the audience is giving the preacher permission to progress to a climax. Without it, the sermon cannot be chanted with much audience enthusiasm.

During the climax, language loses its logical function, assuming a purely poetic one. Propositions, the purpose of prose, are no longer the issue. They have already been negotiated in the preclimactic stages. Form replaces content as primary focus: contextualization decreases until each line becomes a chanted, truncated utterance with unvarying prosody.

In this third stage, the preacher can excite his hearers by running down the aisle, jumping vigorously behind the pulpit, waving his white handkerchief while pounding the lectern at each verse end, or twirling around suddenly, giving the impression that he may at any time fall off the dais—intentional kinesics similar to those found in West African performance of narrative discourse (Fouda 1968: 282). Another means of creating excitement in his hearers is the preacher's verbal artistry, based upon West African principles of verse, namely, the breath group as the basis of poetry. In the text that follows, we see that each line in the latter half of stage three ends with an audible gasp represented by the symbol [*]. This feature is a matter of personal choice. Some preachers prefer the line-end nonsense syllable, such as the "whoa!" that the Mandinka use, as a means of marking the end of the breath group. Others prefer merely waving a white handkerchief to mark this event.

[STAGE THREE]

Each line is followed by audience response [!]
[hovering note finds a tonal center along with two additional notes to create a three-note melody]

> One of these days you won't worry
> You won't worry about tryin' to listen
> You got to give an account one day
> When you stand befo' God for yourself
> All these people you see in here
> Nobody will be with you
> But you better make sure the Lord has heard your cry
> And one thing when the Lord come for ya
> You got to give an account for your ownself
> One thing you won't have somebody to pray for you

[three-tone chant returns to monotone]

Lord, send me, I'll go
[******]

But let me tell ya [*]
The Lord said you might fall [*]
But you better not be cast down [*]
[******]
Some folks come [*]
To the Lord home [*]
To find every possible fault [*]
Everyone they can find [*]
[******]
Let me tell ya [*]
I didn't come to find fault in ya [*]
I want to tell ya what the Lord said
[******]
If you haven't heard the voice of the Lord callin' today [*]
You oughta be able to say to Him now [*]
Where the cross may be, Lord [*]
What you want me to do, I'll do it for ya [*]
[******]
I got a place somewhere in God's Kingdom [*]
One of these days, no mo' suffering down here [*]
No more cryin' down here [*]
And no more lyin' down here [*]

[He stops chanting]

Everyday will be Sunday
And Sabbath will have no end.

During the sermon's climax, this preacher "sculpts" his lines into groups of alternating four- and three-verse clusters, wedged between hummed breath-groups marked by asterisks [******]. In this manner, he creates a 3+4+3+4 stanza pattern instead of a more regular one of 3+3+3+3 or 4+4+4+4 verses. By patterning his discourse this way, the preacher staggers a verbal design reminiscent of narrow-strip cloth patterns in West Africa or additive rhythms found throughout West Africa (Jones 1964: 59; Roberts 1974: 135; Thompson 1983: 209). In West Africa as in the African Western Hemisphere, artistic embellishment in religious ritual is a sign not of personal ability but of divine presence (Deren 1953: 249). The audience's shouting resulting from hearing the sermon as it progresses is a testimony to the divine speaking through the preacher: no mortal could possibly project such a design so far in advance, and so consistently, upon what appears to be spontaneous speech.

Not all preachers stagger their breath groups. Other designs are possible. Each preacher chooses his own form of verbal sculpture. One guest preacher at St. John Progressive simply alternates his chant between lines, such as in the following excerpt from his sermon's climax:

> I know a man [chanted]
> Don't worry [not chanted]
> I know a man [chanted]
> That try to help me [not chanted]
> Oh Lord [chanted]
> It's been alright today [not chanted]
> I know it is [chanted]
> Oh Lord [chanted]
> Oh Lord [not chanted]
> Oh Lord [chanted]
> Oh Lord [not chanted]

By allowing for idiosyncratic artistry, the sermon gives the preacher a freedom that the tightly structured stages of prayer deny the deacon. In such a way, code structuring helps to create a sense of formality or informality.

The existence of co-occurrence rules also helps to create a mood of "seriousness." These rules determine which events can occur together, setting up a consistency between events. For example, chanting occurs much more predictably in the prayers than in the sermon. Having finished his opening proem, the deacon will almost always begin chanting through his thanksgiving and appeals. Not until he comes to the last lines of the peroration will he return to normal speech. The co-occurrence of chant with the prayer's structure, then, is a tight fit. The fit between chanting and the sermon's structure, on the other hand, is much looser. Chanting here usually begins somewhere during the buildup as the use of formulas increases. By the time he reaches his sermon's climax, the preacher is usually chanting. If there are several climaxes, as there sometimes are, the preacher chants anew, having returned with each denouement to normal speech. However, it is quite possible that the preacher may never start chanting, thus turning what was expected to be a sermon into what his hearers will call a "lecture." Pastor Pearson sometimes warns his congregation that he will not "whoop" through his sermon. With this word of caution, he indicates that he will not chant or excite his audience, so that they will hear all of his message instead of going into trance. He reserves these lectures for discussing very delicate church matters.

The co-occurrence of speech and song is much tighter in the Devotion than in the Service. As we have seen, hymn and prayer follow upon each other as automatically as breathing. The ordering of speech and song in the Service, however, is not so predictable. The choir or soloist may sing any number of songs before the pastor delivers his sermon. The preacher may indeed request that a particular song be sung after the choir has finished with its usual number of songs. This looseness of vocal organization, when compared to Devotion, helps to create a less formal ambience in which trance will occur.

Invoking "positional and public, rather than personal, identities" also helps to create the prevailing mood of seriousness in Devotion. In the first frame the deacons are the first to speak or sing, as they begin the hymn-prayer cycle. When the deacon or any other member begins to pray, it is difficult for the congregation to identify the speaker by sight because he has knelt before his bench out of view with his back toward his audience. Although most members can identify each others' voices, the first frame speaker is no longer the private individual he was when he entered the sanctuary. The deacon or congregational member offers himself as a spokesman for the entire congregation as he makes appeals and gives thanks to God on their behalf. His anonymity and invisibility only underscore the importance of his new public role of pray-er.

The role of the preacher in the second frame, however, is different. Unlike the self-effacing speaker in frame one, the preacher exploits his identity as he manipulates rapport with his audience. He is a performer before a congregation that judges his ability to "bring down the Spirit." If the preacher does not actually identify himself in the course of the sermon, he will usually offer some personal anecdote recounting an episode of his private history in order to enhance the rapport between himself and his listeners. The anonymous public speaker in frame one yields to the private, personal figure in frame two, thereby allowing a less formal second frame.

The emergence of a central situational focus, which engages the attention of the whole group, is another factor in the formality in frame one. Although the praying deacon is out of the congregation's visual focus, the audience's attention is nevertheless supposed to be riveted on the event of the prayer or hymn lining. The central focus of the

Devotion is not visual but aural. To insure that this attention is not interrupted, the ushers block the various entrances into the sanctuary to bar anyone from entering or leaving during prayer. Mothers constrain their fidgeting children. Since a prayer may last as long as ten minutes, sitting motionless for that long may seem a test of endurance and patience. Only during Devotion singing do the ushers allow the sanctuary doors to open so that members may enter in time for the next prayer. Impatient children or adults take advantage of the opened door to slip out and catch a breath of fresh air.

During the second frame, attention eventually focuses on the sermon. The sermon's delivery, however, does not demand the same intensity of focus as prayer. The congregation is not forced by rules of decorum to be immobile as in Devotion. No usher bars the doors as the sermon progresses. While eyes are turned to the pulpit, members may comment quite audibly about the preacher's words and performance. While older members may be attentive to the preaching, younger children begin to rustle their church fans, fidget in their seats, play with another child, or exit for the bathroom. In fact, it is not all that uncommon for Pastor Pearson to admonish his young hearers for "keeping up too much noise" as they freely move about while he is preaching.

The congregation's attention also shifts during the Service when another member shouts during the sermon or choir singing. When a member does begin to shout, other members rush to his or her side so that the shouter may not injure anyone. If shouting spreads contagiously through the congregation, central focus becomes kaleidoscopic as eyes, no longer on the pulpit, dart from shouter to shouter. The preacher has momentarily lost control, or at least attention. During such excitement the interrupted sermon will have to wait before its completion, if indeed it is ever finished. If, by some unfortunate circumstance, the preacher is unable to re-establish rapport, he cannot keep their focus on him. Members will turn their focus in all directions, replying to the preacher's lines with a polite but subdued "Amen," indicating to the speaker that he should soon end. Even at its most interesting moments, the Service is not so unidimensionally focused as the Devotion, when eyes may be fixed on the ceiling but ears are glued to the deacon's prayer.

The serious mood of the first Afro-Baptist frame is comparable to that of the African initiation in which future mediums are cleansed and trained. Although the former lacks scarification, physical isolation, and dietary restraints, the use of slow lining and long prayers in archaic speech is highly routinized in both. In Africa and in certain areas of the diaspora, it is not known beforehand which gods will possess which mediums in which order. The possession rites may continue well into the night or the next day until all mediums have gone into trance. Likewise, in the Afro-Baptist Service no observer can foretell with any certainty who among them will shout and in which order. One ritual certainty does exist, though: in Devotion, prayer will follow hymn and no one will shout.

The Service, then, becomes a release not only from hierarchical social structure but from the psychological structure of routine. This release provides the antistructure that Sister Odessa Houston finds so transformative. Describing the change of mood between frames, Sister Odessa says

> You sit there [in Devotion] and want to be dignified, but you can't help yourself. All of a sudden . . . you're smilin'. At first you go to service poised and all . . . then all of a sudden everything is rocking and moving. If you get in with it, then you won't be left out. . . . You go along with the flow of the rhythm.

As on a ship, Sister Odessa is carried along from the calmness of structure to a tumultuous, billowy sea of antistructure, then back to the smooth restructure of the benedictory prayer. The ritual is not only a personal vessel but one that carries all its participants through communitas and spiritual transformation together. When asked how she feels after a good worship service, Sister Pearson answers: "I feel like going on. Feel like you can make it." In a society that exploits one's labor and belittles one's humanity, this answer carries considerable significance.

African Retentions and the Binary Frames

In Brazilian Candomblé as well as in Haitian Vodun, religious syncretism between African powers and Roman Catholic saints occurs. On the other hand, in Afro-Baptist and Trinidadian Spiritual Baptist rituals, where only shouting shows a trace of African retentions, little blending of African and European religions seems to have taken place. When looking at various diaspora rituals from the viewpoint of a binary frame structure, however, the varying extent of African retentions becomes clearer even when rituals appear to be equally syncretistic or to bear no resemblance to each other at all.

Who, for example, would equate the elaborately long Candomblé initiation with the frighteningly wild Kromanti rituals of Suriname? On the level of ritual structure, both are quite similar in that their public possession rites are separate from a period of initiation for mediums. Both involve a separation of future adepts from society to teach them sacred knowledge (Herskovits and Herskovits 1934: 310). Although the names of Candomblé and Kromanti deities belong to different traditions, the separation of the initiation period from the trance rites is African.

On the other hand, the encapsulated, truncated African initiation was attached to the trance ritual in the United States, Jamaica, Haiti, and Trinidad. The answer to this enigma can be found in Herskovits' *Myth of the Negro Past*, in which he outlines four factors influencing the degree of African retentions in the Americas. They are climate (and topography), organization of the plantation, the ratio of whites to blacks, and the amount of contact between the two groups (Herskovits [1941] 1958: 111). In order to explain the binary ritual frames, all four factors and their interaction are important. The Kromanti rituals among the Saramaccans in Suriname will provide an example. These people are descended from Africans brought to Suriname as slaves but who soon escaped into the thick, forbidding jungle. They successfully repelled the Europeans who were intent on recapturing them. Because of their relatively weak exposure to European customs and culture, the Saramaccans, secluded and protected in the bush, continued practicing West African religion uninterrupted by the white man for three centuries.

Why should the Brazilian follower of Candomblé also separate his initiation from the trance rites? The answer may lie at the outset of the Atlantic slave trade when the Portuguese, who initiated it, had not yet found that the trade could be financially rewarding. In fact, Portugal began plantation slavery as a mere experiment with a sugarcane economy to offset Spain's profits from gold mining in her Central American highland territories (Girvan 1975: 3). (This experiment was to serve as an immense stimulus to the slave trade. Cuba, for example, for three centuries was little more than a way station for Spanish galleons enroute to Central America and Spain until the 1804 Haitian Revolution catapulted her into immense sugarcane profits based on African slavery [Fagg 1965: 17–27].)

Without implying that African slavery was more benign in the Iberian colonies, it is likely that a certain amount of laxity existed where a strong demand for constant labor was absent (for a discussion of comparative plantation systems in the Americas, see Tannenbaum [1946] 1963: passim, and Harris 1969: 38–47). Because of this laxity, the Portuguese, and later the Spanish, gave their slaves relative leisure to continue their African ways, especially those relating to religion. Grouped together in *cabildos*, that is, fraternities based on tribal membership, Africans were allowed to continue initiation rituals (Bastide 1971: 91–96; Davis 1969b: 72; Klein 1969: 149; Marks 1972: 49–50).

North American plantations, in contrast to those in Portuguese, Spanish, and French colonies, contained relatively few black laborers when compared to the surrounding white population (Davis 1969a: 67); usually no more than twenty slaves belonged to one plantation (Light 1987: 92; Meier and Rudwick 1966: 56–57; Roberts 1974: 39). By rigorously supervising field hands, slave owners hoped to maximize profits while at the same time suppressing slave revolt. Under such conditions, the African initiation had little chance of survival except in a disguised form. African slavery in North America, as well as in other Anglo-ruled colonies, was the linchpin for agribusiness. From the start slavery was capital-intensive.

Haiti's sugarcane production before the revolution was so intensive that it supported two-thirds of France's gross national product (Davis 1988: 18; James [1938] 1963: vii). Because of its great dependence on slave labor and the overwhelming ratio of slaves to whites, Haiti resembles both the Iberian plantation system and that of the British. With fewer whites to supervise their time, the African in Haiti could continue the initiation tradition more easily than was possible in North America. Because of the amount of time consumed in labor, however, slaves did not have the benefit of conducting the lengthy initiations common in Cuba, Brazil, and Africa. These socioeconomic constraints on the initiation better explain why it is obligatory in Brazil but not in Haiti. One observer of the two cultures believed that the Haitian vodunsi were more constantly involved with the supernatural and therefore did not need initiation as the followers of Candomblé did (Jules-Rosette 1980: 5–6). The position that the frequency of contact with the supernatural world is proportional to the need for initiation is difficult to maintain, however.

In Haiti these conditions, as well as the presence of fugitive slaves, created exceptions to the binary frame ritual. The possibility that escaped slaves, or maroons, could form their own large communities also created the opportunity to continue African religious practices, as the Saramaccans demonstrate in Suriname. In Haiti the Bizango secret rituals are a legacy of maroons. Beginning somewhat like a Vodun ritual, the Bizango *séance ordinaire*, however, lacks the Christian-looking first frame but begins with drumming, dancing, and salutations to Legba, the Trickster. Also unlike the Vodun ritual, the center pole—poteau mitan—is draped in black and red, while a human skull sits ominously in front of it on the ground.

The easy, conversational mood of the opening changes when the president of the society blows a conch shell, announcing that point in the ritual when Bizango rhythms and songs should be heard. Members then disappear only to re-enter, faces behind masks, dressed anew in black suits and red shirts—red gowns for the women. The remaining ritual stresses the work that the anonymous members must complete, and may include ritual healing of one of its members. A central figure during this ritual segment is the ever-present empty coffin in the center of the room into which members cast monetary donations (Davis 1988: 256–65; Laguerre 1980: 153–55). Resembling more a meeting convened to handle mundane rather than metaphysical matters, the séance reflects the origins of the Bizango groups in rebel maroon communities, which now operate as secret paramilitary units to protect peasant lands and villages from the oppressive central Haitian government (see Hurston [1938] 1990: 210–31; Laguerre 1980: 148–49).

The ambivalent nature of plantation slavery in Haiti also provided for an optional initiation into religious secrets. Known as *kanzo*, this separate initiation period takes weeks to complete (Deren 1953: 219–20; Métraux [1959] 1972: 192–95). The kanzo rites test the novices' prowess by requiring them to plunge their hands, while possessed by a loa, into boiling oil to retrieve a ball of dough at the pot's bottom. If truly possessed and protected by supernatural power, the initiate will not be burned. In order to advance to the rank of cult leader, that is, houngan for men and mambo for women, the vodunsi must undergo kanzo (Deren 1953: 219–20).

A similar optional initiation also exists in Trinidad among the Spiritual Baptists, reflecting the fact of a huge ratio of Africans to whites on plantations. Called *mournin'* and *buildin'*, the lengthy initiation is a period of seclusion and food deprivation in which the initiate experiences hallucinatory visions (see Herskovits and Herskovits 1964: 207–9). This costly initiation increases the seeker's knowledge of religious mysteries and control over supernatural forces. It is, therefore, repeatable according to the seeker's ability to pay for each initiation. These individual quests can probably be associated with reinterpretation of Native American vision quests along with Bantu vision quests, such as those found among the Fon (Merriam 1965). Among Orisha followers, initiation into the religion involves a separate period involving days of seclusion. The existence of frame one for Orisha rituals, however, suggests historical as well as socioeconomic similarities between Trinidad and Haiti as plantation societies. Both were settled by the French. As with the rites of kanzo, the rites of buildin' confer status on members and are required for leadership in the group. Since most members in Trinidad and Haiti are too poor to undergo the optional initiations, an initiatory frame one attaches itself to the ritual involving trance. This annexation, as in North America, assures that all participants are cleansed before coming into contact with the spirit world.

It would be naive to conclude that the North American plantation system precluded any attempts at preserving African initiations. Descriptions of bush meetings on seventeenth-century plantations point to the continuation of puberty rites in colonial North America (Fisher 1963: 33–34). Accounts from the Gullah Sea Islands also point to the fact that communicants in the Afro-Protestant ringshouts had to undergo probably months of secret initiation and training in religious doctrine before joining the ring (Creel 1988: 285–97). The fact that there has always been a small ratio of whites to blacks on the Sea Islands underscores the Africans' desire to retain certain cultural values and practices that are focal. Even within the Afro-Baptist church there is a suggestion that a separate, elaborate initiation period existed for those who wanted to become members through baptism (Williams 1982: 69–79). In its description this initiation may have resembled more the Native American vision quest than the African initiation, with the former's emphasis on individual rather than group experience.

With the exigencies of slavery bearing down upon them, enslaved Africans organized their religious practices according to circumstances.

The binary frame structure in some regions of the diaspora attests to their ingenuity. The separate initiation period attests to their ability to continue many of their rites. Like other African-Americans, Afro-Baptists in central Texas have been able to hold on to a significant African ethos. Whether Devotion will continue unaltered, however, is a matter for time to decide. In certain cities in the South, the Devotion found at St. John Progressive has disappeared, replaced by a brief, perfunctory reading of Scripture. Lining of hymns does not occur. When one inquires where the old-time Devotion has gone, the usual response is to the rural hinterland. Surprisingly, in other cities of the nation, such as Oakland, California, the old-time Devotion is very much alive. This situation is not so odd when one considers that black immigrants from states like Texas settled outside of the South, taking their religious practices with them. Slow to change under new conditions, these rituals help preserve the immigrant community's identity.

Whatever the fate of the Afro-Baptist ritual, the two binary frames have made it a spiritual ship carrying its participants along. In a more distant past, however, the image of a ship was a specter that loomed darkly in the African-American mind. For those Africans who found themselves captured on board, their plight was harrowing as they saw their homeland gradually fade away:

> But what happened on those ships, those thousands of ships which took us out into the ocean, away from the sights and smells of our land, beyond even the far-ranging flight of our birds? . . . So it was on the ocean as we moved further from the black shores into the agonies of the middle passage . . . [that] the only possible struggle for most captives was to stay alive. . . . (Harding 1981: 15)

As slave ships moved a continent's population across the seas to a new hemisphere, another ship soon bore some of this population to freedom. Later called the Underground Railroad, the system of escape from slavery often began with a surreptitious note to a prospective runaway, like the one below: "Tell my brothers to be always watching unto prayer, and when the good old ship of Zion comes along, to be ready to step aboard" (Harding 1981: 165).

So the good old ship of Zion transported black fugitives to a dubious freedom in the North where the Fugitive Slave Laws of 1793 and 1850 still permitted the slave owner to track down his chattel (Harding 1981: 119). Because the black church concealed runaways throughout the South, many fugitives succeeded in their escape to a treacherous future. Today, the ship still transports its crew and passengers through rocky times. Sung about in another Dorsey composition, the "old ship of Zion" symbolizes spiritual transformation in ritual. To the congregations of Afro-Baptists across this country, however, it symbolizes the church that has provided both a shelter against the storm of racial oppression and a vessel for sailing through it.

Notes

1. This discussion of the sermon is taken from my article, "West African Poetics in Black Preaching," *American Speech* 64 (Spring 1989): 140–46 (© 1989 by the University of Alabama Press; used by permission). The Reverend Leanza Harris, pastor of Bethel Baptist Church in Tuskegee, Alabama, delivered this sermon, December 27, 1985.

REFERENCES

Alho, Olli. (1976). *The Religion of the Slaves*. Helsinki: Academia Scientarium Fennica.

Allen, W. F. ([1865] 1967). "The Negro Dialect." In *The Negro and His Folklore in Nineteenth Century Periodicals*, edited by Bruce Jackson. Austin: University of Texas Press.

Baer, Hans. (1984). *The Black Spiritual Movement: A Religious Response to Racism*. Knoxville: University of Tennessee Press.

Bailey, Ben. (1978). "The Lined Hymn Tradition." *The Black Perspective in Music* 6:3–7.

Bailey, Guy, and Natalie Maynor. (1985). "The Present Tense of Be in White Folk Speech of the Southern United States." *English World-Wide* 6:199–216.

Baldwin, James. (1963). *Go Tell It on the Mountain*. New York: Dial Press.

Baltzell, E. Digby. (1964). *The Protestant Establishment*. New York: Random House.

Barr, Alwyn. (1973) *Black Texans: A History of Negroes in Texas 1528–1971*. Austin: Jenkins Publishing.

Bastide, Roger. (1971). *African Civilizations in the New World*. Translated by Peter Green. New York: Harper & Row.

Baugh, John. (1983). *Black Street Speech: Its History, Structure, and Survival*. Austin: University of Texas Press.

———. (1984). "Steady: Progressive Aspect in Black Vernacular English." *American Speech* 59:3–11.

Benedict, Ruth. (1934). *Patterns of Culture*. Boston: Houghton Mifflin.

Bickerton, Derek. (1981). *Roots of Language*. Ann Arbor: Karoma Publishers.

Bickerton, Derek, and Aquilas Escalante. (1970). "Palenquero: A Spanish-Based Creole of Northern Colombia." *Lingua* 24:254–67.

Bird, Charles. (1972). "Heroic Songs of the Mande Hunters." In *African Folklore*, edited by Richard Dorson. Bloomington: Indiana University Press.

Blassingame, John. (1979). *Slave Community: Plantation Life in the Antebellum South*. 2d ed. New York: Oxford University Press.

Bontemps, Arna. (1958). "Rock, Church, Rock!" In *The Book of Negro Folklore*, edited by Langston Hughes and Arna Bontemps. New York: Dodd, Mead.

Boyer, Horace. (1983). "Charles Albert Tindley: Progenitor of Black-American Gospel Music." *The Black Perspective in Music* 7:103–32.

Breen, T. H. (1987). "The 'Giddy Multitude': Race and Class in Early Virginia." In *From Different Shores*, edited by Ronald Takaki. New York: Oxford University Press.

Bruce, Dickson. (1974). *And They All Sang Halleluia: Plain-Folk Camp-Meeting Religion, 1800–1845*. Knoxville: Tennessee University Press.

Burnim, Mellonee. (1980). "The Black Gospel Music Tradition: Symbol of Ethnicity." Ph.D. diss., Indiana University.

Campbell, Randolph. (1989). *An Empire for Slavery: The Peculiar Institution in Texas 1821–1865*. Baton Rouge: Louisiana State University Press.

Carmer, C. L. (1934). *Stars Fell on Alabama*. New York: Farrar & Rinehart.

Carter, Harold. (1976). *The Prayer Tradition in Black People*. Valley Forge, Penn.: Judson.

Cassidy, Frederic. (1961). *Jamaica Talk*. London: Macmillan Caribbean.

Chase, Gilbert. (1966). *America's Music from the Pilgrims to the Present*. 2d ed. New York: McGraw-Hill.

Chernoff, John M. (1979). *African Rhythm and Sensibility*. Chicago: University of Chicago Press.

Cone, James H. (1971). "The Black Church and Black Power." In *The Black Church in America*, edited by Hart Nelsen, Raytha L. Yokley, and Anne K. Nelsen. New York: Basic Books.

Coolen, M. T. (1982). "The Fodet: A Senegambian Origin for the Blues." *The Black Perspective in Music* 10:69–84.

Courlander, Harold. (1960). *The Drum and the Hoe: Life and Lore of the Haitian People*. Berkeley: University of California Press.

———. (1976). *Afro-American Folklore*. New York: Crown Publishers.

Creel, Margaret W. (1988). *"A Peculiar People": Slave Religion and Community-Culture Among the Gullahs*. New York: New York University Press.

David, Jonathan C. (1988). "On One Accord: Theology and Iconography of a Ring Shout Service." Unpublished paper presented at the Society for Ethnomusicology. Tempe, Ariz., October.

Davis, David B. (1969a). "The Comparative Approach to American History: Slavery." In *Slavery in the New World*, edited by Laura Foner and Eugene Genovese. Englewood Cliffs, N.J.: Prentice-Hall.

———. (1969b). "A Comparison of British America and Latin America." In *Slavery in the New World*.

Davis, Gerald L. (1985). *I Got the Word in Me and I Can Sing It, You Know: A Study of the Performed African-American Sermon*. Philadelphia: University of Pennsylvania Press.

Davis, Wade. (1988). *Passage of Darkness: The Ethnobiology of the Haitian Zombie*. Chapel Hill: University of North Carolina Press.

Denning, M., and Rudolph, G. (1979). *Voudoun Fire*. St. Paul, Minn.: Llewellyn Publications.

Deren, Maya. (1953). *Divine Horsemen: The Living Gods of Haiti*. New York: Thames & Hudson.

Dillard, J. L. (1972). *Black English: Its History and Usage in the United States*. New York: Random House.

DuBois, W. E. B. ([1896] 1969). *The Suppression of the African Slave Trade*. Baton Rouge: Louisiana State University Press.

———. ([1903] 1973). *Souls of Black Folk*. Millwood, N.Y.: Kraus-Thomson Organization Ltd.

———. (1971). "Of the Faith of the Fathers." In *The Black Church in America*, edited by Hart Nelson, Raytha Yokley, and Ann Nelsen. New York: Basic Books.

Dunham, Philip, and Everett L. Jones. (1965). *The Negro Cowboys*. Lincoln: Nebraska University Press.

Ellison, Mary. (1989). *Lyrical Protest: Black Music's Struggle Against Discrimination*. New York: Praeger.

Erikson, Kia T. (1966). *Wayward Puritans: A Study in the Sociology of Deviance*. New York: John Wiley & Sons.

Fagg, John Edwin. (1965). *Cuba, Haiti, and the Dominican Republic*. Englewood Cliffs, N.J.: Prentice-Hall.

Falcon, R. P. P. (1970). "Religion du Vodun." *Etudes Dahoméennes* 18–19.

Fasold, Ralph. (1981). "The Relation Between Black and White Speech in the South." *American Speech* 56:163–89.

Faulk, John H. (1983). *Fear On Trial*. Austin: University of Texas Press.

Fernandez, James. (1973). "Analysis of Ritual: Metaphoric Correspondences as the Elementary Forms." *Science* 182:1366–67.

———. (1974). "The Mission of Metaphor in Expressive Culture." *Current Anthropology* 15:119–45.

Field, M. J. (1969). "Spirit Possession in Ghana." In *Spirit Mediumship and Society in Africa*, edited by John Beattie and John Middleton. New York: Africana Publishing.

Fisher, Miles Mark. (1963). *Negro Slave Songs in the United States*. Ithaca, N.Y.: Cornell University Press.

Fouda, Basile-Juléat. (1968). "Negro-African Oral Literature." In *Colloquium*. Dakar: Présence Africaine.

Franklin, M. (1982). "The Relationship of Black Preaching to Black Gospel Music." Ph.D. diss., Drew University.

Fredrickson, George. (1981). *White Supremacy: A Comparative Study of American and South African History*. New York: Oxford University Press.

Girvan, Norman. (1975). *Aspects of the Political Economy of Race in the Caribbean and the Americas*. Atlanta: Institute of the Black World Press. (Mona, Jamaica: Institute of Social & Economic Research, University of the West Indies).

Glazier, Stephen. (1983). *Marchin' the Pilgrims Home: Leadership and Decision-Making in an Afro-Caribbean Faith*. Westport, Conn.: Greenwood Press.

Goines, L. (1975). "Africanisms among the Bush Negroes of Surinam." *The Black Perspective in Music* 3 (Spring): 40–44.

Goodman, Felicitas D. (1988). *How About Demons?: Possessions and Exorcism in the Modern World*. Bloomington: Indiana University Press.

Gordon, Robert. (1972). "Negro 'shouts' from Georgia." In *Mother Wit from the Laughing Barrel*, edited by Alan Dundes. Englewood Cliffs, N.J.: Prentice-Hall.

Goreau, L. (1975). *Just Mahalia, Baby*. Waco, Texas: World Books.

Gray, Bennison. (1971). "Repetition in Oral Literature." *Journal of American Folklore* 84:289–303.

Gumperz, John J. (1982). *Discourse Strategies*. New York: Cambridge University Press.

Hancock, Ian F. (1986). "The Domestic Hypothesis, Diffusion and Componentiality: An Account of Atlantic Anglophone Creole Origins." In *Substrata versus Universals in Creole Genesis*, edited by Pieter Muysken and Norval Smith. Amsterdam: John Benjamin.

———. (1993). "Black English in Education—U.S.A." In *The Encyclopedia Of Language And Linguistics*, edited by R. E. Asher. Aberdeen: Pergamon Press and Aberdeen University Press.

Harding, Vincent. (1981). *There Is a River: The Black Struggle for Freedom in America*. New York: Harcourt Brace Jovanovich.

Harris, Marvin. (1969). "The Myth of the Friendly Master." In *Slavery in the New World*, edited by Laura Foner and Eugene Genovese. Englewood Cliffs, N.J.: Prentice-Hall.

Heath, Shirley Brice. (1983). *Ways With Words*. New York: Cambridge University Press.

Heilbut, Anthony. (1985). *The Gospel Sound: Good News and Bad Times*. New York: Limelight.

Herskovits, Melville J. (1937). *Life in a Haitian Valley*. New York: Knopf.

———. (1958). *Myth of the Negro Past*. Boston: Beacon Press.

Herskovits, Melville J., and Frances S. Herskovits. (1934). *Rebel Destiny: Among the Bush Negroes of Dutch Guiana*. New York: Whittlesey House.

———. (1964). *Trinidad Village*. New York: Octagon Books.

Higginson, Thomas W. (1960). *Army Life in a Black Regiment*. East Lansing, Mich.: Michigan State University Press.

Horton, Robin. (1969). "Types of Spirit Possession in Kalahari Religion." In *Spirit Mediumship and Society in Africa*, edited by John Beattie and John Middleton. New York: Africana Publishing.

Houk, James T. (1986). "Patterns of Possession in two Afro-American Religious Groups in Trinidad: The Spiritual Baptists and the Shango Cult." Master's thesis, Louisiana State University.

Hughes, Langston, and Arna Bontemps. (1958). *The Book of Negro Folklore*. New York: Dodd, Mead.

Hughes, Langston, and Milton Meltzer. (1967). *Black Magic: A Pictorial History of the Negro in American Entertainment*. Englewood Cliffs, N.J.: Prentice-Hall.

Hurston, Zora N. ([1934] 1971). *Jonah's Gourd Vine*. Philadelphia: Lippincott.

———. ([1938] 1990). *Tell My Horse: Voodoo and Life in Haiti and Jamaica*. New York: Harper & Row. (Philadelphia: Lippincott for 1938).

Irvine, Judith. (1984). "Formality and Informality in Communicative Events." In *Language in Use*, edited by John Baugh and Joel Sherzer. Englewood Cliffs, N.J.: Prentice-Hall.

———. (1989). "Strategies of Status Manipulation in the Wolof Greeting." In *Explorations in the Ethnography of Speaking*, edited by Richard Bauman and Joel Sherzer. New York: Cambridge University Press.

Jackson, George Pullen. (1943). *White and Negro Spirituals: Their Life Span and Kinship*. New York: DaCapo Press.

Jackson, Joyce M. (1981). "The Black American Folk Preacher and the Chanted Sermon: Parallels with a West African Tradition." In *Discourse in Ethnomusicology II: A Tribute to Alan Merriam*, edited by Caroline Card et al. Bloomington, Ind.: Ethnomusicology Publishing Group.

———. (1988). "The Performing Black Sacred Quartet: An Expression of Cultural Values and Aesthetics." Ph.D. diss., Indiana University.

Jackson, Joyce M., and James Jones. (1987). "Good News for the Motor City: Black Gospel Music in Detroit." In *Festival of American Folklife*. Washington, D.C.: Smithsonian Institution.

James, C. L. R. ([1938] 1963). *Black Jacobins: Toussain Louverture and the San Domingo Revolution*. 2d. ed. New York: Dial.

Johnson, James, and Rosamond Johnson. (1925). *The Book of American Negro Spirituals*. New York: Viking.

Johnson, James W. ([1927] 1975). *God's Trombones: Seven Negro Sermons in Verse*. New York: Viking.

Jones, A. M. (1964). "African Metrical Lyrics." *African Language Studies* 5:52–63.

Jones, Alice. (1942). "The Negro Folk Sermon: A Study in the Sociology of Folk Culture." Master's thesis, Fisk University.

Jones, Charles Colcock. (1842). *Instruction for Negroes in the United States.* Savannah: Thomas Purse.

Jones, Leroi [Amiri Baraka]. (1963). *Blues People: Negro Music in White America.* New York: Morrow.

Jones-Jackson, Patricia. (1987). *When Roots Die: Endangered Traditions on the Sea Islands.* Athens: Georgia University Press.

————. (n.d.) "Prayer from Wadmalaw Island."

Jordon, Terry. (1981). *Trails to Texas: Southern Roots of Western Cattle-Ranching.* Lincoln: Nebraska University Press.

Jules-Rosette, Bennetta. (1980). "Creative Spirituality from Africa to America; Cross-Cultural Influences in Contemporary Religious Forms." Paper presented at the Tenth Annual Meeting of the Popular Culture Association.

Kaslow, Andrew, and Claude Jacobs. (1981). *Prophecy, Healing, and Power: The Afro-American Spiritual Churches of New Orleans.* New Orleans: Jean Lafitte Historical Park.

Klein, Herbert S. (1969). "Anglicanism, Catholicism, and the Negro Slave." In *Slavery in the New World*, edited by Laura Foner and Eugene Genovese. Englewood Cliffs, N.J.: Prentice-Hall.

Knight, Roderick. (1984). "Music in Africa: the Manding Contexts." In *Performance Practice: Ethnomusicological Perspectives*, edited by Gerard Behague. Westport, Conn.: Greenwood.

Laguerre, Michel. (1980). "Bizango: A Voodoo Secret Society in Haiti." In *Secrecy*, edited by Stanton K. Tefft. New York: Human Sciences Press.

Lawless, Elaine. (1982). "Women's Speech in the Pentecostal Religious Service." Ph.D. diss., Indiana University.

————. (1983). "Shouting for the Lord: The Power of Women's Speech in the Pentecostal Religious Service." *Journal of American Folklore* 96:434–59.

Levine, Lawrence. (1977). *Black Culture and Black Consciousness.* New York: Oxford University Press.

Lewin, Olive. (1968). Jamaican Folk Music. *Caribbean Quarterly* 14:49–56.

Light, Ivan. (1987). "Ethnic Enterprise: Japanese, Chinese, and Blacks." In *From Different Shores: Perspectives on Race and Ethnicity in America*, edited by Ronald Takaki. New York: Oxford University Press.

Lipski, John. (1986). "The Negros Congos of Panama." *Journal of Black Studies* 16:409–28.

Logan, Wendell. (1982). "Conversations with Marjorie Whylie, Director of Folk Music Research at Jamaica School of Music, Kingston: Some

Aspects of Religious Cult Music in Jamaica." In *The Black Perspective in Music* 10(1): 85–94.

Lomax, John A. (1947). *Adventures of a Ballad Hunter.* New York: Macmillan.

Lovell, John, Jr. (1972). *Black Song: The Forge and the Flame.* New York: Macmillan.

Marks, Morton. (1974). "Uncovering Ritual Structures in Afro-American Music." In *Religious Movements in Contemporary America*, edited by Irving Zaretsky and Mark Leone. Princeton, N.J.: Princeton University Press.

————. (1982). "You Can't Sing Unless You're Saved." In *African Religious Groups and Beliefs*, edited by Simon Ottenberg. Meerut, India: Archana.

Maultsby, Portia K. (1990). "Africanisms in African-American Music." In *Africanisms in American Culture*, edited by Joseph E. Holloway. Bloomington: Indiana University Press.

Mbiti, John S. (1969). *African Religions and Philosophy.* New York: Frederick A. Praeger.

McCarthy, S. M. W. (1976). "The Afro-American Sermon and the Blues: Some Parallels." *The Black Perspective in Music* 4: 269–77.

McIntyre, Paul. (1976). *Black Pentecostal Music in Windsor.* Ottawa: Canadian Centre for Folk Culture Studies, National Museums of Canada.

Meier, August, and Elliott M. Rudwick. (1970). *From Plantation to Ghetto.* New York: Hill & Wang.

Merriam, Alan P. (1965). "The Importance of Song in the Flathead Indian Vision Quest." *Ethnomusicology* 9:91–99.

Métraux, Alfred ([1959] 1972). *Voodoo in Haiti.* New York: Schocken.

Moore, Joseph. (1979). Music and Dance as Expressions of Religious Worship in Jamacia. In *The Performing Arts: Music and Dance*, edited by John Blacking and Joann Kealiinohomoku. The Hague: Mouton.

Murphy, Joseph M. (1988). *Santería: An African Religion in America.* Boston: Beacon.

Myrdal, Gunner. (1944). *An American Dilemma.* New York: Harper and Row.

Nagashima, Yoshiko. (1984). *Rastafarian Music in Contemporary Jamaica.* Tokyo: Institute for the Study of Languages and Cultures of Asia and Africa.

Oates, Stephen B. (1982). *Let the Trumpet Sound: The Life of Martin Luther King, Jr.* New York: Harper & Row.

Oliver, Paul. (1970). *Savannah Syncopators: African Retentions in the Blues.* New York: Stein & Day.

Oliviera, Jorge de. (1973). *Ritual Prático do Candomblé e Seus Mistérios.* Rio de Janeiro: Editora Espiritualista Ltda.

Owsley, Frank L. ([1949] 1982). *Plain Folk of the Old South*. Baton Rouge: Louisiana State University Press.

Paris, Arthur E. (1982). *Black Pentecostalism: Southern Religion in an Urban World*. Amherst, Mass.: Massachusetts University Press.

Parks, Alfrieta V. (1981). "The Conceptualization of Kinship among the Spiritual Baptists of Trinidad." Ph.D. diss., Department of Religion, Princeton University.

Parrish, Lydia. (1942). "Slave Songs of the Georgia Sea Islands." New York: Creative Age.

Pipes, William. (1951). *Say Amen Brother! Old-Time Negro Preaching: A Study in American Frustration*. New York: William-Frederick.

Pitts, Ann. (1978). "A Prosodic Analysis of a Chanted Formulaic Sermon." *Rackham Literary Studies* 9:89–96.

Pitts, Walter F. (1988). " 'Keep the Fire Burnin': Language and Ritual in the Afro-Baptist Church." *Journal of the American Academy of Religion* 56:77–97.

Plancquaert, M. (1930). *Les Sociétés chez Bayaka*. Louvain: Imprimerie J. Kuyl-Otto.

Puckett, Newbell N. (1926). *Folk Beliefs of the Southern Negro*. Chapel Hill: University of North Carolina Press.

Raboteau, Albert J. (1978). *Slave Religion: The "Invisible" Institution in the Antebellum South*. New York: Oxford University Press.

Randolph, Peter. (1855). *Sketches of Slave Life*. Boston: James H. Earle.

Rigaud, Milo. (1953). *La Tradition Voudou et Le Voudou Haitien*. Paris: Editions Niclaus.

Roberts, John Storm. (1974). *Black Music of Two Worlds*. New York: Morrow.

Roberts, John W. (1989). *From Trickster to Badman: The Black Folk Hero in Slavery and Freedom*. Philadelphia: Pennsylvania University Press.

Rosenberg, Bruce. (1970). *Art of the American Folk Preacher*. New York: Oxford University Press.

Rouget, Gilbert. (1966). "African Traditional Non-prose Forms: Reciting, Declaiming, Singing and Strophic Structure." In *Conference on African Language and Literature*, edited by Jack Berry, Robert Plant Armstrong, and John Povey. Evanston, Ill.: Northwestern University.

———. (1980). *La Musique et La Transe*. Paris: Editions Gallimard.

———. (1985). *Music and Trance: A Theory of the Relations between Music and Possession*. Translated by Brunhilde Biebuyck. Chicago: University of Chicago Press.

Sapp, Jane. (1976). "Origins of Black Gospel Music." In *Black People and Their Culture*, edited by Linn Shapiro. Washington, D.C.: African Diaspora Program.

Seaga, Edward. (1969). "Revival Cults in Jamaica." Reprint from *Jamaica Journal*, v. 3, 2, 1–13.

Sernett, M. C. (1975). *Black Religion and American Evangelism*. Metuchen, N.J.: Scarecrow.

Sherzer, Joel, and Sammie Wicks. (1982). "The Intersection of Music and Language in Kuna Discourse." *Latin American Music Review* 3:147–64.

Silverthorne, Elizabeth. (1986). *Plantation Life in Texas*. College Station: Texas A&M University Press.

Simpson, George E. (1965). *The Shago Cult in Trinidad*. Rio Piedras: University of Puerto Rico, Institute of Caribbean Studies.

———. (1970). *Religious Cults of the Caribbean: Trinidad, Jamaica, and Haiti*. 2d ed. Rio Piedras, P.R.: University of Puerto Rico Press.

———. (1978). *Black Religion in the New World*. New York: Columbia University Press.

Sobel, Mechal. (1979). *Trabelin' On: The Slave Journey to an Afro-Baptist Faith*. Westport, Conn.: Greenwood Press.

Southern, Eileen. (1983). *The Music of Black Americans*. 2d ed. New York: Norton.

Spaulding, Henry George. ([1863] 1969). "Negro 'Shouts' and Shout Songs." In *The American Negro: His History and Literature*, edited by Bernard Katz. New York: Arno.

Stuckey, Sterling. (1987). *Slave Culture: Nationalist Theory and the Foundations of Black America*. New York: Oxford University Press.

Sutton, Brett. (1982). *Primitive Baptist Hymns of the Blue Ridge*. Chapel Hill: North Carolina University Press.

Takaki, Ronald. (1971). *A Pro-Slavery Crusade: The Agitation to Re-open the African Slave Trade*. New York: Free Press.

———. (1979). *Iron Cages: Race and Culture in 19th-Century America*. New York: Knopf

Tallmadge, W. H. (1961). "Dr. Watts and Mahalia Jackson—The Development, Decline, and Survival of a Folk Style in America." *Ethnomusicology* 5:95–99.

Tannenbaum, Frank. ([1946] 1963). *Slave and Citizen: The Negro in the Americas*. New York: Vintage.

Taylor, Douglas. (1963). "The Origin of West Indian Creole Languages." *American Anthropoligist* 65:800–14.

Thompson, Robert Farris. (1983). *Flash of the Spirit: African and Afro-American Art and Philosophy*. New York: Random House.

Torday, Emil. (1906). "Les Sociétés Sécrétes." In *Notes Analytiques sur les Collections Ethnographiques du Musée du Congo* I: 199–207.

Traugott, E. C. (1976). "Pidgins, Creoles, and the Origins of Vernacular Black

English." In *Black English: A Seminar*, edited by Deborah Sears Harrison and Tom Trabasso. New York: John Wiley & Sons.

Trudgill, Peter. (1974). *Sociolinguistics: An Introduction*. New York: Penguin Books.

Turner, Victor (1965). "Betwixt and Between: The Liminal Period in Rites of Passage." In *Reader in Comparative Religion*. 3d ed., edited by William A. Lessa and Evon Z. Vogt. New York: Harper & Row.

———. (1977). *The Ritual Process: Structure and Antistructure*. Ithaca: Cornell University Press.

van Gennep, Arnold. ([1903] 1960). *The Rites of Passage*. Translated by M. Vizedom and G. Caffee. Chicago: University of Chicago Press.

Vansina, Jan. (1955). "Initiation Rituals of the Bushong." *Africa* 25:138–53.

Vaughn-Cooke, Faye. (1972). "The Black Preaching Style: Historical Development and Characteristics." In *Language and Linguistics Working Papers 5*. Washington, D.C.: Georgetown University Press.

Verger, Pierre. (1954). "Rôle joué par l'état d'hébétude au cours de l'initiation des novices aux Cultes des Orisha et Vodun." *Bulletin de l'Institut Français d'Afrique Noir*, v. 16, 3–4, 322–40.

———. (1957). "Notes sur le Culte des Orisha et Vodun." Dakar: I.F.A.N.

———. (1969). "Trance and Convention in Nago-Yoruba Spirit Mediumship." In *Spirit Mediumship and Society in Africa*, edited by John Beattie and John Middleton. New York: Africana Publishing.

Walker, Wyatt T. (1979). *Somebody's Calling My Name: Black Sacred Music and Social Change*. Valley Forge, Penn.: Judson.

Wallace, Anthony F. C. (1966). *Religion: An Anthropological View*. New York: Random House.

Washington, Joseph R. (1971). "Black Politics." In *The Black Church in America*, edited by Hart Nelsen, Raytha L. Yokley, and Anne K. Nelsen. New York: Basic Books.

Waterman, Richard Alan. (1943). "African Patterns in Trinidad Negro Music." Ph.D. diss. Northwestern University.

Welch, David. (1977). "West African Cult Music Retentions in Haitian Urban Vaudou: a Preliminary Report." In *Essays for a Humanist: An Offering to Klaus Wachsman*. Spring Valley, N.Y.: Town House.

Wiley, Electra C., and Robert L. Wiley. (1984). "The Plaintive Sound: The Rhetoric of Despair in Black Churches in Arkansas." *Journal of Communication Studies* 2:5–10.

Williams, Charles. (1982). "The Conversion Ritual in a Rural Black Baptist Church." In *Holding on to the Land and the Lord*, edited by Robert L. Hall and Carol B. Stack. Athens: University of Georgia Press.

Williams, Mervyn R. (1985). "Song from Valley to Mountain: Music and Ritual among the Spiritual Baptists ("Shouters") of Trinidad." Master's thesis, Folklore Department, Indiana University.

Wolfram, Walt, and Ralph W. Fasold. (1974). *The Study of Social Dialects in American English*. Englewood Cliffs, N.J.: Prentice-Hall.

Wright, Richard L. (1976). "Language Standards and Communicative Style in the Black Church." Ph.D. diss., University of Texas at Austin.

Zahan, Dominique. (1960). *Sociétés d'Initiation Bambara: N'domo and Kore*. Paris: Mouton.

———. (1979). *The Religion, Spirituality, and Thought of Traditional Africa*. Chicago: Chicago University Press.

AUDIOGRAPHY

Note: Numbers refer to the year a recording was obtained by the archive, the accession number, and whether it was a field (F) or commercial recording.

Hagaman, Barbara. *Ghana, Northern Region, Lobi and Wala, 1975.* Archives of Traditional Music, Indiana University, #81-099-F.

Herskovits, Melville and Francis. *Trinidad, Port of Spain and Toco, 1939.* Archives of Traditional Music, Indiana University, #67-149-F.

Lomax, Alan. *Haiti, Port Benedet and Leogane, 1951.* Archives of Traditional Music, Indiana University, #73-087-F.

Murray, Laura. *Jamaican, 1960–1961.* Archives of Traditional Music, Indiana University, #61-020-F.

Pitts, Walter. *Alabama 1986, Delaware 1985, Trinidad 1989—African American Religious Services.* Archives of Traditional Music, Indiana University, #89-176-F.

Sapir, J. David. *The Music of the Diola-Fogny of the Casamance, Senegal.* Folkways Records, #FE4323, 1965.

Simpson, George. *Cult Music of Trinidad.* Folkways Records #FE4478, 1960.

INDEX